PARIS
IN YOUR POCKET

A handy directory of restaurants, hotels, museums, theaters, stores, nightlife, famous landmarks—the best of the city's sights, services, and pleasures!

Second Edition

BARRON'S

Woodbury, New York • London • Toronto
Sydney

Credits

Metro map courtesy of RATP.

Book design by Milton Glaser, Inc.
Illustrations by Juan Suarez

All inquiries should be addressed to:
Barron's Educational Series, Inc.
113 Crossways Park Drive
Woodbury, New York 11797

Library of Congress Catalog Card No. 86-22216

International Standard Book No. 0-8120-3756-1

Library of Congress Cataloging in Publication Data

Paris in your pocket

    1. Paris (France)—Description—1975—
—Guide-books   I. Barron's Educational Series, Inc.
DC708.P3125   1987   914.4′36104838   86-22216
ISBN 0-8120-3756-1

PRINTED IN THE UNITED STATES OF AMERICA

789   880   987654321

CONTENTS

Contents

iv

EIFFEL TOWER

PREFACE

A Gallic tribe, the Parisii, were the first to recognize the splendors of what is now Paris when they settled on the Ile de la Cité. They were defeated by the Romans in the first century, and the Romans then civilized the island and called it Lutèce. By the end of the 4th century it was called Paris, and from that time on, its place as an illustrious, often-fought-over center of civilization was assured. Paris developed into a walled city that grew to include monasteries, churches, and cathedrals. Saint-Germain-des-Prés in the 6th century and l'Eglise Saint-Pierre-de-Montmartre and Notre Dame in the 12th century were among the first churches. Schools here produced great artists, scholars, and leaders responsible for the city's awesome architecture, opulent palaces, and expansive urban plan. These people and places were all facets of a society that placed more importance on beauty, style, and pride in its accomplishments than on life itself.

That Paris remains a beautiful, seductive city is accepted as fact. Proud buildings, monuments, and markets still retain their historical essence and verve; the skies change from moment to moment; the cuisine leads the world in quality and style; its butcher shops, bakeries, pastry shops, and cheese shops turn each neighborhood into a movable feast, the city into a constantly changing palette. And there are the careening taxis, the languid street sweepers, the *mobylettes* that whiz through a crosswalk just when you think it's safe; there are the recalcitrant dogs, the groups of meter maids in their sky-blue uniforms (the *oiseaux bleus*), the time of day when everyone in the street seems to be tearing the end off a baguette—all the scenes that are part of a city as majestic in beauty as it is strong in character.

What isn't so obvious about Paris is that it is easy to know, to use, to get around in, to come back to, to take as one's own. Whether it be during the hot, sometimes unbearably humid, tourist-crowded days of July; the delightfully uncrowded days of August, when most Parisians desert Paris for their annual vacations; the quixotic days of fall; the short, gray, bone-chilling days of midwinter; or the robin's-egg-blue skies of spring—Paris is alive, bending, and accommodating the present without losing the past, ready to divulge its wealth to anyone willing to search it out.

The best way to see Paris is by walking—wandering down streets and stumbling onto markets or neighborhood antique shops, houses of fashion or tiny public gardens, hidden courtyards or a family at dinner behind windows flung wide. Each *arrondissement* has its own style, depth of character, and appeal.

This guide is intended for use by tourists, residents, and people who come for a week or who hope to stay for years. We've tried to make it a well-rounded combination of useful, accurate information, hints, and ideas about how best to get around and get to know Paris.

Paris in Your Pocket is arranged alphabetically by category, and listings within each category are also mostly alphabetically arranged. Like any guidebook, it does not attempt to cover every facet of the city, but aims to provide a basis for your own exploration and discovery.

Acknowledgments

We are indebted to Susan Herrmann Loomis for compiling, writing and updating this edition for us, in a way that captures the city best for the English-speaking tourist or traveler. We are also grateful for the help given us by Frédérique Moinard, who assisted in the project.

Before You Go

You must obtain a visa before you leave the U.S. Visas can be obtained either in person from a French consulate (if you live near one) or through the mail. In either case, you will need a valid U.S. passport to apply for a visa. Visa applications are available at travel agents and airline offices, as well as at French consulates. It is impossible to get a visa of any kind once you are in France.

ARRIVAL IN PARIS

If you arrive in Paris by air there are several ways to get into the city from the airports.

Roissy–Charles de Gaulle

By Bus The Air France bus leaves the airport daily, every 15 minutes between 6 AM and 11 PM, going to Porte Maillot, in the 16e. The trip takes one hour, and costs about 34F. The bus stops first at Avenue des Ternes (near the Palais des Congrès and the Méridien Hotel), then at the Place Charles de Gaulle—Etoile (Arc de Triomphe). From Porte Maillot you can get a taxi, bus, or metro to your destination.

City Buses N.350 to Gare de l'Est, 10e, leaves every 15 minutes between 5:30 AM and 10:00 PM. Bus N.351 to Place de la Nation, 12e, leaves every half hour from 5:30 AM to 8:24 PM.

RER (Roissy-Rail) Take a shuttle ride to the express train, which leaves every 15 minutes from 5:30 AM to 11:30 PM, to Gare du Nord, 10e; cost is about 26F.

By Car Take Autoroute A-1 to Porte de la Chapelle, or the A-3 to Porte de Bagnolet.

Orly

By Bus The Air France bus leaves every 12 minutes daily between 6 AM and 11 PM to the Aérogare des Invalides. The trip takes 40 minutes and costs 27F.

City Buses N.215 leaves every 15 minutes between 6:05 AM and 11 PM to Place Denfert-Rochereau, 14e. N.285A leaves every 15 minutes between 4:45 AM and midnight to Porte d'Italie, 13e. N.183A leaves every 30 minutes between 5:30 AM and 8:30 PM to Porte de Choisy, 13e.

RER (Orly-Rail) The express train leaves every 15 minutes between 5:51 AM and 10:51 PM to Gare d'Austerlitz, 5e; Gare St.-Michel, 5e; and Quai d'Orsay, 7e; it costs about 20F.

By Car Take the Autoroute du Sud to Porte d'Orléans, 14e.

Note: City buses are slower and less efficient than the RER and Air France Buses.

Taxis are also available at each airport.

Arrival

Bus service between Roissy-Charles de Gaulle and Orly Airports is available. The trip costs approximately 45F.

You can charter a helicopter from Roissy or Orly by calling Aircharter Darta, (1) 48-62-54-54; telex, 211564F.

Arrival by Train

There are six train stations in Paris, each serving a specific area of the continent and Britain:

Gare d'Austerlitz, 13e. Trains to southwestern France, Spain, Portugal.

Gare de l'Est, 10e. Trains to eastern France, Luxembourg, parts of Switzerland, southern Germany, Austria, and Hungary.

Gare de Lyon, 12e. Trains to southern and southeastern France, parts of Switzerland, Italy, Greece, and points east.

Gare de Montparnasse, 15e. Trains to western France, including Versailles, Chartres, and Brittany.

Gare du Nord, 10e. Trains to northern France, Belgium, the Netherlands, Scandinavia, U.S.S.R., northern Germany, and Britain.

Gare St.-Lazare, 9e. Trains to Normandy, including Le Havre, where ships leave for North and South America and England.

Tourist Offices

Tourist offices at each train station—open year-round except Sundays and holidays—offer information, maps, and hotel reservations; English is spoken. The main tourist office is **Office du Tourisme de Paris**, 127, av. des Champs-Elysées, 8e, Métro: Etoile (47-23-61-72). It is open daily, year-round. A welcome office— **Bureau d'Accueil**, Eiffel Tower, 7e, Métro: Trocadéro—is open daily, May to September.

Changing Money

Bureaux de change or banks at airports and train stations are generally open from 7 AM to 10 PM six days a week, closed Sundays. *Bureaux* open year-round are: Gare de Lyon, 12e; Gare du Nord, 10e; Gare St.-Lazare, 9e. You must have your passport with you to change money. Other reliable places to change money are: **American Express** 11, rue Scribe, 9e. Métro: Opéra.

Arrival

Banque Nationale de Paris (BNP) 2, bd. des Italiens, 9e. Métro: Richelieu-Drouot.
Crédit Commercial de France (CCF) 115–117, av. des Champs-Elysées, 8e. Métro: Etoile.
Crédit Lyonnais 22, bd. St.-Michel, 6e. Métro: St.-Michel.
Société Générale 29, bd. Haussmann, 9e. Métro: Chaussée d'Antin.
Union de Banques à Paris 154, av. des, Champs-Elysées, 8e. Métro: Etoile.

Credit Cards

Many more places accept credit cards now, but check beforehand or, if in doubt, carry enough cash. Abbreviations used in this book are: AE—American Express; DC—Diners Club; EC—Eurocard or Mastercard; V—Visa.

Note: When prices are mentioned in this guide, "F" (for example, "50F") refers to French francs. Smaller denominations are distinguished from the franc by a comma. For example, "50,50F" means 50 francs, 50 centimes. The comma is the equivalent of the English decimal point. On the other hand, large denominations are distinguished with a period. For example, 1,000 francs would be shown as 1.000F.

Timely Information

In Paris, some businesses close between noon and 2 PM, and most small shops and grocery stores are closed on Mondays.

The French use the 24-hour clock. Therefore, 8 AM is "8 *heures*," and 8 PM is "20 *heures*." A simple rule: subtract 12 to find out what time it is.

FINDING YOUR WAY AROUND PARIS

North, south, east, and west are far less important than left and right in Paris. The Seine River divides the city in two; the Right Bank (*Rive Droite*), includes the Champs-Elysées, the Grands Boulevards, the Opéra, Montmartre, and Pigalle; the Left Bank (*Rive Gauche*), has Paris' bohemia of Boulevard Saint-Michel, Saint-Germain-des-Prés, Montparnasse, and the residential Les Invalides area.

Arrondissements

Paris is divided into 20 numbered *arrondissements*, as it has been since Napoléon's urban planner, Baron Haussmann, redesigned the city in the mid-19th century. Numbering begins in the center of the city. The "first," which includes the Louvre and Châtelet, starts a spiral that turns clockwise, ending at the 20th in the east part. Each *arrondissement* has its own personality, and serves as a reference point for everything within that sector.

Numbers at the end of Parisian addresses refer to the *arrondissement*—for example, on an envelope, 75008 denotes the "eighth"; it's "*8ème Arr.*" on a street sign, elsewhere "8*e*," or plain "8." The addresses in this book have been abbreviated in the French manner. Therefore, you will see the following abbreviations, with these meanings:

av.—avenue
bd.—boulevard
bis—literally "repeat," meaning 2 buildings with same number
pl.—place

The building number precedes the designation of "street" (*rue*) or "avenue" (*av.*) and is separated from it by a comma. The word *niveau* means "level": niveau-1 is Level 1.

Arrondissements are unofficially divided into *quartiers*, or neighborhoods, that depict more specifically the character of the neighborhood. They are roughly divided into:

Opéra—1er, 2e, 9e
Les Halles—1er
Marais—3e, 4e
Ile St.-Louis—4e
Latin Quarter—5e
Saint-Germain—6e
Champ de Mars/Invalides—7e

Around Town

4 quatre (*kah-truh*)

Etoile/Faubourg-St.-Honoré—8e
Parc de Monceau—17e
Montparnasse—14e, 15e
Victor Hugo/Palais de Chaillot—16e
Montmartre—18e
Belleville/Ménilmontant—19e, 20e

A note about addresses and locations. In France, the ground floor is called the *rez-de-chaussée*; the next story up—what Americans would call the second floor—is referred to as the first floor, or *1er étage*.

Maps

You can get maps that show a general layout of the city's streets and monuments free from tourist offices and many department stores. For a detailed map that will make any visit infinitely easier, get a small book called either *Plan de Paris* or *Taride*, available at any bookstore or newsstand. It has everything in it, from the tiniest alley to maps of bus and métro routes, detailed maps of each *arrondissement*, and lists and locations for churches, post offices, and libraries, all carefully indicated.

Transportation in the City

Paris is a walkers' city, laid out on a very human scale. There is really no better way to experience the city than on foot. You'll become embroiled in the constant drama of Paris and get to know its best. But when your feet give out there are several efficient alternatives.

The Métro Paris' métro is one of the best in the world, and usually the fastest way to get around. There are 13 métro lines, and the name of each line refers to the last stop in the direction you are traveling. Thus, if you are going to the Jardin des Plantes, 5e, and you want to get off at métro stop Jussieu coming from the north, find the stop on the map and follow the line to the end: Mairie d'Ivry-Kremlin-Bicêtre. That is your direction. If you are coming from the south, follow the direction Fort d'Aubervilliers. To make a transfer, check on your map where the two lines intersect, get off at the stop, and look up at the orange and white sign labelled "*Correspondance*" to find your direction.

You should carry a large métro map with you, but if you don't have one, there is one in this book and there are large maps outside each station and on the walls inside each station. Free maps are available at most métro stations. Note that the first métro leaves at 5:30 AM, the last at 12:45 AM.

There is a first and a second class on the métro. First-class cars, marked with the number 1, are open to everyone before 9 AM and after 5 PM but at other times, beware. If a ticket inspector finds you in the wrong class you'll be fined, no matter how inadvertent your error.

There are ticket packages for every need, all of them at considerable savings on the price of a single ticket. All tickets are good on the métro, inner-city RER, and bus routes, unless otherwise mentioned. Bring a couple of small black and white photos of yourself with you; you will need them for certain passes.

Tickets: Single, *carnet* (10); *coupon Jaune* (weekly pass); *carte orange* (monthly pass); *carte sésame* (tourist pass)—first class only for 2, 4, or 7 days. *Cartes sésame* are good on the métro, RER, and buses in and outside of Paris. Remember to keep your tickets until you've left the métro.

Taxis Taxi drivers in Paris are generally helpful and willing to get you to your destination in record time. There is no reason to fear; they are crack drivers. You can catch a taxi at a taxi stand, identified by signs that say *Tête de Station* and/or *Taxi*, on a first-come, first-served basis. If both roof lights are lit, it's available; if just one is lit, it's taken. You can call for taxis—42-05-77-77 or 42-03-99-99 are two of many numbers to call—but getting a taxi in the street is usually faster. Many taxi drivers will not pick up more than three people, and there will be surcharges for extra bags. It helps to have the address of your destination clearly written down for the driver.

ANTIQUES

See SHOPPING.

Around Town

ANNUAL EVENTS

These events help determine Paris' busiest times of year. Paris is the least crowded in March, April, May, August, and October. For specific dates and information, call the **Office du Tourisme de Paris**, 47-23-61-72.

January

Fashion shows (summer collection).

February

Bread and Pastry Exposition.

March

Palm Sunday—Prix du Président de la République at Auteuil race course, Bois de Boulogne.

April

April to May—Paris Fair (commercial exhibition) at Parc des Expositions.
Early April to early October—Son et Lumière at les Invalides.

May

May to September—illuminated fountains at Versailles.
Mid-May—Paris marathon (footrace around Paris).
Mid-May to end of June—Versailles music and drama festival.
End of May to early June—French Open Tennis Championships, Roland Garros Courts, 16e.
Foire à la Ferraille, à la Brocante et aux Jambons (antiques and regional food fair).

June

Early June—Paris Air Show (odd years only), Le Bourget Airport.
Early June to mid-July—Marais Festival (music, drama, exhibitions).
Throughout June—a festival of music, drama, and dance at Saint-Denis.

Mid-June—Grand Steeplechase de Paris at Auteuil race course, Bois de Boulogne.
Mid-June—Fête du Pont-Neuf (booths and street performers on the bridge and in the Place Dauphine).
June 24—Feux de la Saint-Jean (fireworks) at Sacré Cœur.
End of June—Grand Prix de Paris, Longchamp race course, Bois de Boulogne.

July

July 14—Bastille Day (celebrations throughout the city and military display in the Champs-Elysées).
Mid-July—Finish of the Tour de France cycle race in the Champs-Elysées.
Fashion shows (winter collections).
Mid-July to mid-September—Festival Estival de Paris (classical music, concerts, and recitals throughout the city).

September

Festival de Montmartre.
End of September to early December—Festival d'Automne (music, drama, ballet, exhibitions).
Foire à la Ferraille, à la Brocante et aux Jambons (antiques and regional food fair).

October

First Sunday—Prix de l'Arc de Triomphe at Longchamp race course, Bois de Boulogne.
Early October—Montmartre wine festival. Paris motor show at Parc des Expositions (even years only).
End of October to early November—Festival de Jazz de Paris.

November

November 11—Armistice Day ceremony at Arc de Triomphe.

December

Christmas Eve—midnight mass at Notre-Dame.
New Year's Eve—street celebrations throughout the city.

ART GALLERIES

See GALLERIES.

BABYSITTERS

Rates for babysitters run from 22F to 24F an hour, plus a nominal fee for the agency (approx. 40 F). Those listed below claim they can provide bilingual babysitters:

American College 31, av. Bosquet, 7e. 45-55-9. 73. You must call at least 2 days in advance.
Baby-sitting Service 18, rue Tronchet, 8e. 46-37-51-24 or 47-42-69-02.
Catholic Institute 21, rue d'Assas, 6e. 45-48-31-70.
General Association of Paris Medical Students 105, bd. de l'Hôpital, 13e. 45-86-19-44.
Kid Service 17, rue Molière, 1er. 42-96-04-16.

BANKS AND BANKING

See ARRIVAL IN PARIS.

BARS

While bars are not typically Parisian, they do exist. Some of the best are in the city's grand hotels.

Crillon 10, pl. de la Concorde, 8e. Métro: Concorde. 42-96-10-81.
George V 31, av. George -V, 8e. Métro: George-V. 47-23-54-00.
Hilton 18, avenue Suffren, 15e. Métro: Bir-Hakeim. 42-73-92-00.
Intercontinental 3, rue Castiglione, 1er. Métro: Tuileries. 42-60-37-80.
Plaza Athénée 25, av. Montaigne, 8e. Métro: Franklin D. Roosevelt. 47-23-78-33.
Rhumerie 166 bd. Saint-Germain-des-Prés, 6e. Métro: St.-Germain. 43-54-28-94.
Ritz 15, pl. Vendôme, 1er. Métro: Pyramides. 42-60-38-30.

If you're homesick for an American bar:
Harry's Bar 5, rue Daunou, 2e. Métro: Opéra. 42-61-71-14.

Beer Bars

The following beer bars—casual, cheerful, neighborhood spots—offer up to 400 varieties of beer from all over the world, many of them served in their own specially designed glass. Food in beer bars ranges from bread and *charcuterie* to mussels and crispy *frites*, or specialties cooked with beer.
Académie de la Bière 88 bis, bd. de Port-Royal, 5e. Métro: Port-Royal. 43-54-66-65.
Bar Belge 75, av. de St.-Ouen, 17e. Métro: Guy-Moquet. 46-27-41-01.
Gueuze 19, rue Soufflot, 5e. Métro: Luxembourg. 43-54-63-00.
Mort Subite 20, rue Mouffetard, 5e. Métro: Monge. 43-31-41-48.
Pinte 13, Carrefour de l'Odéon, 6e. Métro: Odéon. 43-26-26-15.
Pub St.-Germain 17, rue de l'Ancienne Comédie, 6e. Métro: Odéon. 43-29-38-70.

BICYCLE RENTALS

Bicycle rental is very reasonable in Paris, and within the past two years, bicycle lanes—designated by turquoise lines painted on many of the city's streets—have made bicycling, if not safer, at least official.
Bois de Boulogne Rental at the restaurant Le Relais du Bois, route de Suresnes, 16e. Métro: Porte Maillot, bus N.244, stop Pré Catelan. Bicycles available every day in the summer months; Wednesday, Saturday, Sunday, and holidays during the school year (September through June).
RATP "Roue Libre dans le Rer" Bicycles available year-round on Saturday, Sunday, and holidays at RER stops: Châtelet-Les-Halles, St.-Germain-en-Laye, Courcelle-sur-Yvette (direction St.-Rémy-Les-Chevreuse), Noisiel-Le-Luzard (direction Marne-La-Vallée), Vincennes. Ask for directions at the ticket windows.

BOAT TRIPS

All of these boat trips operate year-round, departing approximately every half hour. Generally they don't operate between noon and 2 PM.

Seine Trips

Bateaux Mouches Pont de l'Alma, 8e (Rive Droite). Métro: Alma-Marceau. 42-25-96-10. Also offers meals daily April–October. Reduced schedule November–March. Lunch cruises at 1 PM in season; Saturday afternoon tea year-round. Closed in February.

Bateaux Parisiens Pont d'Iéna, Port de la Bourdonnais, 7e (Rive Gauche). Métro: Trocadéro. Telephone for reservations: 47-05-50-00.

Bateaux Vedettes de Paris Ile-de-France Port de Suffren, 7e (Rive Gauche). 47-05-71-29. Métro: Bir-Hakeim or Iéna.

Bateaux Vedettes Pont-Neuf Pont-Neuf, Square du Vert-Galant, 1er. Métro: Pont-Neuf. 46-33-98-38 or 43-29-86-19.

Canal Trips

Reservations necessary.

Canauxrama 5 bis, quai de la Loire, 19e. Métro: Jean-Jaurès. 46-24-86-16.

Patache Eaurobus—Canal St.-Martin et la Seine Quai Anatole France, 7e. Métro: Solférino. 48-74-75-30. Guided cruises in English, May to November daily.

BOOKS

Guides to Paris

Gault et Millaut Guide In French or English, published every two years. Food, drinks, rated restaurants, hotels, shopping. Everything about Paris for the consumer.

Michelin Red Guide *Paris et Environs* Published yearly in French and English. Rates restaurants and hotels.

Michelin Green Guide *Paris and Suburbs* Historic information, in French or English editions.

Paris Pas Cher Shopping, hotels, restaurants at low prices, published yearly in French only.

And some weekly newspaper-type guides:

L'Officiel des Spectacles Entertainment in Paris, in French.

Pariscope Entertainment in Paris, in French.

Paris Passion Entertainment, arts, calendar of events, published monthly in English.

Before you go and while you're there, read:

Food Lover's Guide to Paris Everything about food in Paris, in English.

BOOKSTORES (ENGLISH LANGUAGE)

Albion 13, rue Charles-V, 4e. Métro: St.-Paul. 42-72-50-71. Classic and contemporary Anglo-American literature, some history and science. Closed Sunday and Monday morning, and August.

Attica 34, rue des Ecoles, 5e. Métro: Maubert-Mutualité. 43-26-09-53. Old and contemporary Anglo-American literature. Closed Sunday and Monday morning.

Brentano's 37, av. de l'Opéra, 2e. Métro: Pyramides. 42-61-52-50. Anglo-American literature, art books, newspapers, and magazines. Closed Sunday.

Galignani 224, rue de Rivoli, 1er, Métro: Tuileries. 42-60-76-07. Books, newspapers, magazines, guidebooks, and maps. Closed Sunday.

Librairie de l'Unesco 9, pl. de Fontenoy, 7e. Métro: Ségur. 45-68-10-00. Large collection of newspapers and UNESCO publications (Education and Science). Closed Saturday and Sunday.

Nouveau Quartier Latin 78, bd. St.-Michel. Métro: Luxembourg. 43-26-42-70. Anglo-American literature, paperbacks, guidebooks. Closed Sunday.

Shakespeare and Company 37, rue de la Bûcherie, 5e. Métro: St.-Michel. 43-26-96-50. Books in many languages. Large selection of used books. Poetry readings Monday evenings. Open daily.

Village Voice 6, rue Princesse, 6e. Métro: Mabillon. 46-33-36-47. Eclectic selection of books in English. Closed Sunday and Monday.

W.H. Smith 248, rue de Rivoli, 1er. Métro: Concorde. 42-60-37-97. Part of a large British bookstore chain, they stock Anglo-American literature, newspapers, cookbooks, maps, and guidebooks. English tea room upstairs. Closed Sunday.

BOOKSTORES (FRENCH)

These stores have wonderful selections of books of every kind, occasionally also in English. They are fun to poke around in, and the books make wonderful gifts.

In addition, the **bouquinistes** (bookstalls) along the quais of the Seine are fun and full of surprises. You can find rare books, new books, art books—you name it.

FNAC Forum des Halles, 1, rue Pierre Lescot, 1er. Métro: Les Halles. 42-61-81-18. Closed Sunday and Monday morning. Also at 136, rue de Rennes, 6e. Métro: Montparnasse. 45-44-39-12; and 26, av. de Wagram, 17e. Métro: Etoile. 47-66-52-50. Both stores closed Sunday and Monday. Huge selection of everything, with 5 percent discount for everyone.

Gilbert Jeune 27, quai St.-Michel, 5e. Métro: St.-Michel. 43-54-57-32. They have Anglo-American literature and everything else under the sun. Closed Sunday.

The following are specialized bookstores:

Art and Architecture

Artcurial 9, av. Matignon, 8e. Métro: Franklin D. Roosevelt. 42-99-16-19. A huge stock of books on fine arts from around the globe: painting, graphic design, architecture, photography. Closed Sunday and Monday.

Delamain 155, rue St.-Honoré, 1er. Métro: Palais-Royal. 42-61-48-78. Founded in 1880, this historic, cozy shop specializes in art old and new, French literature, and cookbooks among others. Closed Sunday.

Dupré Octante 42, rue de Berri, 8e. Métro: St.-Philippe-du-Roule. 45-63-10-11; 39, rue d'Artois, 8e. Métro: St.-Philippe-du-Roule. 45-63-15-30. This store has books for graphic artists, architects, designers, jewelers. Some decorative, some technical books and a collection of posters and magazines.

Hune 170, bd. St.-Germain, 6e. Métro: St.-Germain-des-Prés. 45-48-35-85. One of the best-known bookstores in Paris. It specializes in international art books, avant-garde literature, graphic design, and much more. Open until midnight and always packed. Closed Sunday.

Librairie du Musée d'Art Moderne de la Ville de Paris 11, av. du Président Wilson, 16e. Métro: Iéna. 47-23-61-27. Specializes in books on 19th- and 20th-century art. Closed Monday.

Comic Books

Album 6–8, rue Danté, 5e. Métro: Maubert-Mutualité. 43-25-85-19. French comic books old and new, including Flash Gordon, Felix the Cat, Schtroumpfs, and Astérix. Closed Sunday.

Chambre d'Horus 14, rue Blot, 17e. 43-87-46-71. Métro: Place Clichy. Specialists in Tintin. This is a shop for real collectors. Open daily.

Pellucidar 25, rue de la Reynie, 4e. Métro: Châtelet. 45-08-13-02. Large choice of comic books and old children's books, as well as newspapers and books on every subject from film to fashion. Closed Sunday and Monday.

Film and Photography

Feux de la Rampe 2, rue de Luynes, 7e. Métro: Rue-du-Bac. 45-48-80-97. Everything on films, from start to finish. Closed Sunday and Monday.

Gastronomy

Au Bain Marie 20, rue Hérold, 1er. Métro: Bourse. 42-60-94-55. Closed Sunday.

Edgar Soete 5, quai Voltaire, 7e. Métro: Rue du Bac. 42-60-72-41. Closed Saturday and Sunday.

Gueule et Gosier 8, rue du Bourg-Tibourg, 4e. Métro: Hôtel-de-Ville. 42-78-58-50. A small shop filled with books all about food, and a genial proprietor who is

BOOKSTALLS ON QUAI VOLTAIRE

happy to answer questions. Open Monday through Saturday, 11 AM–8 PM.

Gilbert Jeune 5, pl. St.-Michel, 5e. Métro: St.-Michel. 43-25-70-07. Closed Sunday.

Tuile à Loup 35, rue Daubenton, 5e. Métro: Censier-Daubenton. 47-07-28-90. Closed Monday.

Verre et l'Assiette 1, rue du Val-de-Grace, 5e. Métro: Port-Royal. 46-33-45-96. Closed Sunday.

Music

Arioso 10, rue Geoffroy-Marie, 9e. Métro: Montmartre. 42-46-86-50. Large selection of classical sheet music and music dictionaries in many languages. Closed Sunday.

Librairie Musicale de Paris 68 bis, rue Réaumur, 3e. Métro: Réaumur-Sébastopol. 42-72-30-72. Old and new sheet music from throughout the world, and a selection of books about music. Closed Sunday and Monday.

Originals

Thierry Bodin 45, rue de l'Abbé-Grégoire, 6e. Métro: St.-Placide. 45-48-25-31. Historic manuscripts, original letters of renowned authors, original musical scores by well-known composers. Closed Saturday and Sunday.

Rare Books

Coulet et Faure 5, rue Drouot, 9e. Métro: Richelieu-Drouot. 47-70-84-87. This store hasn't changed much since it opened in 1880. Many old books and some contemporary ones, including illustrated originals. Closed Saturday afternoon, Sunday, and August.

Lardanchet 100, rue du Faubourg-St.-Honoré, 8e. Métro: Miromesnil. 42-66-68-32. Downstairs is a selection of art books and new releases; upstairs, a gallery specializing in engravings, as well as a collection of rare and old originals from the personal libraries of historic French figures. Closed Sunday and August.

Sports

Au Vieux Campeur 2, rue Latran, 5e. Métro: Maubert-Mutualité. 43-29-12-32. If you're planning a hiking, climbing, camping, bicycling, or car-touring trip, or just a stroll in Paris environs, this is the place to come for maps and guides. Closed Sunday and Monday.

Travel

Michelin 46, av. de Breteuil, 7e. Métro: St.-François-Xavier. 45-39-25-00. Everything this respectable house prints is available here: maps, green guides, red guides. In French or English, except for books about France. Closed Saturday and Sunday.

BOUTIQUES

See FASHION; DISCOUNT CLOTHING.

BREAD AND BOULANGERIES

See FOOD.

BUSES TO AIRPORT

See ARRIVAL IN PARIS.

BUS TOURS

The following companies offer day and night tours year-round.

American Express Cityrama counter, 11, rue Scribe, 9e. Métro: Opéra. 42-66-09-99.

Cityrama 4, pl. des Pyramides, 1er. Métro: Pyramides. 42-60-30-14. AE/DC/EC/V

Paris-Vision 214, rue de Rivoli, 1er. Métro: Tuileries. 42-60-31-25. AE/DC/EC/V

The RATP (the Parisian transportation system) also sponsors bus tours in the Ile-de-France, the area surrounding Paris. Tourist Office, open April to November, pl. de la Madeleine (near flower market), 8e. Métro: Madeleine. 42-65-31-18. AE/DC/EC/V.

BUSINESS SERVICES

The following luxury hotels offer conference rooms and secretarial services on request to their clients. See also HOTELS.

Concorde–La Fayette 3, pl. du Général Koenig, 17e. Métro: Porte Maillot. 47-58-12-84. Telex: 650892. 1,000 rooms. AE/DE/EC/V.

Hilton 18, av. de Suffren, 15e. Métro: Bir-Hakeim. 42-93-92-00. Telex: 200955. 450 rooms. AE/DC/EC/V.

Inter-Continental 3, rue de Castiglione, 1er. Métro: Tuileries. 42-60-37-80. Telex: 220114. 500 rooms. AE/DC/EC/V.

Meridien 81, bd. Gouvion-St.-Cyr, 17e. Métro: Porte Maillot. 47-58-12-30. Telex: 290952. 1,023 rooms. AE/DC/EC/V.

Montparnasse-Park Hotel 19, rue du Commandant René Mouchotte, 14e. Métro: Montparnasse. 43-20-15-51. Telex: 200135. 993 rooms. AE/DC/EC/V.

Nikko 61, quai de Grenelle, 15e. Métro: Javel. 45-75-62-62. Telex: 260012. 797 rooms. AE/DC/EC/V.

Plm Saint-Jacques 17, bd. St.-Jacques, 14e. Métro: Glacière. 45-89-89-80. Telex: 270740. 812 rooms. AE/DC/EC/V.

Sofitel Bourbon 32, rue St.-Dominique, 7e. Métro: Solférino. 45-55-91-80. Telex: 250019. 112 rooms. AE/DC/EC/V.

Sofitel de Paris 8-12, rue Louis-Armand, 15e. Métro: Porte de Versailles. 45-54-95-00. Telex: 200432. 600 rooms. AE/DC/EC/V.

Business Services and Office Rentals

Boss Buro Express 91, rue du Faubourg-St.-Honoré, 8e. Métro: St.-Philippe-du-Roule. 42-66-90-75. Telex: 642066. Closed weekends. They offer multilingual secretaries, offices for rent by the hour, day, week, month, year; telex, some interpreting, and other services.

Ibos 15, av. Victor-Hugo, 16e. Métro: Charles-de-Gaulle-Etoile. 45-02-18-00. Telex: 620893. Closed Saturday afternoon and Sunday. They offer bilingual services by the hour; offices to rent by the half day, day, and month; telex; answering service; photocopying service.

Office de Tourisme *Service Congrès*; 127, av. des Champs-Elysées, 8e. Métro: Charles-de-Gaulle-Etoile. 47-23-61-72. They will provide addresses for all your business and conference needs in Paris.

P.A.T. (Permanence d'Assistance Téléphonique) Telephone answering services. 46-09-95-95. Telex: 270560. Offers 24-hour answering service and mailing address. Bilingual staff.

CABARETS

Reservations are necessary at most of the following spots and encouraged at all of them.

Au Lapin Agile 22, rue des Saules, 18e. Métro: Lamarck-Caulaincourt. 46-06-85-87. A bit touristy, but still a reasonable facsimile of its former self, when the Montmartre artists spend their evenings there.

Caveau des Oubliettes 11, rue St.-Julien Le Pauvre, 5e. Métro: St.-Michel. 43-57-94-97. Lively French songs in the cellar of this 14th-century building. No meals. Open daily.

Chez Félix 23, rue Mouffetard, 5e. Métro: Cardinal-Lemoine. 47-07-68-78. Meals and Brazilian orchestra for dancing. Closed Sunday and Monday.

Club des Poètes 30, rue de Bourgogne, 7e. Métro: Varenne. 47-05-06-03. Poetry reading, occasionally in English, and hearty meals. AE/V. Closed Sunday.

Don Camilo 10, rue des Sts.-Pères, 7e. Métro: St.-Germain-des-Prés. 42-60-25-46. Dinner theater with local actors. AE/DC/EC/V. Open daily.

Limelight Boys International 14, rue St.-Denis, 1er. Métro: Châtelet. 45-08-96-25.Open nightly.(For gays.)

Mendigotte 80, quai de l'Hôtel-de-Ville, 4e. Métro: Pont-Marie. 42-72-19-76. Closed Monday. (For gays.)

Palace 8, rue du Faubourg-Montmartre, 9e. Métro: Montmartre. 42-46-10-87. Tea dance for men Sundays.

Régine 49–51, rue de Ponthieu, 8e. Métro: Champs-Elysées. 43-59-21-13. Private club. International membership cards required.

CAFES

Cafés are extensions of the Parisian living room, places to drink a quick *exprès* in the morning, have a sandwich at lunchtime, a *café crème* and a newspaper in the afternoon. If you stand at the bar, drinks are less expensive. If it's mealtime and the tables are set with cloths (or paper), those are reserved for diners. At cafés the tip is always included in the bill.

Some cafés are more expensive than others, depending on location and clientele. Being "chic" has a price, sometimes incredibly high!

Bar le 1900 56, rue d'Argout, 2e. Métro: Etienne-Marcel. 45-08-10-17. Nightly. (For gays.)

Café Costas 4, rue Berger (Square des Innocents), 1er. Métro: Les Halles. 45-08-54-39. This used to be the quaint, old-fashioned Café l'Innocent. But while it still serves typical café fare—espresso, *ballons* of red wine, *tisanes*, and *croque-monsieur*. Always packed with an equally chic clientele, many of whom linger on the simulated leather banquettes for hours. The entrance surely must have been inspired by a love of theater.

Café le Dôme 108, bd. du Montparnasse, 14e. Métro: Vavin. 43-54-53-61. Less chic than the nearby La Coupole, nonetheless a popular, late-night, neighborhood café. Closed Monday.

Café de Flore 172, bd. St.-Germain, 6e. Métro: St.-Germain-des-Prés. 45-48-55-26. The café to see and be seen in. Jam-packed with people who seem eternally involved in lengthy, serious discussions, with pauses now and then to check out the most recent arrival. Open daily, closed July.

Café de la Mairie 8, pl. St.-Sulpice, 6e. Métro: St.-Sulpice. 43-26-67-82. A neighborhood café.   you can sit and enjoy the dimension and calm of the austere Place Saint-Sulpice. Closed Monday.

Café de la Paix pl. de l'Opéra, 9e. Métro: Opéra. 47-42-97-02. A true institution, this famous sidewalk café is a perfect spot for "people-watching."

Closerie des Lilas 171, bd. du Montparnasse, 14e. Métro: Port-Royal. 43-26-70-50. Sit outside and absorb the chic atmosphere. You may catch a glimpse of a French film star. There is a restaurant inside. Open daily.

Cafés

Clown Bar 114, rue Amelot, 11e. Métro: Filles-du-Cal-vaire. 47-00-51-18. Slightly grubby but this is where performers from the nearby Cirque d'Hiver hold court. Closed Saturday.

Cochon à l'Oreille 15, rue Montmartre, 1er. Métro: Les Halles. 42-36-07-56. A flavor of old Les Halles. Closed Sunday.

Coupole 102, bd. du Montparnasse, 14e. Métro: Vavin. 43-20-14-20. The enclosed terrace in front is the café, filled with well-coiffed elderly women and young escorts, actors, models, and tourists. Open daily, closed August.

Deux Magots 170, bd. St.-Germain, 6e. Métro: St.-Germain-des-Prés. 45-48-55-25. A former Hemingway haunt. You can see it all from this vantage point in the heart of St.-Germain-des-Prés—from musicians to street vendors. Open daily, closed August.

Deux Saules 91, rue St.-Denis, 1er. Métro: Les Halles. 42-36-46-57. An oasis in Les Halles where waiters in long, blue aprons brusquely take orders, and picnic tables accommodate groups of young people taking a break from the frantic pace. Open daily.

Grande Cascade Allée de Longchamp, 16e. Nearest métro: Porte Maillot, bus N.244 from Porte Maillot. 47-72-66-00. The opulent Belle Epoque decor is magnificent; a jewel amidst the trees and pathways of the Bois de Boulogne. Open daily in the afternoons.

Le Fouquet's 99, avenue des Champs-Elysées, 8e. Métro: Etoile. 47-23-70-60. A "must" in Paris. Enjoy the view from the famous outdoor café: the Arc de Triomphe and, in the background, the Obelisk of the Place de la Concorde. Another option is to study the menu and make your choice before dining upstairs in the highly rated restaurant.

Ma Bourgogne 19, pl. des Vosges, 4e. Métro: St.-Paul. 42-78-44-64. A solid, refined café with excellent *café crème*, under the arcades of the Place des Vosges in the Marais. Get there early and you can watch them haul up buckets full of freshly cut potatoes for lunchtime *frites*. Closed Monday.

Palette 43, rue de Seine, 6e. Métro: Mabillon. 43-26-68-15. Situated as it is amidst the tourist rush of Saint-Germain-des-Prés, this friendly café that spills out into the sidewalk remains a strictly Parisian preserve. An artists' café, the walls are covered with tableaux, payment in kind for all manner of sustenance. Open daily, closed August.

Cafés

Papillons 129, rue Mouffetard, 5e. Métro: Censier-Daubenton. 43-31-66-50. The charm of this café is the clientele. Vendors from the Mouffetard market come here to share the woes, gossip, and triumphs of the early morning over generous ham or pâté sandwiches and beer, when most people are just opening their eyes over coffee and croissants. Closed Monday.

Sling 10, rue du Perche, 3e. Métro: Filles-du-Calvaire. 42-71-57-88. Nightly. (For gays.)

The Look 49, rue St.-Honoré, 1er. Métro: Louvre. No phone. Closed Monday. (For gays.)

Verre à Pied 118 bis., rue Mouffetard, 5e. Métro: Censier-Daubenton. 43-31-15-72. A tiny, spotless café with smiling *patron* and general good will amidst the Mouffetard market bustle. Closed Monday.

CAR RENTALS

See DRIVING IN PARIS.

CATHEDRALS

See SIGHTS AND TOURS—CHURCHES.

CEMETERIES

There are cemeteries tucked away throughout Paris, many of them providing oases of quiet and calmness, with a profusion of ceramic flowers, photographs, and memorabilia. Two of the most historically interesting are:

Montmartre 20, av. Rachel, 18e. Métro: Blanche. Many literati are interred here including Baudelaire, Dumas Père, and the painter Fragonard.

Père Lachaise 16, rue du Repos, 20e. Métro: Père Lachaise. Groupies have been known to cluster around the graves of their idols, including Honoré de Balzac, Colette, Gertrude Stein, Victor Hugo, Edith Piaf, Marcel Proust, Jim Morrison, and Oscar Wilde. Map available from caretaker at entrance.

Cemeteries

CHARCUTERIES

See FOOD.

CHEESE AND FROMAGERIES

See FOOD.

CHILDREN'S FASHIONS

Artisanat Monastique 68 bis, av. Denfert-Rochereau, 14e. Métro: Port-Royal. 43-35-15-76. Beautiful handmade clothing, stuffed animals, baby gifts, embroidery, and lace. Open afternoons, closed Sunday and August.

Baby-Dior 28, av. Montaigne, 8e. Métro: Alma-Marceau. 47-23-54-44. Miniature designer fashions, just like mom's and dad's. Some teeny baby clothes. Closed Sunday. AE/DC/V.

Bonnes Fées 57, av. Mozart, 16e. Métro: Ranelagh. 42-88-14-22. Every child in the family can get the same outfit here no matter the size or number. Closed Sunday.

Bonpoint 67, rue de l'Université, 7e. Métro: Solférino. 45-55-63-70; 64, av. Raymond Poincaré, 16e. Métro: Victor-Hugo. 47-27-60-81; 184, rue de Courcelles, 17e. Métro: Péreire. 47-63-87-49. Elegant, refined clothes with style for the child up to 18 years. Closed Sunday. AE/DC/V.

See also SHOES.

Kids' Fashions at Discount

Nuage Rouge 26, rue des Canettes, 6e. Métro: St.-Sulpice. 43-26-52-32. Closed Sunday and Monday morning.

Petit Mouton 10, rue St.-Placide, 6e. Métro: Sèvres-Babylone. 45-48-86-26. Closed Sunday and Monday morning.

Children's Fashions

CHILDREN'S PARIS

Almost every park and square in Paris has at least a sandbox, and many of them—from small neighborhood squares to large parks—also have slides, swings, merry-go-rounds, even puppet shows and donkey rides. Parks are open year-round, though hours vary. Generally they are open from dawn to dusk. Organized activities—toy-boat rentals, puppet shows, donkey rides—correspond with school vacations. They're generally available daily during July and August, at other times on weekends and Wednesdays.

Zoos, Aquariums, Farms

Aquarium du Trocadéro Jardin du Palais de Chaillot, 16e. Métro: Trocadéro. 47-23-62-95. Every fish that swims in France is here. Open daily, 10 AM to 5:30 PM.

Jardin d'Acclimatation Bois de Boulogne, 16e. Métro: Les Sablons. 46-24-10-80. A zoo, a Norman farm, playground, miniature train (from Porte Maillot), doll museum. Open daily, 10 AM to 6 PM.

Jardin des Plantes 57, rue Cuvier, 5e. Métro: Jussieu. 43-36-14-41. Zoo, small farm, aquarium, reptiles, and insects. Also, beautiful flower and herb gardens. Open daily 9 AM–5 PM.

Parc Zoologique de Paris 53, av. de St.-Maurice, 12e. (In the Bois de Vincennes). Métro: Porte Dorée. 43-43-84-95. Almost 28 acres of zoo, plus an aquarium. Visitors can help feed the animals at mealtime. Open daily, 9 AM to 6:00 PM (to 5:30 from October 15 to February 28).

Parks

The following parks all have puppet shows, in French only.

Champ de Mars 7e. Métro: Ecole-Militaire. 46-37-07-87.

Jardin du Luxembourg 5e. Métro: Luxembourg. 43-26-46-47. Shows in the afternoons. Also, donkey rides, toy-boat rentals.

Jardin des Tuileries 8e. Métro: Concorde. 42-64-05-19. Shows in the afternoons. Also, merry-go-round, swings, donkey rides, toy-boat rentals.

Parc des Buttes Chaumont Théatre Guignol Anatole, 19e. Métro: Laumière. 43-87-13-12. Shows hourly from 3 PM to 5 PM.

Movies

For movies throughout the city, consult the *Pariscope* "Pour les Jeunes" section.

See **Movies**, page 94 for further information.

Circuses

Cirque Gruss 211, av. Jean-Jaurès, 19e. Métro: Porte de la Villette. 42-45-85-85. In Paris from October to the end of February.

Cirque d'Hiver 110, rue Amelot, 11e. Métro: Filles-du-Calvaire. 47-00-12-25. The only permanent circus in Paris; open school holidays, Wednesdays, and weekends. Consult the *Pariscope* or *L'Officiel des Spectacles* for specific programs.

The following circuses travel throughout France during the year, making yearly appearances in Paris. Consult the *Pariscope* or *L'Officiel des Spectacles* for specific dates and programs.

Cirque Jean Richard
Cirque de Paris
Ecole Nationale du Cirque

CHOCOLATE
See FOOD.

CREDIT CARDS
See ARRIVAL IN PARIS.

CHURCH AND SYNAGOGUE SERVICES (IN ENGLISH)

American Cathedral 23, av. George-V, 8e. Métro: Alma-Marceau. 47-20-17-92. Episcopal, but welcomes anyone.

American Church in Paris 65, quai d'Orsay, 7e. Métro: Invalides. 47-05-07-99. Nondenominational.

Great Synagogue 44, rue de La Victoire, 9e. Métro: Le Peletier. 42-85-71-09.

St.-Joseph's Church 50, av. Hoche, 8e. Métro: Etoile. 45-63-20-61. Roman Catholic.

St.-Michael's Church 5, rue d'Aguesseau, 8e. Métro: Madeleine. 47-42-70-88. Church of England.

Union Libérale Israelite Synagogue 24, rue Copernic, 16e. Métro: Boissière. 47-04-37-27. English rabbi.

CHURCHES

See SIGHTS AND TOURS.

CONCERTS

The following is a list of free concerts. For other concerts consult the *Pariscope*, *L'Officiel des Spectacles*, or call La Maison de la Radio at 45-24-18-18 for information.

American Church in Paris 65, quai d'Orsay, 7e. Métro: Invalides. 47-05-07-99. Concerts on Sundays at 6:30 PM all year 'round, except August. Call for programs.

Carillon du Beffroi de la Mairie du 1er 4, pl. du Louvre, 1er. Métro: Louvre. 42-60-38-01. Concert of bells in the bell tower of the Mairie, Wednesdays at 5 PM in summer, at 1:30 PM in winter.

Eglise Saint-Merri 76, rue de la Verrerie, 4e. Métro: Hôtel-de-Ville. 42-71-93-93. Concerts—from piano recitals to orchestras—Saturdays at 9 PM and Sundays at 4 PM. Consult *L'Officiel des Spectacles* or *Pariscope* for details.

Musée d'Art Moderne 11, av. du Président-Wilson, 16e. Métro: Alma-Marceau. 47-23-61-27. Jazz concerts twice a week (call for schedule) and poetry readings Wednesdays at 7:15 PM.

Notre-Dame de Paris pl. du Parvis Notre Dame, 4e. Métro: Cité. 43-26-07-39. Organ concerts on Sundays and holidays at 5:45 PM.

Public Gardens From May to September there are many free concerts in Paris' parks. Call 46-51-71-20 for information.

Radio France-Maison de la Radio 116, av. du Président-Kennedy, 16e. Métro: Passy. 45-24-18-18. Concerts throughout the week. Call for information.

CONVERSIONS

Weight

1 kilo = 2.2 pounds
A half-kilo is a *demi-kilo* or a *livre*.

Length-Distance

1 meter = 3.28 feet
1 kilometer = 0.62 mile

Capacity

1 litre = 0.265 U.S. gallon
A full bottle of wine is normally 75 centilitres.

Temperature

CENTIGRADE	FAHRENHEIT
−10°	14°
− 5°	23°
0°	32°
5°	41°
10°	50°
20°	68°

Clothing

Sizes may vary considerably, depending on designer or brand.

WOMEN						
France	38	40	42	44	46	48
U.S.	08	10	12	14	16	18

MEN'S SLACKS					
France	42	44	46	48	50
U.S.	32	34	36	38	40

SHOES									
France	36	37	38	39	40	41	42	43	44
U.S.	5	6	7	7½	8	9	10	10½	11

MEN'S SHIRTS						
France	37	38	39	40	41	42	43
U.S.	14½	15	15½	15¾	16	16½	17

COOKING AND WINE SCHOOLS

Académie du Vin 24, rue Boissy d'Anglas (at Cité Berryer), 8e. Métro: Madeleine. 42-66-28-45. Wine classes in English and French.

Cooking Schools

Centre de Formations Technologiques Ferrandi 11, rue Jean Ferrandi, 6e. Métro: St.-Placide. 45-44-38-18. Unique 9-month restaurant and hotel program, including wine restaurant service and cheese classes. In English.

Cordon Bleu 24, rue du Champ-de-Mars, 7e. Métro: Ecole-Militaire. 45-55-02-77. Registration: 40, av. Bosquet, 7e. Métro: Ecole-Militaire. Classes and afternoon cooking demonstrations. French only.

Ecole de Cuisine la Varenne 34, rue St.-Dominique, 7e. Métro: Invalides. 47-05-10-16. Classes and afternoon demonstrations with English translations.

Ecole Lenôtre 40, rue Pierre Curie, Zone Industrielle Les Gâtines, 78370 Plaisir. 40-55-81-12. Take the train to Versailles from Montparnasse, then a bus to Plaisir. Professional-quality classes, in French only.

Marie-Blanche de Broglie Cooking School 18, av. de la Motte-Picquet, 7e. Métro: Ecole Militaire. 45-51-36-34. Cooking, cheese, and wine classes. Afternoon demonstrations. In French and English.

Martha Rose Shulman 20, rue du Vieux Colombier, 6e. Métro: St.-Sulpice. Five-class series of cooking classes limited to 6 students; offered in English. A series of food-related seminars also available.

Paris en Cuisine 78, rue de la Croix-Nivert, 15e. Métro: Commerce. 42-50-04-23. Food-related tours and classes in English.

Pot au Feu 14, rue Duphot, 1er. Métro: Madeleine. 42-60-00-94. Daily cooking classes. In French only.

DANCING

Balajo 9, rue de Lappe, 11e. Métro: Bastille. 47-00-07-87. Tango, waltz, rumba, cha-cha. Open Monday, Friday, Saturday, 10 PM–4:30 AM, daily 3 PM–6:30 PM.

Club 79 79, av. des Champs-Elysées, 8e. Métro: George-V. 47-23-68-75. Disco on weekends; waltz, tango during the week. Open nightly.

Coupole 102, bd. du Montparnasse, 14e. Métro: Montparnasse-Bienvenue. 43-20-14-20. Tango, waltz, classical dancing, downstairs from restaurant. Open nightly.

Gibus 18, rue du Faubourg-du-Temple, 11e. Métro: République. 47-00-78-88. Live music, rock, new wave. Closed Sunday and Monday.

La Scala de Paris 188 bis, rue de Rivoli, 1er. Métro: Palais Royal. 42-61-64-00. Rock, disco. Open nightly.

Main Jaune pl. de la Porte de Champerret, 17e. Métro: Porte-de-Champerret. 47-63-26-47. Roller disco. Open nightly.

Palace 8, rue du Faubourg-Montmartre. 9e. Métro: Montmartre. 42-46-10-87. Disco, rock, funk, new wave, and concerts (information on concerts in the *Pariscope* and *L'Officiel des Spectacles*). Open nightly.

Saint-Hilaire 24, rue Vavin, 6e. Métro: Vavin. 43-26-86-38. Disco, rock, reggae. Punk evening is Wednesday. Closed Monday.

Salle Wagram 39, av. de Wagram, 17e. Métro: Ternes. 43-80-30-03. Rock, hard rock, funky. Friday and Saturday nights only.

Whisky à Gogo 57, rue de Seine, 6e. Métro: St.-Germain. 46-33-74-99. Disco, rock. Open nightly.

DAY TRIPS

Chantilly Half-hour train ride from Gare du Nord and a walk through the village to the chateau. Chantilly is known for its horse races, sweetened whipped *crème fraîche*—"*crème Chantilly*"—and chateau. The chateau, built on a very human scale, is surrounded by ponds and contains a rich collection of paintings, furniture, tapestries, and memorabilia from the 15th and 16th centuries. Closed Tuesday.

Chartres 45-minute train trip from Gare Montparnasse. Worth a trip to see the cathedral and its renowned stained glass windows where "Chartres blue" predominates. The town of winding streets, many steps, and old buildings is small and quaint.

Fontainebleau 50-minute train trip from Gare de Lyon, then a short bus trip to the chateau. The 34,000-acre forest, the former hunting grounds for French royalty, is now popular with day and weekend hikers. The chateau appeared first in history in 1137, though it was reconstructed by Henry IV and François I in the 16th century. Closed Tuesday.

Malmaison RER line A, stop Rueil-Malmaison and a 10-minute walk to chateau. Visit Napoléon's and Joséphine's lovely country home and the stables, which now house a carefully preserved collection of antique carriages. Closed Tuesday and holidays.

Moret-sur Loing A 1-hour train trip from Gare de Lyon, stop Moret/Veneux-les-Sablons. On the banks of the gentle Loing river, this former walled medieval town has just two of its 14th-century gates still standing. Sisely and Pissaro both painted here, and it is still a favorite spot for artists.

Musée de l'Air et de l'Espace Aéroport du Bourget. 838-9111. RER line B-3 or B-5, then bus N.350 to the museum. Aircraft from 1919 on, and audiovisual programs, all in the former Le Bourget airport. Closed Monday.

Musée Claude Monet Giverny (16–32) 51-28-21. Fifty-five-minute train trip from Gare St.-Lazare, stop Vernon, then 6 km from train station; taxis available. The restored house, which contains Monet's extensive Japanese art collection, and the sumptuous gardens (with lily ponds), are open to visitors from April to November, 10 AM–6 PM. Closed Monday.

Parc de Sceaux RER line B-4, stop Parc de Sceaux and a short walk to the park. The *Musée de l'Ile de France* (46-61-04-71) and an *Orangerie* sit amidst a beautiful and impeccably manicured park with ponds and paths, perfect for picnics, jogging, walking. In autumn you'll see the guards hunting wild mushrooms throughout the park. Concerts in the Orangerie (46-60-07-79) on Saturday and Sunday at 7:30 PM, July–September. Museum closed Tuesday.

Rouen 1½-hour train-trip from Gare St.-Lazare. A charming, historic town of ancient leaning timbered homes, progressive architecture, and an astounding cathedral. The central shopping district, much of it closed to cars, surrounds the Gros Horloge, a clock set into a 16-century gate house. Joan of Arc was burned in the Place du Vieux Marché.

Saint-Germain-en-Laye RER line A-1, stops in front of the chateau that houses the *Musée des Antiquités Nationales* (34-51-53-65)—an archeological museum. A walk around town is also worthwhile; though close to Paris, Saint-Germain-en-Laye feels like a provincial town. Museum closed on Tuesday and holidays.

Versailles 15-minute trip on the RER C line, stop Versailles RG (Rive Gauche) and follow the crowd. A full-day trip to see the magnificent chateau, the Trianon, the gardens with their fountains that play on the 1st and 3rd Sunday from May through September. Chateau closed Monday and holidays. Park open year-round.

DEPARTMENT STORES

See FASHION.

DESIGNERS

See FASHION.

DISCOUNT CLOTHING

The rue St.-Placide is one of the best-known shopping streets, lined with small boutiques selling all manner of inexpensive, usually trendy, clothing. You may not find designer stock there, or at any of the following boutiques, but much of it is chic, fun, and *à la mode*.

Annexe 46, rue St.-Placide, 6e. Métro: Sèvres-Babylone. 45-48-82-85. For men. Closed Sunday and Monday morning. V.

King Soldes 24, rue St.-Placide, 6e. Métro: St.-Placide. 42-22-39-40. Women only. Closed Sunday and Monday morning.

Mouton à Cinq Pattes 8, rue St.-Placide, 6e. Métro: Sèvres-Babylone. 45-48-86-26. For women. Closed Sunday and Monday morning. V.

Pilou 9, rue St.-Placide. 6e. Métro: St.-Placide. 45-48-86-02. Women only. Closed Sunday. V.

For those who don't mind searching for a good deal:

Clef Des Soldes 99, rue St.-Dominique, 7e. Métro: La-tour-Maubourg. 47-05-04-55. For men and women. Closed Sunday and Monday morning.
Club des Dix 43, rue du Faubourg-St.-Honoré, 3rd floor, 8e. Métro: Concorde. 42-66-43-61. Men and women. Closed Sunday and Monday. V.

Don't forget in your wanderings to check out *Les Boutiques du Métro*. There is a network of merchants who sell their wares—anything from handy leather coin purses to belts, scarves, jewelry, beauty products—in the little fold-down stalls provided by the RATP or even from the top of an overturned cardboard box. These "boutiques" can be great spots to pick up a trendy accessory. Incidentally, merchants come and go in the métro selling seasonal fruits (avocados, melons, and such) and fresh flowers. The flowers are always a good deal, the fruit usually not.

DRIVING IN PARIS

Driving in Paris isn't as bad as it looks. Everyone drives fast but according to rules, written and un-written. Written rules make seatbelts obligatory, and give the car on the right the right of way at all times, even in traffic circles. Otherwise it is a matter of quick thinking, quick reactions, and absolute concentration so you can either hang back or shoot ahead, depending on what's happening around you.

Car Rentals

You must be at least 23 and have a valid U.S. drivers' license, at least one year old, to rent a car and drive in Paris.
Avis 5, rue Bixio, 7e. Métro: Ecole-Militaire. 45-50-32-31; 60, rue de Ponthieu, 8e. Métro: George-V. 43-59-03-83. Agencies at airports.

Budget 3, rue de l'Arrivée, 15e. Métro: Montparnasse-Bienvenue. 45-38-71-60; 4, av. Franklin D. Roosevelt, 8e. Métro: Franklin D. Roosevelt. 42-25-79-89. Agencies at airports and all train stations.

Europcar and National Rent-A-Car 42, av. de Saxe, 7e. Métro: Ségur. 45-67-10-26; 145, av. Malakoff, 16e. Métro: Porte Maillot. 45-00-08-06.

Hertz Aérogare des Invalides, 7e. Métro: Invalides. 45-51-20-37.

Paris Edison Location 176, av. d'Italie. 13e. Métro: Place d'Italie. 45-88-45-00 (one of the least expensive in the city).

Chauffeured Cars

If you want to do everything first-class, try these chauffeured cars, most of them Mercedes:

Bernard Durand et Cie 2, rue de l'Eglise, 92200 Neuilly-sur-Seine. 46-24-37-27.

FAST International 42, av. d'Iéna, 16e. Métro: Iéna. 47-23-88-92.

Murdoch Associates 59, av. Marceau, 16e. Métro: George-V. 47-20-63-28.

See also PARKING.

ELECTRICITY

All the electric current is 220 volts, and plugs are round, 2-pin, standard for Europe. You will need plug adaptors for any 110-volt appliances—hair dryers, razors and so on—and transformers (*transformateurs*), which you can get at the following stores in Paris, or before you leave home:

Bazar de l'Hôtel de Ville 52, rue de Rivoli, 4e. Métro: Hôtel-de-Ville. 42-74-90-00. Closed Sunday.

Galeries Lafayette 40, bd. Haussmann, 9e. Métro: Chaussée-d'Antin. 42-82-34-56. Closed Sunday.

Samaritaine 19, rue de la Monnaie, 1er. Métro: Pont-Neuf. 45-08-33-33. Closed Sunday.

EMBASSIES AND CONSULATES

While embassies generally have higher profiles than consulates, consulates offer far more services to the visitor. Embassies are almost strictly concerned with diplomatic affairs.

Australian Embassy and Consulate 4, rue Jean-Rey, 15e. Métro: Bir-Hakeim. 45-75-62-00.

Canadian Embassy and Consulate 35, av. Montaigne, 8e. Métro: Franklin D. Roosevelt. 47-23-01-01. Tourist services offered.

Canadian Cultural Center 5, rue de Constantine, 7e. Métro: Invalides. 45-51-35-73. Has library, small café, and a bulletin board with housing and job information.

New Zealand Embassy, Consulate, and Cultural Center 7 Ter, rue Léonard-de-Vinci, 16e. Métro: Victor-Hugo. 45-00-24-11.

United Kingdom Embassy 35, rue du Faubourg-St.-Honoré, 8e. Métro: Concorde. 42-66-91-42. *Consulate* 2, Cité du Retiro (3rd floor), 8e. Métro: Concorde. 42-66-91-42. *Cultural Center* 9, rue de Constantine, 7e. Métro: Invalides. 45-51-95-95.

United States of America Embassy 2, av. Gabriel, 8e. Métro: Concorde. 42-96-12-02. *Consulate and Cultural Center* 2, rue St.-Florentin, 8e. Métro: Concorde. 42-61-80-75. Has an American Services Department for those who have lost passports, want to declare stolen possessions, or wish to report any injuries or emergencies. The Cultural Center offers books and newspapers.

EXERCISE SPOTS

The exercise craze has hit Paris, and it's well established. The following is a list of spots where you can dance, stretch, jump, bound yourself into fitness.

Club Harmonie Centre Galaxie, 30, av. d'Italie, 13e. Métro: Tolbiak. 45-80-34-16. Open daily. 100F per day, or 10 tickets for 400F and one ticket is good for one day. Aerobics, Nautilus, sauna, Jacuzzi, swimming pool, tanning. There are 9 Clubs Harmonie throughout Paris. Call here for information.

Le Samouraï 26, rue de Berri, 8e. Métro: George-V. 43-59-04-58. Daily. Gymnastics, aerobics, yoga, modern dance, exercise classes. 200F per week.

Les Gymnases Club Maillot 17, rue du Débarcadère, 17e. Métro: Porte Maillot. 45-74-14-04. Open daily. 100F per day or book of 10 tickets for 400F. Aerobics, boxing, rock and modern dance, golf, sauna, tanning. There's a bar where fruit juices are served. Daycare facilities available. There are nine of these clubs throughout Paris. Call here for information.

Nadine Birtchansky 6, rue St.-Florentin, at the back of the courtyard, 1er. Métro: Concorde. 42-61-66-05. Closed weekends. Gymnastic dance to disco. Price depends on the number of visits.

FABRICS, SEWING ACCESSORIES

If you don't want to buy designer fashions ready-made, you can always buy fabrics and more at the following shops:

Madame Coupon 125, rue Cambronne, 15e. Métro: Vaugirard. 47-34-70-44. Roll ends of Saint-Laurent, Chanel, and other designers. Closed Saturday and Sunday.

Marché-Saint-Pierre 2, rue Charles Nodier, 18e. Métro: Anvers. 46-06-56-34. Four floors of fabrics from synthetics to designer fabrics, pure cotton, wool, and silk. Also, an entire floor of household linens including pure cotton sheets, pillow cases, quilt covers, and kitchen towels. Closed Sunday and Monday morning.

Mendes Tissus 140, rue Montmartre, 2e. Métro: Montmartre. 42-36-02-39. Last year's, or more recent, Saint-Laurent fabrics—all at reduced prices.

Sewing Accessories

Roi du Bouton 19, av. de Clichy, 17e. Métro: Place-Clichy. 45-22-37-76. Closed Sunday and Monday morning.

Ultramode Confection 32, rue Boinod, 18*e*. 42-58-68-38. Métro: Quatre-Septembre. Closed Sunday and Monday.

FASHION

It seems that everyone in Paris dresses well, from those who prefer top designer fashions to students who wear anything from trendy to sloppy, but always coordinated, clothes. There are clothing stores for every taste, pocketbook, and desire. The boutiques listed here are just a small selection of what Paris offers.

Designer shops are scattered throughout the city. Stroll down rue du Faubourg-Saint-Honoré, 8*e*, to see elegant, often astonishing clothes—truly the stuff of which fashion fantasies are made. Walk toward the Place Vendôme, 1*er*, where you'll see the world's most noted jewelers' shops. If you continue far enough down rue Saint-Honoré, 1*er*, you'll get to les Halles, where boutique after boutique offer everything from the latest punk fashion to designer sweatshirts, ultra-trendy shoes, and casual, American-style jeans and sports clothes. Whatever your taste, you can spend hours checking out the stylish, extremely individualist boutiques or racks of used or very inexpensive flea-market type fashions on the street. Go into the depths of the Les Halles shopping mall and, though it lacks the charm of a Parisian street, you will find some of the best names in fashion.

Saint-Germain-des-Prés is a neighborhood tailor-made for shopping, with literally hundreds of shoe stores and individual boutiques to explore for hours. Avenue Victor-Hugo drips with class and style, and many of the more important names have small boutiques there. And there's Avenue Montaigne, for the *haute, haute couture*, in opulent stores with display windows that make even a window-shopping trip a must.

If you want everything in one place, there are the *grands magasins*: Galeries Lafayette, Printemps, Au Bon Marché, Aux Trois Quartiers. These are huge department stores with individual designer sections, so you can get the variety you're after under one roof.

See also SHOES.

Fashion

CHAMPS-ELYSEES AND ARC DE TRIOMPHE

Department Stores

Au Bon Marché 22, rue de Sèvres, 7e. Métro: Sèvres-Babylone. 42-60-33-45. Closed Sunday. AE/DC/V.

Aux Trois Quartiers 17, bd. de la Madeleine, 1er. Métro: Madeleine. 42-60-39-30. Closed Sunday. AE/DC/EC/V.

Brummel 102, rue de Provence, 9e. Métro: Havre-Caumartin. 42-82-50-00. Closed Sunday. This is Le Printemps for men. AE/DC/EC/V.

Galeries Lafayette 40, bd. Haussmann, 9e. Métro: Chaussée-d'Antin. 42-82-34-56. Also at the Tour Montparnasse, 17, rue de l'Arrivée, 15e. Métro: Montparnasse. 45-38-52-87. Both stores closed Sunday. AE/DC/EC/V.

Madelios 10, pl. de la Madeleine, 8e. Métro: Madeleine. 42-60-39-30. This is Aux Trois Quartiers for men. Closed Sunday. AE/DC/EC/V.

Marks and Spencer 35, bd. Haussmann, 9e. Métro: Opéra. 47-42-42-91. Closed Sunday. From England, their favorite department store.

Printemps 64, bd. Haussmann, 9e. Métro: Havre-Caumartin. 42-82-50-00. Closed Sunday. AE/DC/EC/V.

Haute Couture

Carven 6, Rond-Point, 8e. Métro: Champs-Elysées-Clémenceau. 42-25-66-50.

Chanel 31, rue Cambon, 1er. Métro: Concorde. 42-61-54-55.

Christian Dior 30, av. Montaigne, 8e. Métro: Franklin D. Roosevelt. 47-23-54-44.

Courrèges 40, rue François-1er, 8e. Métro: Franklin D. Roosevelt. 47-20-70-44.

Emanuel Ungaro 2, av. Montaigne, 8e. Métro: Franklin D. Roosevelt. 47-23-61-94.

Givenchy 3, av. George-V, 8e. Métro: Alma-Marceau. 47-23-81-36.

Grès 1, rue de la Paix, 2e. Métro: Opéra. 42-61-58-15.

Guy Laroche 29, av. Montaigne, 8e. Métro: Franklin D. Roosevelt. 47-23-78-72.

Hanae Mori Paris 17, av. Montaigne, 8e. Métro: Franklin D. Roosevelt. 47-23-52-03.

Jean-Louis Scherrer 51, av. Montaigne, 8e. Métro: Alma-Marceau. 43-59-55-39.

Fashion

Jean Patou 7, rue St.-Florentin, 8e. Métro: Concorde. 42-60-17-92.

Lanvin 22, rue du Faubourg-St.-Honoré, 8e. Métro: Madeleine. 42-65-14-40.

Louis Féraud 88, rue du Faubourg-St.-Honoré, 8e. Métro: St.-Philippe-du-Roule. 42-65-32-84.

Nina Ricci 39, av. Montaigne, 8e. Métro: Franklin D. Roosevelt. 47-23-78-88.

Pierre Balmain 44, rue François-1er, 8e. Métro: Franklin D. Roosevelt. 47-20-35-34.

Pierre Cardin 29, rue du Faubourg-St.-Honoré, 8e. Métro: Champs-Elysées Clémenceau. 42-66-92-25.

Ted Lapidus 35, rue François-1er, 8e. Métro: Franklin D. Roosevelt. 47-20-69-33.

Torrente 9, rue du Faubourg-St.-Honoré, 8e. Métro: 42-66-14-14.

Yves Saint Laurent 5, av. Marceau, 8e. Métro: Alma-Marceau. 47-23-72-71.

Discount Designers

The following shops sell designer clothing at reduced prices, sometimes by as much as 50 percent off. They are often last year's styles, but not always. Since they're classics, it doesn't matter anyway, and there are great bargains to be had.

Cacharel Stock 114, rue d'Alésia, 14e. Métro: Alésia. 45-42-53-04. For men and women. Closed Sunday. AE/DC/V.

Courrèges 7, rue de Turbigo, 1st floor, 1er. Métro: Etienne-Marcel. 42-33-03-57. For women. Closed Sunday.

Dorothée Bis Stock 74, rue d'Alésia, 14e. Métro: Alésia. 45-42-40-68. For women. Some sportswear as well. Closed Sunday. AE/DC/V.

Mendes 65, rue Montmartre, 2e. Métro: Sentier. 42-36-83-32. For women. Closed Sunday.

Mic Mac Stock 13, rue Laugier, 17e. Métro: Ternes. 46-22-58-19. For men and women. Closed Sunday. AE/DC/V.

Rodier 11, bd. de la Madeleine, 1er. Métro: Madeleine. 42-61-51-55. For men and women. Closed Saturday and Sunday. AE/DC/V.

Stock Austerlitz Daniel Hechter 16, bd. de l'Hôpital,

13e. Métro: Austerlitz. 47-07-88-44. For men and women. Closed Sunday and Monday morning V.

Other Fashions

Au Petit Matelot 27, av. de la Grande-Armée, 16e. Métro: Argentine. 45-00-15-51. French sailors' clothes, beautiful woolens for men, women and children. Closed Sunday and Monday morning.

Benetton 63, rue de Rennes, 6e. Métro: St.-Sulpice. 45-48-80-92; 13, rue Tronchet, 8e. Métro: Madeleine. 42-66-63-77; 75, rue de Passy, 16e. Métro: La Muette. 42-88-54-10; 82, av. Victor-Hugo, 16e. Métro: Victor-Hugo. 47-27-73-73. All stores closed Sunday. Men's and women's clothes.

Cacharel 74, av. des Champs-Elysées, 8e. Métro: Franklin D. Roosevelt. 45-63-23-09; 34, rue Tronchet, 9e. Métro: St.-Lazare. 47-42-11-46. Both stores closed Sunday. Men's, women's, and children's clothes. AE/DC/V.

Chloé 3, rue de Gribeauval, 7e. Métro: Bac. 45-44-02-04; 60, rue du Faubourg-St.-Honoré, 8e. Métro: Concorde. 42-66-01-39. Both stores closed Sunday. Women's clothes only. AE/DC/V.

Courrèges 49, rue de Rennes, 6e. Métro: St.-Germain-des-Prés. 45-48-08-71; 40, rue François-1er, 8e. Métro: George V. 47-20-70-44. Closed Sunday. Men's and women's clothes. There are several other Courrèges boutiques in Paris. AE/DC/V.

Daniel Hechter 146, bd. St.-Germain, 6e. Métro: Odéon. 43-26-96-36. Closed Sunday. Men's and women's clothes. AE/DC/V.

Dorothée Bis 33, rue de Sèvres, 6e. Métro: Sèvres-Babylone. 42-22-00-45. Closed Sunday. Women only. There are several other Dorothée Bis boutiques in Paris.

Issey Miyake 201, bd. St.-Germain, 7e. Métro: Bac. 45-44-60-88. Closed Sunday. Men's and women's clothes. AE/DC/V.

Kenzo 3, pl. des Victoires, 2e. Métro: Palais-Royal. 42-36-81-41. Closed Sunday. Men's and women's clothes. AE/V.

Laura Ashley 94, rue de Rennes, 6e. Métro: Rennes. 45-48-43-89; 95, av. Raymond-Poincaré, 16e. Métro: Victor-Hugo. 45-01-24-73. Both stores closed Sunday and Monday morning. Women's clothes only. V.

Fashion

quarante et un (*kah-rahn-tay-uhn*) **41**

Mic Mac 13, rue de Tournon, 6e. Métro: Odéon. 43-54-44-99; 46, av. Victor-Hugo, 16e. Métro: Charles-de-Gaulle-Etoile. 45-01-87-52; Forum Les Halles, niveau-1, Porte Rambuteau, 1er. Métro: Les Halles. 42-96-91-44. Men's and women's clothes. Women's only at the Victor-Hugo address. Closed Sunday. AE/V.

Montana 31, rue de Grenelle, 7e. Métro: Sèvres-Babylone. 42-22-69-56. Women's clothes only. Closed Sunday. AE/DC/V.

Sonia Rykiel 6, rue de Grenelle, 6e. Métro: Sèvres-Babylone. 42-22-43-22; 70, rue du Faubourg-St.-Honoré, 8e. Métro: Concorde. 42-65-20-81. Both stores closed Sunday. Men's and women's clothes. AE.

Yohji Yamamoto 47, rue Etienne-Marcel, 1er. Métro: Etienne-Marcel. 45-08-82-45. Closed Sunday. Women's clothes only. AE/DC/V.

FLOOR SHOWS

Alcazar de Paris 62, rue Mazarine, 6e. Métro: Odéon. 43-29-02-20. Dinner at 8:30 PM, floor show at 10 PM, and disco dancing afterwards. AE/DC/EC/V.

Belle Epoque 36, rue des Petits-Champs, 2e. Métro: Pyramides. 42-96-33-33. French cabaret acts and singers in a 1900s decor. Preceded by dinner. AE/DC/EC/V.

Cabaret L'Ane Rouge 3, rue Laugier, 17e. Métro: Ternes. 47-66-45-12. Dinner and show afterwards. French cancan, magicians, and impersonators. Open daily.

Cabaret Michou 80, rue des Martyrs, 18e. Métro: Pigalle. 46-06-16-04. Burlesque show. Open daily.

Canne à Sucre 4, rue Ste.-Beuve, 6e. Métro: Vavin. 42-22-23-25. Orchestra from the Antilles, Créole cuisine, show, and dancing. Closed Sunday and Monday. AE/DC/V.

Chez Hippolyte 23, av. du Maine, 14e. Métro: Montparnasse. 45-44-64-13. Clowns on roller skates serve dinner; floor show and dancing afterwards. Closed Tuesday. AE/DC/V.

Crazy Horse Saloon 12, av. George-V, 8e. Métro: Alma-Marceau. 47-23-32-32. A floor show, considered one of the best. No meals. AE/DC/EC/V.

Etoile de Moscou 6, rue Arsène-Houssaye, 8e. Métro: Etoile. 45-63-63-12. Russian and Tzigane music and dancing. Open daily. AE/DC/V.

Lido 116 bis, av. des Champs-Elysées, 8e. Métro: George-V. 45-63-11-61. Dinner at 8 PM. Lots of sound and light and dancing between shows. AE/DC/V.

Paradis Latin 28, rue du Cardinal Lemoine, 5e. Métro: Cardinal Lemoine. 43-25-28-28. Both dinner theater and champagne theater, staged with skill. AE/DC/V.

FLEA MARKETS

See MARKETS.

FLOWER MARKETS

See MARKETS.

FOOD

Paris is a temple to food—a temple built by armies of bakers, many of whom still rise in the dead of night to fire up ovens so bread is baked by dawn; by legion butchers who are at their craft with the first ray of light; by pastry chefs, *confiseurs* (candy makers), *charcutiers* who work diligently behind closed doors, their products speaking for their dedication. The quality of life in Paris is due in large part to the flavors, scents, and sights of golden pastries, hearty pâtés, and beautiful breads that illuminate so many windows throughout the city.

For information on food markets, see MARKETS.

For specialty foods, see SHOPPING.

Bread

Bread is the ever-present ingredient of every French meal. Whether it be a crisp-crusted, creamy white baguette, a hearty golden *pain au levain*, or a round, light *pain de campagne*, its eternal presence complements each dish, sops up sauces, cleans utensils, fills in the gaps, provides a foil for cheese.

The quality of bread in France has suffered in recent years. Many bakers are trying to change that by resisting modern technology that cuts down on time but adversely affects quality. More bakers are returning to traditional methods, perhaps charging a bit more but producing better-quality bread.

Look for a blue-and-white sign on bakery windows showing a stylized baker holding a bread paddle and leaning into an oven. While it's no guarantee of quality, it means the baker is aspiring to the "good bread movement." A key characteristic of good bread is a creamy instead of a bright white dough filled with lots of irregular holes, and a good, crisp crust.

Bread Glossary

Baguette The thin, long loaf synonymous with Paris. Its weight is standard (250 grams—4 ounces), its price regulated, its ingredients uniform (flour, salt, yeast, water). Ideal for sandwiches.

Ficelle (or Flûte) A very thin loaf, mostly crust. For a special breakfast treat, cut the loaf lengthwise and spread with *beurre des Charentes* (a type of salted butter).

Pain au Son Bran bread.

Pain au Levain (*Cuit au Feu de Bois*) The epitome of country bread when it's well made—a sourdough loaf with a thick crust (baked in wood-fired ovens).

Pain Brioché Eggs, milk, and sugar are added to baguette dough.

Pain Complet Whole-wheat bread.

Pain de Campagne Usually a round loaf (called "*miche*") that can be anything from a glorified baguette dough to a satisfying country loaf.

Pain de Fantaisie Bread sold by the piece, not by the loaf.

Pain Noir A combination of buckwheat and rye bread.

Pain de Seigle Rye bread.

Pain Viennois A baguette, though milk and sugar are added to the dough.

Petit Pain A small roll made with flour, salt, yeast, and water.

Bakeries

A la Petite Marquise 91, rue de la Convention, 15e. Métro: Boucicaut. 45-54-50-20. Closed Sunday. Also 3, pl. Victor-Hugo, 16e. Métro: Victor-Hugo. 45-00-77-36. Closed Sunday.

Food

Boulangerie Moderne 16, rue des Fossés-St.-Jacques, 5e. Métro: Luxembourg. 43-54-12-22. Closed Saturday afternoon and Sunday.

Boulangerie Perruche 68, rue du Cardinal Lemoine, 5e. Métro: Cardinal-Lemoine. 43-26-34-62. Closed Sunday and Monday.

Boulangerie Vacher 55, bd. Gouvion-St.-Cyr, 17e. Métro: Porte Maillot. 45-74-04-50. Open 7 AM to 8 PM. Closed Wednesday and Thursday.

Boutique du Pain 11, rue Gustave-Flaubert, 18e. Métro: Ternes. 47-63-75-68. Open 7:30 AM to 8:30 PM. Closed Sunday and Monday.

Gourmet Pressé 16, pl. de la Nation, 12e. Métro: Nation. 43-07-62-87. Closed Sunday.

Lionel Poilâne 8, rue du Cherche-Midi, 6e. Métro: Sèvres-Babylone. 45-48-42-59. Closed Sunday. Also 49, bd. de Grenelle, 15e. Métro: Bir-Hakeim/Grenelle. 45-79-11-49. Closed Monday.

Max Poilâne 87, rue Brançion, 15e. Métro: Porte de Vanves. 48-28-45-90. Closed Monday.

Panetier Lebon 10, pl. des Petits-Pères, 2e. Métro: Bourse. 42-60-90-23. Closed weekends.

Place Monge Market Stall 61, Place Monge, 5e. Métro: Monge. Open Wednesday, Friday and Sunday morning.

Roger Barré 69, rue Léon-Frot, 11e. Métro: Charonne. 43-79-55-56. Closed Friday and Saturday.

Charcuteries and Take-Out Food

There are hundreds—even thousands—of *charcuteries* throughout Paris that sell everything from pâtés, sausages, cooked, smoked or aged hams, foie gras, and pigs feet to carrot salads, cooked artichokes, steaming *choucroute*, usually hot right at lunchtime, for a fine take-out meal or a picnic to go. Some *charcutiers* make their own products, searching the country far and wide for good-quality ingredients; others buy from small producers; still others sell industrially produced products. The following is a short list of *charcuteries* that either make their own products or go to considerable effort to find small producers who make good-quality *charcuterie*. These shops also offer everything from sweet and savory pastries to entire take-out meals.

A la Ville de Rodez 72, rue Vieille-du-Temple, 4e. Métro: St.-Paul. 48-87-79-36. Closed Sunday and Monday.

Bonney-Comestibles-Salaisons 112, rue Mouffetard, 5e. Métro: Censier-Daubenton. 47-07-98-19. Closed Monday.

Boucheries Bernard 19, rue Danielle-Casanova, 1er. Métro: Pyramides. 42-61-57-57. Closed Sunday and Monday.

Caviar Kaspia 17, pl. de la Madeleine, 8e. Métro: Madeleine. 42-65-33-52. Closed Sunday. Caviar, smoked salmon, and blinis to go.

Chedeville et Bourdon 12, rue du Marché-St.-Honoré, 1er. Métro: Tuileries. 42-61-11-11. They also have a shop at the Roissy–Charles de Gaulle and Orly-Ouest airports. This house supplies many of Paris' grand restaurants.

Chez Teil 6, rue de Lappe, 11e. Métro: Bastille. 47-00-41-28. Closed Monday.

Coesnon 30, rue Dauphine, 6e. Métro: Odéon. 43-26-56-39. Closed Sunday and Monday.

Dalloyau 101, rue du Faubourg-St.-Honoré, 8e. Métro: Champs-Elysees. 43-59-18-10. Open daily. 69, rue de la Convention, 15e. Métro: Javel. 45-77-84-27. Closed Monday. Centre commercial Beaugrenelle 36, rue Linois, 15e. Métro: Charles-Michels. 45-75-59-92. Closed Sunday. 2, pl. Edmond-Rostand, 6e. Métro: Luxembourg. 43-29-31-10. Open daily.

Fauchon 26, pl. de la Madeleine, 8e. Métro: Madeleine. 47-42-60-11. Closed Sunday; just the pastry shop is open on Monday. AE/DC/V. Fauchon's huge picture windows are filled with glorious presentations of classic *charcuterie*—pâtés, salads, poached salmon, roast duck, exotic fruit. And across the street are the equally beautiful pastries.

Flo Prestige 42, pl. du Marché-St.-Honoré, 1er. Métro: Pyramides. 42-61-45-46. Open daily. AE/DC/V. Also, 61, av. de la Grande-Armée, 16e. Métro: Argentine. 45-00-12-10. Open daily. AE/DC/V. Impeccable presentation and quality of cheeses, pâtés, foie gras, and smoked salmon in a sophisticated, ultramodern setting. Foods to take away, perfect for an elegant picnic.

Galoche D'Aurillac 41, rue Lappe, 11e. Métro: Bastille. 47-00-77-15. Closed Sunday and Monday.

Gargantua 284, rue St.-Honoré, 1er. Métro: Tuileries. 42-60-63-38. Closed Sunday. AE/V. A *charcuterie* with everything from pâtés to nuts—even a small bar in the back for coffee and delicious pastries.

Food

Hédiard 21, pl. de la Madeleine, 8e. Métro: Madeleine. 42-66-44-36. Closed Sunday. This old and fashionable shop offers exotic fruits, their own coffees, teas, *confitures* (jams), spices, and their specialty—*pâtés de fruits* (fresh-fruit gum bonbons that are rolled in sugar). There are several other Hédiard shops in Paris.

Lenôtre 44, rue d'Auteuil, 16e. Métro: Michel-Ange-Auteuil. 45-24-52-52. Open daily. 49, av. Victor-Hugo, 16e. Métro: Victor-Hugo. 45-01-71-71. Closed Monday. 3, rue du Havre, Métro: St.-Lazare. 45-22-22-59. Closed Sunday. 121, av. Wagram, 17e. Métro: Ternes. Closed Monday. 44, rue du Bac, 7e. Métro: Bac. 42-22-39-39. Closed Monday.

Maison Pou 16, av. des Ternes, 17e. Métro: Ternes. 43-80-19-24. Closed Monday and Sunday. AE/DC/V.

Paul Corcellet 46, rue des Petits-Champs, 2e. Métro: Pyramides. 42-96-51-82. Closed Sunday and Monday.

Peletier 66, rue de Sèvres, 7e. Métro: Vaneau 47-34-06-62. Closed Monday.

Petrossian 18, bd. de Latour-Maubourg, 7e. Métro: Invalides. 45-51-70-64. Closed Sunday and Monday. Their specialties are caviar, which they travel to Russia to choose themselves, and melt-in-your-mouth Norwegian salmon, which they smoke themselves. They also sell foie gras, vodka, pastries to take away, and tea.

Produits d'Auvergne-Graineterie 46–48, rue Daubenton, 5e. Métro: Censier-Daubenton. 43-31-52-92. Closed Monday.

Schmid 41, rue Legendre, 17e. Métro: Villiers. 47-63-31-04. Closed Monday.

Vaudron 4, rue de la Jonquière, 17e. Métro: Guy-Moquet. 46-27-96-97. Closed Monday.

Cheese

The cheeses found in Paris—more than 150 kinds from every part of France—are astounding. Whether pyramid-shaped, ash-dusted goat cheeses or huge rounds of Beaufort, sharp yet creamy Roquefort, or logs of smooth Bleu d'Auvergne, they grace *fromagerie* (cheese shop) shelves throughout the city. While more and more French cheese is made with pasteurized milk, which detracts from its flavor and texture, there is still much cheese available that is made with good, raw milk and according to traditional methods.

When buying cheese, look or ask for *fromage au lait cru* or *fromage fermier* and you'll get the real thing, made with unpasteurized milk.

If you want a delicious Camembert cheese, ask for "Camembert moulé à la louche," which is made in Normandy for cheese connoisseurs and is only available in France.

Alain Dubois 80, rue de Tocqueville, 17e. Métro: Villiers. 42-27-11-38. A vast selection of raw milk cheeses, particularly goat cheeses. Closed Sunday afternoon and Monday.

Androuët 41, rue d'Amsterdam, 8e. Métro Liège. 48-74-26-90. M. Androuët is the master of cheeses, and his more than 300 varieties are some of the best in the city. A restaurant on the first floor offers a sumptuous, seven-course cheese *dégustation*, or tasting. Reservations necessary. Closed Sunday. AE/DC.

Assiette aux Fromages 2, rue Mouffetard, 5e. Métro: Monge. 45-35-14-21. Open daily. V. This is a sparkling new addition to the cheese scene in Paris, featuring cheese from throughout France, something for everyone. They concentrate on quality, raw-milk offerings, but you'll find "La Vache Qui Rit" also. A pleasant, airy restaurant located at the back of the shop, on a small courtyard, features hearty, regional dishes, many made with cheese.

Ferme Saint-Hubert 21, rue Vignon, 8e. Métro: Madeleine. 47-42-79-20. A chic spot to buy excellent quality cheese. The restaurant next door offers two cheese *dégustations*, one of goat cheeses, the other a variety that changes according to the seasons. Closed Sunday and Monday.

Ferme Sainte-Suzanne 17, rue Le Marais, 16e. Métro: Luxembourg. 42-88-00-66. This pretty little *fromagerie* tucked away on a tiny street has a small restaurant in back that offers a modest, but very good quality, cheese *dégustation*. Closed Saturday and Sunday.

Jean Carmes et Fils 24, rue de Lévis, 17e. Métro: Villiers. 47-63-88-94. These people love cheese and their busy shop is filled with regulars who come for the high quality and personal attention. Closed Sunday afternoon and Monday.

Tachon 38, rue de Richelieu, 1er. Métro: Palais-Royal. 42-96-08-66. This is an eye-catching shop, with its shelf-upon-shelf of excellent cheese and old-fashioned appeal. Closed Sunday and Monday.

Chocolate

French chocolates are some of the best in the world. The French revere chocolate, and for every season, every holiday, there are small monuments in chocolate on display throughout the city. The following shops have been chosen for the quality of the ingredients in their chocolates, their freshness and their flavor.

Chocolats de Puyricard 27, av. Rapp, 7e. Métro: Alma-Marceau. 47-05-59-47. Closed Sunday. A favorite with Parisians, who line up starting at about 11 each morning, for the fresh, good-quality chocolates.

Lenôtre 44, rue du Bac, 7e. Métro: Bac. 42-22-39-39; 5, rue du Havre, 9e. Métro: St.-Lazare. 45-22-22-59; 49, av. Victor-Hugo, 16e. Métro: Victor-Hugo. 45-01-71-71; 41, rue d'Auteuil, 16e. Métro: Michel-Ange-Auteuil. 45-24-52-52. Beautiful shops, impeccable and elegant chocolates with subtle but substantial chocolate punch. Shops closed Monday except rue d'Auteuil.

Maison du Chocolat 225, rue du Faubourg-St.-Honoré, 8e. Métro: Ternes. 42-27-39-44. Looking like a box of chocolates itself, this shop offers the best handmade chocolates in Paris. Closed Sunday and Monday.

Marquise de Sévigné 32, pl. de la Madeleine, 8e. Métro: Madeleine. 42-65-19-47. Closed Sunday. An elegant shop with a tea shop in back where you can sample their pastries with a cup of coffee, before—or after—you've chosen your chocolates. Also at 1, pl. Victor-Hugo. Métro: Victor-Hugo. 45-00-89-68.

Millet 103, rue St.-Dominique, 7e. Métro: Latour-Maubourg. 45-51-49-80. Closed Monday. They make chocolates that are sold by some of the biggest shops in town, as well as stocking their own shop with rich, lovely chocolates.

Petite Fabrique 19, rue Daval, 11e. Métro: Bréguet-Sabin. 48-05-82-02. This is a funny little shop that offers a small selection of rustic, handmade chocolates, all of good quality. Closed Sunday and Wednesday.

Weiss Palais des Congrès, Porte Maillot, 17e. Metro: Porte-Maillot. 47-58-21-55. Noted for their truffles, considered by many to be the best in Paris.

Frites (French Fries)

It is said that the first *frites*—then called *pommes Pont-Neuf*—were sold from roving carts on the Pont-Neuf in 17th-century Paris. Pommes Pont-Neuf are still available; they are thin, dainty *frites* usually accompanying the grilled meats served in cafés, bistros, and brasseries, or with sausages bought from a sidewalk stand. More and more *frites* are, sadly, the precut, frozen variety. But there are still some holdouts, those hearty folk who cut their own and fry them in good, fresh oil. If you like your *frites* crisp and crunchy, ask for them *bien cuites*.

Frite Stand 49, rue du Mazarine, 6e. Métro: Odéon. Perhaps the best *frites* in Paris—discs of crunchy fried potatoes generously served in a paper cone.

Gueuze 19, rue Soufflot, 5e. Métro: Luxembourg. 43-54-63-00.

Ma Bourgogne 19, pl. des Vosges, 4e. Métro: St.-Paul. 42-78-44-64. *Frites* are great here with beer, or with nothing else but the view onto the Place des Vosges.

Mort Subite 20, rue Mouffetard, 5e. Métro: Monge. 43-31-41-48. Try *steak frites* or just *frites* with an oversized bottle of Mort Subite.

Ice Cream

On a warm day in Paris you can see people from one end of the city to the other lapping up delicious ice cream. And it is available at almost every pastry shop—usually from a stand right outside the front door—in signature flavors of *cassis* (black currant), *noisette* (hazelnut), and of course *chocolat* (chocolate), *vanille* (vanilla), and *fraise* (strawberry).

Berthillon 31, rue St.-Louis-en-l'Ile, 4e. Métro: Pont-Marie. 43-54-31-61. The undisputed king of ice cream in Paris. Closed Monday and Tuesday.

Clichy 5, bd. Beaumarchais, 3e. Métro: Bastille. 48-87-89-88. Closed Monday.

Lenôtre 44, rue du Bac, 7e. Métro: Bac. 42-22-39-39. Closed Monday. (For other Lenôtre addresses, see FOOD—CHOCOLATE).

Peletier 66, rue de Sèvres, 7e. Métro: Vaneau. 47-34-06-62. Closed Monday.

Pastries

Ah, Paris and her pastries. Window after window of irresistible *croissants* (butter-layered, yeast-dough breakfast pastry), *pains au chocolat* (pillow-shaped *croissant* pastry with a stick—sometimes two—of

Food

chocolate inside), *brioche* (butter-and-egg–rich cake-like bread), *chaussons-aux-pommes* (puff pastry apple turnovers), gleaming fruit tarts and cream-filled cakes, dainty *madeleines* and almond *financiers*. Look for pastry shops displaying the *pur beurre* sign in the window; it means everything is made with butter only. If you see *au beurre*, it means they use butter, but not exclusively. When asking for a croissant, specify *croissant au beurre* unless you want one made with margarine (*croissants ordinaires*). The following *pâtisseries* have been included in this list because of the high quality and appeal of their pastries.

Bonbonnière de Buci 12, rue de Buci, 6e. Métro: Mabillon. 43-26-97-13. Their specialty is a chocolate *oursin*—a small tart mounded high with creamy, rich chocolate. Closed Tuesday.

Fremont 24, pl. de la Nation, 12e. Métro: Nation. 43-43-77-36. Their specialties are coffee, chocolate, nut macaroons, and *madeleines*. Closed Monday.

Hellegouarch 185, rue de Vaugirard, 15e. Métro: Pasteur. 47-83-29-72. Worth a special trip for the mouthwatering *croissants* and *pains au chocolat*. Closed Monday and August.

Hellegouarch/Pâtisserie Montmartre 81, rue du Mont-Cenis, 18e. Métro: Jules-Joffrin. 46-06-39-28. Excellent *pain au chocolat*, and a small *salon de thé* for light meals. Open daily.

Lerch 4, rue du Cardinal Lemoine, 5e. Métro: Cardinal-Lemoine. 43-26-15-80. Monsieur Lerch is known for his fresh fruit tarts, but his *madeleines* and *kougelhopf* are worth a detour. Closed Monday and Tuesday.

Lubré 18, rue Surcouf, 7e. Métro: Invalides. 45-55-50-25. Huge, delicious *croissants*, inventive cakes (sometimes a carrot cake), and good *sablés* (butter cookies). Closed Sunday.

Millet 103, rue St.-Dominique, 7e. Métro: Latour-Maubourg. 45-51-49-80. Some of the finest *croissants* and *pains au chocolat* in Paris, not to mention their honey *madeleines*, *financiers* and luscious *gâteaux Opéra*. Closed Monday and August.

Moule à Gâteau 111, rue Mouffetard, 5e. Métro: Censier-Daubenton. 43-31-80-47; 10, rue Poncelet, 17e. Métro: Ternes. 47-63-06-49. Both shops are closed Monday. The pastries in these shops—part of a growing group under the same management—are all made with butter, and are sparkling delicious. They use lots of nuts in their cakes, which are all available by the slice. The *croissants* and *pains au chocolat* melt in your mouth, especially first thing in the morning.

Peletier 66, rue de Sèvres, 7e. Métro: Vaneau. 47-34-06-62. For inventive, beautiful, elegant cakes, this is the place. There's a small bar in back that serves coffee to enjoy with the fresh pastry of your choice. Closed Monday.

Poujauran 20, rue Jean Nicot, 7e. Métro: Latour-Maubourg. 47-05-80-88. Pound cake with fruits and nuts, gingerbread, *financiers*. Closed Saturday and Sunday.

Saint-Paul 4, rue de Rivoli, 4e. Métro: St.-Paul. 48-87-87-16. Beautiful pastries that are always impeccable in presentation and taste. Try their *Quatre-quarts* (pound cake). Closed Monday and Tuesday.

Wine

The best way to learn about France's wines is to taste them. If you're serious about learning, you can go into many wine shops and discuss what you are looking for with the proprietor. You'll pick up some good advice, including hints on what wine goes with which food and what's best that year for storing in your wine cellar.

Cave de Georges Duboeuf 9, rue Marbeuf, 8e. Métro: Alma-Marceau. 47-20-71-23. This shop has a good selection of, among others, Monsieur Duboeuf's beaujolais. Closed Sunday, Monday, and August.

Cave Michel Renaud 12, pl. de la Nation, 12e. Métro: Nation. 43-07-98-93. M. Renaud specializes in small wines at reasonable prices; he also has some well-known wines. Open daily.

Jean Danflou 36, rue du Mont-Thabor, 1er. Métro: Concorde. 42-61-51-09. You can make an appointment for a personal tasting tour of Monsieur Danflou's selection of *eaux-de-vie* (clear fruit-based brandies), which he dispenses with generosity and much information. Closed weekends and August 1–15.

Lucien Legrand Filles et Fils 12, Galerie Vivienne, 2e. Métro: Bourse. 42-60-07-12. Some of Monsieur Legrand's wines, most of them from small productions, are available for tasting. English spoken. Closed Sunday and Monday.

Printemps Nation 25, cours de Vincennes, 20e. Métro: Nation. 43-71-12-14. There is quite an impressive wine department at this department-cum-specialty store.

Food

Steven Spurrier-Caves de la Madeleine 25, rue Royale (Cité Berryer), 8e. Métro: Madeleine. 42-65-92-40. This shop, started and still owned by English proprietors, is tucked away in the lively Cité Berryer. They offer a wide assortment of wines from their specialty—Burgundies—to selections from Provence, Italy, and Spain. They also have a variety of *eaux-de-vie*. Closed Sunday.

Use the following wine card to help you choose the vintage.

COMPARATIVE QUALITIES OF THE WINES OF FRANCE

★ EXCEPTIONAL VINTAGES : 1921, 1928, 1929, 1945 ★

VINTAGE	Red Bordeaux	White Bordeaux	Red Burgundy	White Burgundy	Côtes du Rhône Growths	Alsace	Pouilly s/Loire Sancerre	Anjou Touraine	Beaujolais
1947	★	••••	••••		★			★	
1949	★	••••	★		••••			••••	
1955	★	••••	••••	•••	••••			••••	
1959	•••	••••	★	•••	•••	★		★	
1961	★	★	★	••••	••••	••••		•••	
1962	••••	•••	•••	••••	••••	••		•••	
1964	•••	••	••••	•••	•••	•••			
1966	••••	•••	••••	••••	••••	••••			
1967	•••	★	•••	•••	••••	••••			
1969	•	••	••••	••••	•••	•••			••••
1970	★	•••	•••	★	★	•••			
1971	••••	•••	••••	••••	••••	★		•••	
1973	•••	•••	••	•••		••••		••	
1974	••	•••	•••	•••				••	
1975	••••	••••	•••	••	••••	••••		•••	
1976	••••	••••	••••	••••	••••	★		••••	
1977	••	••	••	•••		••		•••	
1978	••••	•••	★	••••	★	••		•••	
1979	••••	••••	•••	★	••••	••••		•••	
1980	••	••	•••	•••	•••	••	•••	••	•
1981	••••	•••	••	•••	•••	••••	••	•••	•••
1982	★	•••	•••	••••	••	•••	••••	••••	•••
1983	••••	••••	••••	••••	•••	★	••••	••••	★
1984	••	••	•••	•••	••	••	••	•••	••
1985	Abundant harvest of very fine quality								

Average vintage •   Medium vintage ••   Good vintage •••   Great vintage ••••   Exceptional vintage ★

Food

FRENCH COURSES

There are almost as many possibilities for French classes in Paris as there are aspiring students who want to learn French. The following is a list of the most recognized schools and organizations.

Alliance Française 101, bd. Raspail, 6e. Métro: Notre-Dame-des-Champs. 45-44-38-28. Make an appointment to take the obligatory entrance exam. A passport and personal photo, plus the monthly fee, are all that are necessary to enroll. They offer regular or intensive courses. Students can sign up at any time during the year.

Eurocentre 13, passage Dauphine, 6e. Métro: Odéon. 43-25-81-40. Offers 3-week, 4-week, or 1-month sessions for beginning and advanced students, 6 hours a day; 5 days a week obligatory. No visa required.

France Langues 2, rue Sfax, 16e. Métro: Victor-Hugo. 45-00-40-15. Offers 4- to 12-week sessions. Classes have 20 to 30 students each.

Institut Catholique de Paris 21, rue d'Assas, 6e. Métro: Rennes. 42-22-41-80. Classes divided into 2 semesters, from mid-October to mid-February, and from mid-February to mid-June. Offers grammar, phonetics, translation, French civilization, commercial French.

Institut Français de Langues Vivantes 46, bd. St.-Michel, 6e. Métro: St.-Michel. 43-26-08-70. Offers private tutors to small groups, at all levels. Students can register at any time during the year.

La Sorbonne 47, rue des Ecoles, 5e. 43-29-12-13. This famous university offers extensive French language and civilization courses at all levels. There are 16-week sessions and summer programs of varying lengths. A high school diploma is required. For an application, write to the Cours de Civilisation Française, La Sorbonne (address above).

Paris American Academy 9, rue des Ursulines, 5e. Métro: Luxembourg. 43-29-38-83. Offers all levels of classes from October to May.

For more information about French courses, go to the Centre d'Information et de Documentation Jeunesse, 101, quai Branly, 15e. Métro: Bir-Hakeim. 45-66-40-20. If you're self-motivated, you can learn French on your own by using the French language tapes at the Centre Georges Pompidou library. Entrance to and use of the library is free. You can stay as long as you like, but you must give up your booth after an hour and wait in line again. The collection of tapes is excellent, the staff very helpful, and the crowd there to use the facility truly international. It's best to get there early. It's a popular place to study and space is limited. Open noon to 10 PM Monday and Wednesday through Friday; open 10 AM to 10 PM Saturday and Sunday.

GALLERIES

The majority of galleries are located in basically three neighborhoods in Paris. If your time is limited you can choose the type of art to see, and go to the appropriate neighborhood.

The plush, well-established galleries that show primarily 19th- and 20th-century figurative work, most exclusively by masters of the Ecole Française both living and dead, are on the Right Bank, along the rue du Faubourg-Saint-Honoré and avenue Matignon.

Galleries on the Left Bank tend to represent new and international art movements. You can find rich naïf (naïve) collections, contemporary and ancient engravings, many galleries specializing in Asian art, and some in art from Africa. The galleries are grouped primarily on the streets that begin at the Place de l'Odéon (6e) and run toward the Seine—rue de Seine, rue des Beaux-Arts, rue Bonaparte, rue Mazarine, and rue Jacob.

The following is not a complete list of galleries in Paris. There are literally hundreds, and many of them open and close with regular frequency. While the artists mentioned here with each gallery may not currently have works on display, they are listed to give a specific idea of the nature of each gallery. For up-to-date information, buy *L'Officiel des Galeries*, available at any kiosk. Note that most galleries are closed Sunday, Monday, and the entire month of August.

Right Bank

André Pacitti 174, rue du Faubourg-St.-Honoré, 8e. Métro: Ternes. 45-63-75-30. Works by Edmond Ceria, Martin Dieterle, Jean Dureuil, Lapicque, Mulh.

Arcadia 54, rue du Faubourg-St.-Honoré (Cour des Antiquaires), 8e. Métro: St.-Philippe-du-Roule. 42-66-55-20. Works by Rozzolini, Goetz, Poliakoff, Vieira da Silva.

Ariel 140, bd. Haussmann, 8e. Métro: Miromesnil. 45-62-13-09. Appel, Doucet, Gillet, Tabuci, Weidemann, Alechinsky, Bitran, Dubuffet, Hartung, Jorn, Poliakoff, Debré, Lindström, Marfaing.

Artcurial 9, av. Matignon, 8e. Métro: Franklin D. Roosevelt. 42-99-16-16. An art bookstore and gallery. Primarily the 20th-century masters: Arp, DeChirico, Max Ernst, Magritte, Zadkine, sculptures by Dubré, Signori.

Art France 36, av. Matignon, 8e. Métro: Franklin D. Roosevelt. 43-59-17-89 or 45-62-80-37. Sculptures by Jean Carton, Fusans, Genis.

Bernheim Jeune 83, rue Faubourg-St.-Honoré, 8e. Métro: Franklin D. Roosevelt. 42-66-60-31. Bonnard, Derain, Kisling, Laurencin, Marquet, Vallotin, Zingg. Closed Saturday, Sunday, and Monday.

Cailleux 136, rue du Faubourg-St.-Honoré, 1er. Métro: St.-Philippe-du-Roule. 43-59-25-24. 18th-century French artists: Fragonard, Boucher, Watteau, Lancret.

Drouart 16, rue de la Grange-Batelière, 9e. Métro: Richelieu-Drouot. 47-70-52-90. Small 19th-century masters, Asian art, Marc Serret, and Cavanna.

Hervé Odermatt 85, rue du Faubourg-St.-Honoré, 8e. Métro: St.-Philippe-du-Roule. 42-66-92-58. Léger, Picasso, Renoir, Germaine Richier, Rouault, Kuper, Penalba, Velickovic, Thierry Leproust, Utsimiya.

Louise Leiris 47, rue de Monceau, 8e. Métro: Villiers, 45-63-28-85. Elie Lascaux, Léger, Picasso, Rouvre.

Maeght-Lelong 13 and 14, rue de Téhéran, 8e. Métro: Miromesnil. 45-63-13-19. Arakawa, Bazaine, Chagall, Miró, Bram van Velde, Calder, Giacometti.

Marumo 243, rue St.-Honoré, 1er. Métro: Tuileries. 42-60-08-66. Artists from the Barbizon School, including Le Grec, Albert, Malet, Raumann.

Mathias Fels 138, bd. Haussmann, 8e. Métro: Miromesnil. 45-62-21-34. Arman, Fontana, Hains, Klasen,

PLACE DE LA CONCORDE

Spoeri, Taule, Télémaque, Rotella, Rancillac. Closed
Sunday and Monday.

Maurice Garnier 6, av. Matignon, 8e. Métro: Franklin
D. Roosevelt, 42-25-61-65. Primarily Bernard Buffet.

Robert Schmidt 396, rue St.-Honoré, 1er. Métro: Madeleine. 42-60-12-24. Impressionism—Renoir, Boudin, and all the masters.

Wally Findlay Galerie Internationale 2, av. Matignon,
8e. Métro: Franklin D. Roosevelt. 42-25-70-74. Impressionists and sculptors—Adamoff, Le Pho, Maik, Nessi.

Left Bank

Adrien Maeght 42, rue du Bac, 7e. Métro: Rue du Bac.
45-48-45-15. Gérard Gasiorowski, Olivier Garand,
Poli, Klasen, Kuroda, Télémaque, Voss.

Albert Loeb 10, rue des Beaux Arts, 6e. Métro: St.-
Germain-des-Prés. 46-33-06-87. Works by Arp, Balthus, Korab, Henriette Lambert, Matisse, Picasso, Ra-
mires, Theimer, Tova, Caballera, Cuartas.

Chardin 36, rue de Seine, 6e. Métro: Mabillon. 43-26-
99-38. Paul Charlot, Claude Schurr, Mouly, Jean Mar-
zelle, Fontanarosa, and Volti (sculptures).

Claude Bernard 7–9, rue des Beaux Arts, 6e. Métro:
St.-Germain-des-Prés. 43-26-97-07. Francis Bacon,
Balthus, Barthélémy, Bourdelle, D'Haese, Estève,
Freundlich, Hockney, Laurens, Lindner, Manzu,
Mompo, Rodin, Sagui, Giacometti, Léger.

Daniel Gervis 14, rue de Grenelle, 7e. Métro: St.-Sul-
pice. 45-44-41-90. Sonderberg, Debré, Malaval, Blom-
stedt, Benrath, Bettencourt.

Demeure 26, rue Mazarine, 6e. Métro: Odéon. 43-26-
02-74. Signed tapestries from Saint-Saëns, Lagrange,
Lurcat, Arp, Thomas Gelb, Grau-Garriga.

Denise René 196, bd. St.-Germain, 7e. Métro: Bac. 42-
22-77-57. Agam, Max Bill, Le Parc, Soto, Schoffer,
Heurtaux, Jacobsen (sculptures).

Dina Vierny 36, rue Jacob, 6e. Métro: St.-Germain-des-
Prés. 42-60-23-18. Drawings by Cézanne, Degas, Matisse, Pascin; and sculptures by Maillol.

Furstemburg 8, rue Jacob, 6e. Métro: St.-Germain-des-
Prés. 43-25-89-58. Bellmer, DeChirico, Leonor Fini,
Kandinsky.

Galarte 13, rue Mazarine, 6e. Métro: Odéon. 43-25-90-
84. Patrice Jordan, Raymondo Sesma.

Galerie Breteau 70, rue Bonaparte, 6e. Métro: St.-Ger-

Galleries

main-des-Prés. 43-26-40-96. Hollis Jeffcoat, Martine Boileau (sculpture).

Galerie du Dragon 19, rue du Dragon, 6e. Métro: St.-Germain-des-Prés. 45-48-24-19. Velickovic, Cremonini, Hultberg, Klusemann, Matta.

Hune 14, rue de l'Abbaye, 6e. Métro: St.-Germain-des-Prés. 43-25-54-06. Jean-Claude le Floch, Ionesco.

Isy Brachot 35, rue Guénégaud, 6e. Métro: Odéon. 46-34-02-36. Delvaux, Magritte, Labisse, Dado, Yuba, Rustin, Liz Santos Silva.

Jacques Damase 61, rue de Varenne, 7e. Métro: Varenne. 47-05-55-04. Robert Delaunay, Uriburu, Calder, Man Ray. Also a library with books primarily about fashion.

Jeanne Bucher 53, rue de Seine, 6e. Métro: Odéon. 43-26-22-32. Stael, Vieira da Silva, Dubuffet, Tobey, Amadou Nallard, Louise Nevelson (sculptures), Moser, Aguayo. Closed Sunday and Monday.

Karl Flinker 25, rue de Tournon, 6e. Métro: Odéon. 43-25-18-73. Thalmann, Martial Raysse, Arroyo, Gafgen, Moninot, Pichler, Kandinsky, Klee, Magnelli.

Lara Vincy 47, rue de Seine, 6e. Métro: Mabillon. 43-26-72-51. Pascal Le Gras, Hervé Vachez.

Lucien Durand 19, rue Mazarine, 6e. Métro: Odéon. 43-26-25-35. Michael Lechner, Rouan, Voss, Bertholo, Nadaud, Leccia.

Marcel Lecomte 17, rue de Seine, 6e. Métro: Mabillon. 43-26-85-47. Drawings and engravings of 20th-century French artists—Daumier, Rousseau, Lautrec, Chahine.

Paul Proute 74, rue de Seine, 6e. Métro: Mabillon. 43-26-89-80. Drawings from 16th to 20th centuries.

Point Cardinal 3, rue Jacob, 6e. Métro: St.-Germain-des-Prés. 43-54-32-08. Henri Michaux, Cárdenas, Louis Pons, Sima.

Plateau Beaubourg/Marais

Alain Blondel Galerie II 550, rue du Temple, 3e. Métro: Rambuteau. 42-71-85-86. Tony Crag, Bazile, and Bustamante.

Alain Oudin 28 bis, bd. de Sébastopol, 4e. Métro: Hôtel-de-Ville. 42-71-83-65. Sculpture and architecture—Biet, Boin, Goberne, Luc Chapelain.

Beaubourg 23, rue du Renard, 4e. Métro: Châtelet-les-Halles. 42-71-20-50. Schlosser, Arman, Louis Cane, César, Dado, Bernard Dufour, Degottex, Mathieu, Messagier, Schneider, Bettencourt.

Galleries

Bellint 28 bis, bd. de Sébastopol, 4e. Métro: Châtelet. 42-78-01-91. Jacques Poncet, Bellmer, Moumeester, Debré, Koenig, Lansky, Poliakoff, Salvado, Vieira da Silva. Some sculpture also.

Daniel Templon 30, rue Beaubourg, 3e. Métro: Rambuteau. 42-72-14-10. De Kooning, Warhol, Lichtenstein, Stella, Olivier Debré, Richard Serra.

Espace Latino-Américain 44, rue du Roi de Sicile, 4e. Métro: St.-Paul. 42-78-25-49. Horacio Garcia Rossi, some photography.

Farideh Cadot 77, rue des Archives, 3e. Métro: Artset-Métiers. 42-78-08-36. Georges Rousse, Meret Oppenheim, Gorchov, Robbins, Sonneman, Bowen, Salomé, Castelli, Laget, Boisrond, Trambley.

Galerie Alain Blondel 4, rue Aubry-Le-Boucher, 4e. Métro: Châtelet-Les-Halles. 42-78-66-67. Albert Brenet, Claude Yvel, Bruno Schmeltz.

Galerie de France 50–52, rue de la Verrerie, 4e. Métro: Hôtel-de-Ville. 42-74-38-00. Judy Rifka, Zao Wou Ki, Alechinsky, Gonzalez, Manessier, Poliakoff.

Liliane et Michel Durand-Dessert 3, rue des Haudriettes, 3e. Métro: Rambuteau. 42-77-63-60. Parmentier, Ger Van Elk, Richler, Hauxe, Beuyes.

Yvon Lambert 5, rue du Grenier-St.-Lazare, 3e. Métro: Rambuteau. 42-71-09-33. Sol Lewitt, Cy Twombly, Oppenheim, Christo, Tuttle.

HAIRCUTS

You can go where the stars go, go for the adventure, or go where the chic, trendy, or bizarre go, but wherever you go for your Paris cut, call first and make an appointment.

Alexandre de Paris 3, av. Matignon, 8e. Métro: Franklin D. Roosevelt. 42-25-57-90. Chic, well-known, and expensive. For women only. Closed Sunday and Monday.

Carita and Carita Messieurs 11, rue du Faubourg-St.-Honoré, 8e. Métro: Madeleine. 42-65-79-00. Chic, inventive coiffures for men and women. Closed Sunday and Monday. AE/DC/V.

Jean-Marc Maniatis 35, rue de Sèvres, 6e. Métro: Sèvres-Babylone. 45-44-16-39. Closed Sunday and

Monday; 18, rue Marbeuf, 8e. Métro: Franklin D. Roosevelt. 47-23-30-14. Closed Saturday and Sunday. Also 89, av. Raymond Poincaré, 16e. Métro: Victor-Hugo. 45-01-28-55. Forum Les Halles, niveau -1, 1er. Métro: Les Halles. 42-96-90-95. Both stores closed Sunday and Monday. Creative cuts that complement facial features for men and women.

Michel Caro 10, rue de Bourgogne, 7e. Métro: Chambre-des-Députés. 45-51-36-51. The politicians' coiffeur—it's just behind the Assemblée Nationale. For men only. Closed Sunday and Monday.

Mod's Hair 57, av. Montaigne, 8e. Métro: Franklin D. Roosevelt. 43-59-06-50. Closed Saturday and Sunday. V. 90, rue de Rennes, 6e. Métro: St.-Sulpice. 45-44-47-02. Closed Sunday and Monday. V. 156, av. Victor-Hugo, 16e. Métro: Rue de la Pompe. 47-97-76-83. Closed Sunday. V. Trendy salon but you will get the cut you want. For men and women.

Many of the better known *Salons de Coiffure* hold regular training sessions for their staff, who are already well-trained professionals. They need models to practice on, and they charge very little, if anything at all, to give a professional haircut. The only disadvantage is that they decide whom they will work on, and what they will do.

Harlow 70, rue du Ranelagh, 16e. Métro: Ranelagh. 45-24-04-54. Every other Thursday. 24, rue St.-Denis, 1er. Métro: Châtelet. 42-33-61-36. Every other Tuesday; 6, rue de Sèze, 9e. Métro: Madeleine. 47-42-40-67. Wednesday night sessions only. Stop by to make an appointment.

Sébastien Aubril 132, rue de Courcelles, 17e. Métro: Courcelles. 47-63-34-12. Avant-garde cuts for men and women. Stop by to make an appointment for the first and third Wednesday of the month.

HISTORY OF PARIS

52–51 B.C. The Romans conquered the village of the tribe Parisii, and named it Lutèce.

3rd or 4th Century A.D. Lutèce was named Paris.

280 After a Barbarian invasion, the first wall was built around Paris.

355 The Emperor Julius was named *César*, lord of the Gauls.

451 Sainte Geneviève turned Attila the Hun away from Paris.

Around 508 Christian King Clovis of the Merovingians resided in Paris. The church of St. Etienne du Mont in the 5e, rue de la Montagne-Sainte-Geneviève, was founded.

8th Century The Carolingians left Paris.

9th Century The Normans raided Paris repeatedly but were defeated by Count Eudes and Bishop Gozlin in 885–884.

888 Count Eudes was elected king of France.

987 Hugues Capet, Count of Paris, was elected king of France, and he established the Capetian dynasty.

1163 Beginning of construction on Notre Dame.

1183 Philippe Auguste passed an ordinance which called for paving the major streets of Paris. He was also responsible for the first construction of Paris' central marketplace, Les Halles.

1180–1215 The Louvre and a wall around Paris were built by Philippe Auguste; Paris' population was 70,000. He was also responsible for the foundation of the University of Paris.

1223–1248 Reigns of Louis VIII, Louis IX, and Philippe III. The Sainte-Chapelle was built to house relics purchased by Louis IX, who was later canonized.

1250 Completion of the Notre Dame façade.

1253 The Sorbonne was established.

1254 The hospital *Quinze-Vingts* built by Louis IX for 300 (15 × 20 = *quinze vingts*) blind patients.

1268 The association of water merchants in Paris adopted the motto *Fluctuat nec mergitur*, "She is tossed but does not sink," which became the motto of the city of Paris.

1302 Philippe IV Le Bel, "the fair," called the first *états-généraux* in Paris.

1367–1383 Construction by Charles V of a wall on the Right Bank, beyond the Philippe Auguste wall.

1420–1436 The English captured and stayed in Paris.

1461–1483 The first school of medicine was opened and the city's first printing press was set up at the Sorbonne.

1475 The city's population was more than 300,000.

1489 The first street markers were installed.

1533 Pierre Viole, merchants' provost, laid the cornerstone of the new Hôtel de Ville.

History

1546 Beginning of work on the Louvre Palace by architect Pierre Lescot, who was helped by the sculptor Jean Goujon.

1594 Henry IV came to Paris. Under his reign, Place des Vosges was created, Pont-Neuf completed, and the Louvre and Tuileries expanded; permission was granted to begin construction of the Palais Royal.

1607 The Place Dauphine, 1er, was built.

1610 Henry IV was assassinated in Paris.

1622 Paris became an independent bishopric. The 17th century was known as *Le Grand Siècle*.

1643 The reign of the Sun King, Louis XIV. Versailles was built, and Gobelins, the Salpiêtre, the Comédie Française, and the Louvre colonnade was constructed.

1649 *La Fronde* uprising against centralized power.

1667 The former Gobelins brothers manufacturing company became the Royal Manufacturers of furniture and tapestries.

1670 Construction of the Hôtel des Invalides for invalid soldiers.

1680 Louis XIV moved permanently to Versailles.

1688 The population of Paris reached 425,000 inhabitants. The Collège des Quatre Nations (the future Institute of France)—founded by Mazarin—was opened.

1718 Elysée Palace, 8e, was erected for the Count of Evreux.

1728 Metal street signs, with the name of the street written on them, put at the corner of each street in Paris.

1753 The beginning of work on the Place de la Concorde.

1760 The Ecole Militaire (7e), where Napoleon gained his military knowledge, was opened.

1764 Louis XV laid the cornerstone of the Panthéon, 5e.

1787–1797 Another wall, the Farmer's General Wall, was erected in Paris as a customs barrier.

July 14, 1789 The storming of the Bastille and the beginning of the French Revolution.

July 17, 1789 The French flag, *le tricolore*, was adopted.

October 6, 1789 The Royal Family moved into the Tuileries.

1790 Celebration of the taking of the Bastille—*la Fête de la Fédération*—at the Champ de Mars, 7e.

1792 Tuileries taken; fall of the Royal Family.

1793 Louis XVI executed.

History

1793–1794 Reign of Terror.

1804 Napoleon I crowned at Notre Dame.

1805 The Vendôme column built. Houses in Paris given numbers—even numbers on the right, odd on the left when walking away from the Seine.

1814 The Allies occupied Paris.

1830 The end of the Bourbon Dynasty, by revolution.

1832 A cholera epidemic killed 19,000 Parisians.

1837 First railway from Paris to Saint-Germain was built.

1842 The church of the Madeleine was completed.

1848 Revolution and the fall of Louis Philippe. Declaration of the Second Republic. Workers' uprising.

1849 Louis Napoleon, president of the Republic, moved into the Elysée Palace.

1854 Baltard built the renowned Les Halles market building.

1855 Universal Exposition on the Champs-Elysées.

1859 The 20 *arrondissements* officially created. Paris had 526,000 inhabitants.

1860 Baron Haussmann, the prefect of Paris, completely redesigned the city as it appears today—new boulevards, parks, gardens, new bridges, fountains, a pipe system for carrying drinking water.

1870 The Third Republic proclaimed at Hôtel de Ville.

1871 Uprising of the Commune of Paris—burning of the Hôtel de Ville and the Tuileries.

1874–1881 The Hôtel de Ville was rebuilt.

1878 Universal Exposition—world's fair.

1885 Death of Victor Hugo.

1889 Eiffel Tower built for Universal Exposition.

1900 First métro line built from Porte Maillot to Porte de Vincennes, 6.2 miles. The Grand Palais, Petit Palais, and the Pont Alexandre III were built for the Universal Exposition.

1940–1944 Paris was occupied by the German army.

August 25, 1944 Liberation of Paris. Général de Gaulle led the provisional government.

1946 The Fourth Republic and a new constitution. Government by a coalition of Socialists, Communists, Radicals, and Catholic Democrats.

1958 Charles de Gaulle formed the Fifth Republic.

1962 France granted independence to Algeria after 4 years of occupation.

1968 The city of Paris was made into its own "département" of 2,590,771 inhabitants. Famous student riots in the streets of Paris.

History

1969 Georges Pompidou was elected president of France. Under him much of Paris' modern architecture was constructed. The market of Les Halles was moved to the suburb of Rungis.

1970 The Place de l'Etoile, around the Arc de Triomphe, was named after Charles de Gaulle.

1977 Jacques Chirac was elected mayor of Paris, the first since 1871.

1981 François Mitterand was elected president of France, leader of a socialist government.

1982 Each *arrondissement* in Paris was made into a municipality governed by its own mayor, under the direction of the major of Paris.

1986 Jacques Chirac, a neo-Gaullist, was elected to serve as prime minister in François Mitterand's opposing Socialist regime, to create France's first "cohabitation" government.

HITCHHIKING

Hitchhiking is legal in France, though it is strictly forbidden on autoroutes. Stand in the following places if you're hitchhiking out of Paris:

To go North (Belgium and The Netherlands)—Porte de la Chapelle.
To go South-central and Southwest—Porte d'Orléans.
To go Southeast (Lyon)—Porte de Gentilly.
To go East (Metz-Alsace)—Porte de Bercy.
To go West (Normandy)—Porte d'Auteuil.

These organizations will put together riders and drivers going in the same direction:

Allostop 84, passage Brady, 10e. Métro: Strasbourg-St.-Denis. 42-46-00-66. Closed Sunday. Participants pay a nominal fee and share driving expenses. Staff speaks English. It is best to stop by for an appointment.

France Stop 35, rue Jacob, 6e. Métro: St.-Germain-des-Prés. 42-60-42-09. Closed Sunday. Participants must buy an annual subscription for a nominal fee and share driving expenses.

(PUBLIC) HOLIDAYS

Though times are changing, many shops, restaurants, museums, even the corner bakery, close on public holidays. Be aware of these dates, and plan accordingly.
January 1—New Year's Day (*Jour de l'An*).
End of March or early April—Easter Monday (*Lundi de Pâques*).
May 1—Labor Day (*Fête du Travail*).
May 8—V.E. Day (*Armistice 1945*).
Five weeks after Easter—Ascension Day (*Ascension*).
July 14—Bastille Day (*Fête Nationale*).
August 15—Assumption (*Assomption*).
November 1—All Saints' Day (*Toussaint*).
November 11—Armistice Day (*Armistice 1918*).
December 25—Christmas (*Noël*).

HORSE RACING

If you are a horse-racing enthusiast and you want to place a bet on your favorite, you can do so at any café displaying the P.M.U. (*Pari Mutuel Urbain*) sign, from 8:30 A.M. to 1 P.M. the day of the race, or right at the Hippodrome, at the P.M.H. (*Pari Mutuel Hippodrome*).

Major horse races throughout the year are listed here. For other races get a copy of the *Paris Turf*, a daily newspaper available at all newsstands, or call the Fédération des Sociétés de Courses, 42-66-92-02. You'll find all race results in the *Paris Turf*.

Major Horse Races

Last Sunday of January—Grand Prix d'Amérique, Hippodrome de Vincennes.
First Sunday of October—Prix de l'Arc de Triomphe, Hippodrome de Longchamp.
End of March—Prix du Président de La République, Hippodrome d'Auteuil.

Hippodromes

Hippodrome d'Auteuil 16e. Métro: Porte d'Auteuil. Walk to hippodrome. 45-27-12-25.

Holidays

Hippodrome de Chantilly 16, av. du Général-Leclerc. Chantilly. Gare-du-Nord, stop Chantilly. 5-minute walk from train station. (16) (4) 44-57-21-35.

Hippodrome d'Enghien Place Henri Foulon, Soisy-Sous-Montmorency. Gare-du-Nord, 10e, stop Hippodrome d'Enghien. 49-89-00-12.

Hippodrome d'Evry Société de Sports de France, Route Départementale 31, Evry. Gare-de-Lyon, 12e, stop Orangis-Bois-de-l'Epine, then take shuttle *hippodrome d'Evry*. 40-77-82-80.

Hippodrome de Longchamp 16e. Bois de Boulogne, 16e. Porte Maillot or Porte d'Auteuil, then bus N.234, stop Carrefour du Moulin. 47-72-57-33.

Hippodrome de Maisons-Laffitte 1, av. de la Pelouse, Maisons-Laffitte, Gare-St.-Lazare, 9e, direction Cergy, stop Maisons-Laffitte, then bus *hippodrome de Maisons-Laffitte*. 49-62-90-95.

Hippodrome de Saint-Cloud 1, rue du Camp Canadien, St.-Cloud, Gare St.-Lazare, 9e, stop Gare de St.-Cloud, then bus N.431 to hippodrome. 47-71-69-26.

Hippodrome de Vincennes Bois de Vincennes, 12e. RER line A-2, stop Joinville-Le-Pont, 10-minute walk to hippodrome. Or: Métro: Château-de-Vincennes, 12e, then shuttle to hippodrome (on race days only). 43-68-35-39.

HOSPITALS

The only hospital in France with 100% reimbursement by the Empire Blue Cross/Blue Shield program is the American Hospital in Paris. A senior citizen (or any other citizen) hospitalized elsewhere will be reimbursed for 80% of the amount of the bill if an itemized bill is submitted in English to Empire Blue Cross/Blue Shield.

The American Hospital 63, bd. Victor-Hugo, Neuilly. 47-47-53-00. Take bus N.82, stop American Hospital. 24-hour emergency and maternity service. Staff speaks English.

Hertford British Hospital 48, rue de Villiers, 92 Levallois-Perret. Métro: Anatole-France. 47-57-24-10. 5-

minute walk to the hospital or Bus N.83, stop Villiers. 24-hour emergency and maternity service. Staff speaks English.

For Children

Groupe Hospitalier Necker 141–161, rue de Sèvres, 15e. Métro: Duroc. 45-55-92-80. 24-hour emergency service. Staff and doctors speak English; interpreters are also available upon request; mention when making an appointment.

HOTELS

From true palaces to modest, family-run residences, Paris has hotels for every taste. In this selection the hotels are rated on a standard star system, with 4 stars being the ultimate in luxury, convenience and price, to one or no stars for establishments that offer clean, though simple accommodations.

Many hotels charge extra for breakfast. Breakfast generally consists of coffee with milk, tea, or chocolate; a *croissant*, and a piece of *baguette* with butter and jam. The price of the room and what it includes will be posted in the room. (*T.T.C.* means that all the taxes are included in the price.)

You should try to have a reservation for your first night in Paris. If you don't have one, **Les Hôtesses de Paris** can give you information about hotels once you have arrived. They generally speak English, and you will find them at the following locations:

Office du Tourisme de Paris 127, av. des Champs-Elysées, 8e. Métro: Etoile. 47-23-61-72. Open daily.
Gare d'Austerlitz 55, quai d'Austerlitz, 13e. Métro: Gare d'Austerlitz. Closed Sunday.
Gare de l'Est pl. du 11 November 1918, 10e. Métro: Gare de l'Est. Closed Sunday.
Gare de Lyon 20, bd. Diderot, 12e. Métro: Gare de Lyon. Closed Sunday.
Gare du Nord 18 rue de Dunkerque, 10e. Métro: Gare du Nord. Closed Sunday.

Four-Star Luxury Hotels

These generally range in price from 1200F to 3500F for a room.

Bristol 112, rue du Faubourg-St.-Honoré, 8e. Métro: St.-Philippe-du-Roule. 42-66-91-45. There are 205 rooms and 35 suites available with beautiful antiques, huge bathrooms. A heated pool on the sixth floor with a view of Paris and a very international guest list. AE/DC/EC/V. Telex: 280961.

Crillon 10, pl. de la Concorde, 8e. Métro: Concorde. 42-65-24-24. Who could lose with such a location, right on the Place de la Concorde? 157 rooms or 48 suites available and a 2-star restaurant right in the hotel. Conference rooms available. AE/DC/V. Telex: 290204.

George V 31, av. George-V, 8e. Métro: Franklin D. Roosevelt. 47-23-54-00. This old, elegant palace offers 293 rooms and 48 suites. Conference rooms, secretarial services, and audio-visual equipment available. AE/DC/EC/V. Telex: 650082.

Meurice 228, rue de Rivoli, 1er. Métro: Tuileries. 42-60-38-60. Some of the 32 suites have views of the Tuileries. All of the 188 rooms are accustomed to the lines of royalty who have visited the hotel for centuries. Conference rooms, secretarial services available. AE/DC/EC/V. Telex: 230673.

Plaza Athénée 25, av. Montaigne, 8e. Métro: Franklin D. Roosevelt. 47-23-78-33. This is where the stars stay when they come to Paris, 218 rooms, 38 suites. AE/DC/EC/V. Telex: 650092.

Prince de Galles 33, av. George-V, 8e. Métro: Franklin D. Roosevelt. 47-23-55-11. This hotel always has flowers at the windows. The 160 rooms are elegant and discreet. Conference rooms and secretarial services available. AE/DC/EC/V. Telex: 280627.

Ritz Hotel 15, pl. Vendôme, 1er. Métro: Tuileries. 42-60-38-30. If you stand outside you may see some familiar faces being driven up in chauffeured limousines, to stay in one of the 163 rooms or suites. Conference rooms and secretarial services available. AE/DC/EC/V. Telex: 220262.

Four-Star Hotels

Baltimore 88, bis av. Kléber, 16e. Métro: Boissière. 45-53-83-33. Beautiful view of the large avenue with the Arc de Triomphe at one end and the Trocadéro at the other end. Near the Eiffel Tower and Avenue Victor Hugo, one of the most exclusive shopping areas in Paris. 118 rooms. Small conference rooms available. Telex 611591.

Frantel-Windsor 14, rue Beaujon, 8e. Métro: Etoile. 45-63-04-04. Near the Champs-Elyseés. 135 rooms. Conference rooms available. Very reasonable price considering the desirable location. AE/DC/EC/V. Telex 650902.

Hilton 18, av. de Suffren, 15e. Métro: Bir-Hakeim. 42-73-92-00. 450 rooms and 29 suites. Wonderful location facing the Eiffel Tower in a very quiet section of Paris. International clientele. Large, modern rooms with marble bathrooms. Conference rooms are available, as well as parking under the hotel. AE/DC/MC/V/EC. Telex 200955.

Holiday Inn 10, pl. de la République, 11e. Métro: République. 43-55-44-34. 316 rooms and 17 suites. AE/DC/EC/V. Telex 210651.

Inter-Continental 3, rue Castiglione, 1e. Métro: Tuileries. 42-60-37-80. Near the American Consulate and the Place de la Concorde. 460 rooms and 40 suites. Conference rooms available. AE/DC/EC/V. Telex 220114.

La Trémoille 14, rue La Trémoille, 8e. Métro: Alma-Marceau. 47-23-34-20. Former mansion located on a quiet little street between av. George-V and av. des Champs-Elysées. 97 rooms and 14 suites. AE/DC/EC/V. Telex 640344.

Le Grand Hôtel 2, rue Scribe, 9e. Métro: Opéra. 42-68-12-13. Located near the Opéra and American Express, and above the famous Café de la Paix. 537 rooms and 19 suites. Conference rooms available. AE/DC/EC/V. Telex 220875.

P. L. M. St.-Jacques 17, bd. St.-Jacques, 14e. Métro: Glacière and St.-Jacques. 45-89-89-80. 783 rooms and 14 suites. Conference rooms and parking facilities available. There are two restaurants and a coffee shop. AE/DC/EC/V. Telex 270740.

Regent's Garden 6, rue Pierre Demours, 17e. Métro: Ternes/Wagram. 45-74-07-30. Charming little hotel with some rooms overlooking a garden, an unusual feature for Paris. Located on an old and very narrow street, walking distance from the Place des Ternes. Reservations should be made at least a month in ad-

Hotels

vance due to the limited number of rooms (47) and the price (from 550F to 850F). Parking facilities available. Telex 640127.

Sofitel-Bourbon 32, rue St.-Dominique, 7e. Métro: Invalides, Solférino or Ecole-Militaire. 45-55-91-80. Located on a typical commercial, narrow street in this exclusive section of Paris. 112 rooms. Parking available. AE/DC/ EC/V. Telex 250019.

Three-Star Hotels (Tourist)

These range from about 450F to 600F for a room.

Abbaye Saint-Germain 10, rue Cassette, 6e. Métro: Mabillon. 45-44-38-11. There are 45 rooms that come with breakfast in this calm, quiet hotel which was once a convent. There's a garden in the courtyard.

Alison 21, rue Surène, 8e. Métro: Madeleine. 42-65-54-00. There are 35 functional, modern rooms in this centrally located hotel right near the Madeleine, the American Embassy, and the Place de la Concorde. Prices are quite reasonable. AE/DC/EC/V.

D'Angleterre 44, rue Jacob, 6e. Métro: St.-Germain-des-Prés. 42-60-34-72. Long ago this was the British Embassy in Paris. Now it is a hotel with 27 rooms and 4 suites; breakfast is extra. Benjamin Franklin refused to set foot inside it when it was British territory, and Hemingway once lived here.

Colisée 6, rue du Colisée, 8e. Métro: Franklin D. Roosevelt. 43-59-95-25. Right near the Champs-Elysées, this hotel has 45 rooms, and rumor has it those whose number ends in 8 are the biggest. AE/DC/EC/V.

Courcelles 184, rue de Courcelles, 17e. Métro: Péreire. 47-63-65-30. Not far from the lovely Parc Monceau, which is perfect for an early morning run, 42 rooms with breakfast, color television, a small winter garden, and a library. AE/DC/V. Telex: 642252.

Deux Iles 59, rue St.-Louis-en-l'Ile, 4e. Métro: Pont-Marie. 43-26-13-35. 17 rooms, breakfast extra, color television. Right in the center of the Ile Saint-Louis.

Hôtel des Grands Hommes 17, pl. du Panthéon, 5e. Métro: Luxembourg. 46-34-19-60. 32 rooms with color television, and breakfast included, small bar; right on the beautiful square of the Panthéon, in the midst of the *Quartier Latin*. AE/DC/V.

Hotels

Hôtel de Seine 52, rue de Seine, 6*e*. Métro: Odéon. 46-34-22-80. There are 30 rooms with breakfast included, at this comfortable hotel that is in the midst of the lively rue de Seine market. AE/DC/V.

Kléber 7, rue de Belloy, 16*e*. Métro: Kléber. 47-23-80-22. 21 rooms and one suite, breakfast included. A very modern hotel right near Trocadéro with a bar on the ground floor. AE/V. Telex: 612830.

Métropole Opéra 2, rue de Gramont, 2*e*. Métro: Quatre-Septembre. 42-96-91-03. 53 rooms relatively spacious, and decorated in discreet, classic style. AE. Telex: 212276.

Modern-Hôtel-Lyon 3, rue Parrot, 12*e*. Métro. Gare-de-Lyon. 43-43-41-52. 53 rooms in this small, family-run hotel. It is right near the Gare-de-Lyon. AE/V. Telex: 230369.

Montana Tuileries 12, rue St.-Roch, 1*er*. Métro: Tuileries. 42-60-35-10. 25 spacious rooms near the Tuileries. Each floor is decorated in a different color.

Rond-Point De Longchamp 86, rue de Longchamp, 16*e*. Métro: Pompe. 45-05-13-63. Some of the 59 rooms are contemporary style, some are redone Louis XV style. There is a bar, billiard room and restaurant as well. AE/DC/EC/V. Telex: 620652.

Victor Hugo 19, rue de Copernic, 16*e*. Métro: Boissière. 45-53-76-01. The 76 rooms and 1 suite have small bars and marble bathrooms. Breakfast is extra, color television included. The rooms on the upper floors have views of the lush neighborhood. AE/DC/EC/V. Telex: 630939.

Two-Star Hotels (Modest)

These range from 100F (rare) to 300F for a room.

Ducs d'Anjou 1, rue Ste.-Opportune, 1*er*. Métro: Châtelet. 42-36-92-24. There are 38 completely redone rooms, breakfast included. Though this hotel overlooks the animated Place Sainte-Opportune, the rooms are quiet and fresh, if rather small.

Family Hotel 35, rue Cambon, 1*er*. Métro: Madeleine. 42-61-54-84. 25 rooms, breakfast extra. Some of the modest rooms in this calm, quiet hotel, have a view of the Place Vendôme.

Hôtel des Célestins 1, rue Charles-V, 4*e*. Métro: Sully-Morland. 48-87-87-04. A wonderful neighborhood surrounds this newly redone hotel. Tastefully decorated, efficient and comfortable.

Hôtel du Vieux Paris 9, rue Gît-Le-Coeur, 6e. Métro: St.-Michel. 43-54-41-66. 21 rooms in this charming hotel, which is decorated in 15th-century style. All the rooms are different, breakfast is included, and in summer the small terrace abounds with flowers.

Kensington 79, av. de la Bourdonnais, 7e. Métro: Ecole-Militaire. 47-05-74-00. 26 cheerful rooms, breakfast extra. In the quiet seventh *arrondissement*, this offers small rooms, right near the Champ-de-Mars. AE/V.

Pavillon 54, rue St.-Dominique, 7e. Métro: Latour-Maubourg. 45-51-42-87. Once a convent, now a hotel with 20 rooms, breakfast not included. A simple hotel of character, with a welcoming entryway. V.

Résidence Etoile-Péreire 146, bd. Péreire, 17e. Métro: Péreire. 42-67-60-00. There are 15 rooms with breakfast included in this hotel, which shares an entrance with the apartment building. There is also a small patio, and a friendly atmosphere. AE/DC/EC/V. Telex: 250303.

Saint-Louis 75, rue St.-Louis-en-l'Ile, 4e. Métro: Pont-Marie. 46-34-04-80. Another charmer with 25 rooms, most of them with bath or shower.

One- or No-Star Hotels (Economy)

The following hotels fall into the "simple" category. Most of them offer some rooms with a bath or shower, and all of them offer bath or shower facilities for a small additional fee. Rooms range from 75F to 250F.

Esmeralda 4, rue St.-Julien-Le-Pauvre, 5e. Métro: St. Michel. 43-54-19-20. The 19 rooms in this 17th-century building are dramatically decorated: plush velvet, heavy antiques, low ceilings. It is right near the center of the Latin Quarter, and 2 steps from the Seine; some rooms have a view of the Viviani Square and the edge of Notre Dame.

Hôtel International 6, rue Auguste-Barbier, 11e. Métro: Goncourt. 43-57-38-07. This neighborhood is slightly off the beaten track but a very French part of Paris, and the rooms in this hotel are charming and well equipped. Breakfast is extra.

Hôtel Lion d'Or 5, rue de la Sourdière, 1er. Métro: Tuileries. 42-60-79-04. Very centrally located near the Louvre, Palais Royal, and the Seine. Breakfast is extra. English is spoken.

Molière 14, rue de Vaugirard, 6e. Métro: Luxembourg. 46-34-18-80. 15 small, tidy, comfortable rooms, all with a bath or shower. There's a cheerful breakfast room downstairs, and the hotel is 2 steps from the Jardin du Luxembourg.

If you want to try bed-and-breakfast arrangements or to rent a studio, an independent furnished room, even a whole house or a barge in Paris, call or write to:

Paris Accueil 485 Madison Ave., Suite 1310, New York, N.Y. 10022, (212) 838-2444, or

Paris Accueil 23, rue de Marignan, 8e. Métro: Franklin D. Roosevelt. 42-56-04-61. They are certified by the Office du Tourisme, and all lodging is guaranteed to have standard levels of comfort.

For hotels that offer secretarial services, see BUSINESS SERVICES.

HOUSEWARES

See SHOPPING.

ICE CREAM

See FOOD.

ILLUMINATIONS

Paris' monuments, already magnificent by day, light up at night. From June 1 until July 14, while daylight in Paris often lasts until 10:30 P.M., 155 monuments are lit from 10 P.M. until midnight during the week, and until 1 A.M. on weekends. The rest of the year, monuments are lit from dusk until midnight during the week, and until 1 A.M. on weekends.

Since January 1, 1986, the *Tour Eiffel* (Eiffel Tower), 7e, has had a sparkling new outfit. The Mairie de Paris replaced 1,290 incandescent light bulbs that shone on the Eiffel Tower from its base, with 292 high-pressure sodium light bulbs wired right into the structure. When the lights go on at night now, they really shine, emitting "five times better, for five times less the price," according to a city engineer.

LA MADELEINE

For a dramatic nighttime stroll, walk along the quai de Montebello near **Notre Dame**, going toward the **Pont-Neuf**. Continue on until the **Pont du Carrousel**, then across the Seine to the quai du Louvre. Continue to the **Place de la Concorde**, which feels a bit like the center of the universe with its lights and whirling traffic. Stand in the *Place* and look one way up the glittering **Champs-Elysées** to the **Arc de Triomphe**, which is bathed in light, or look the other way to the **Louvre**, through the **Place du Carrousel** and the small **Arc de Triomphe du Carrousel**.

Some other illuminated monuments are:

Basilique du Sacré Cœur, 18*e*
Bastille, 4*e*
Column and Place Vendôme, 1*er*
Conciergerie, 1*er*
Ecole Militaire, 7*e*
Eglise de la Madeleine, 8*e*
Eglise de la Sainte-Chapelle, 1*er*
Eglise Saint-Germain-des-Prés, 6*e*
Eglise Saint-Gervais-Saint-Protais, 4*e*
Hôtel des Monnaies, 6*e*
Hôtel de Ville, 4*e*
Institut de France, 6*e*
Invalides, 7*e*
Musée de Cluny and Gardens, 5*e*
Palais de Chaillot, 6*e*
Panthéon, 5*e*
Petit Palais, 8*e*
Place de la République—statue, 11*e*
Pont-Marie, 4*e*
Pont-Alexandre III, 7*e* and 8*e*
Statue de la Liberté, 15*e*
Statue du Triomphe de la République, Place de la Nation, 12*e*
Théâtre du Rond-Point, 8*e*
Théâtre National de l'Opéra, 9*e*
Tour Saint-Jacques, 4*e*

From mid-November until mid-January, windows in the **haute couture boutiques** on and around Avenue Montaigne are transformed into opulent gilt, gold, satin, fur, and silver fairylands. The theme carries out into the street, where all the trees are draped with tiny, elegant white lights, as is the entire Champs-Elysées.

Illuminations

Boulevard Haussmann (8e), behind the Opéra and flanked by **Galeries Lafayette** and **Printemps**, is part of a children's fantasy world: the store windows are filled with intricate and wonderful automated Christmas scenes, and glittering Christmas decorations dance in the night sky above the crowds' heads throughout the Christmas season. The windows at **Au Bon Marché** (7e) and **Aux Trois Quartiers** (8e), too, take on the Christmas frivolity of lights, fancy, and fun.

INFORMATION ABOUT PARIS

See ARRIVAL IN PARIS.

JAZZ CLUBS

Calavados 40, rue Pierre-ler-de-Serbie, 8e. Métro: George-V. 47-20-31-39. Open day and night for jazz; restaurant and American-style bar. AE/DC.

Cambridge 17, av. de Wagram, 17e. Métro: Charles-de-Gaulle-Etoile. 43-80-34-12. One of the best-known clubs in town for jazz. Restaurant on ground floor. Closed Sunday night.

Caveau de la Huchette 5, rue de la Huchette, 5e. Métro: St.-Michel. 43-26-65-05. Music every night until 2:30 AM.

Diner's Jazz 28, rue de la Montagne-Ste. Geneviève, 5e. Métro: Maubert-Mutualité. 46-34-57-03. Jazz, restaurant, and bar. Closed Sunday. AE/DC/EC/V.

Ecume 99, bis, rue de l'Ouest, 14e. Métro: Pernety. 45-42-71-16. Open nightly.

Furstemberg 28, rue de Buci, 6e. Métro: Odéon. 43-54-79-51. Well-known club with traditional jazz. Open nightly until 3 AM.

New Morning 79, rue des Petites Ecuries, 10e. Métro: Château d'Eau. 45-48-93-08. Jazz and American-style bar, nightly.

Patio (Hôtel Méridien) 81, bd. Gouvion-St.-Cyr, 17e. Métro: Porte Maillot. 47-58-12-30. Traditional jazz nightly until 2 AM.

Petit Journal 71, bd. St.-Michel, 5e. Métro: Luxembourg. 43-26-28-59. Music Monday through Saturday nights until 3 AM. Restaurant also.

Petit Opportun 15, rue des Lavandières-St.-Opportun, 1er. Métro: Châtelet. 42-36-01-36. Jazz daily and nightly until 3 AM.

Twenty-One 21, rue Daunou, 2e. Métro: Opéra. 42-60-40-51. Jazz, American-style bar, and restaurant. Nightly from 11 PM to 3 AM.

For specific programs, consult *L'Officiel des Spectacles* or *Pariscope* under "jazz."

JEWELRY

Jewelry in Paris is like fashion—there are shops for every taste, every style, every look imaginable. Most of the big names are on the Place Vendôme, their windows glittering with a wealth of precious gems, gold, and silver. But rue du Faubourg-Saint-Honoré has its share of top stores, as does the area around the Opéra.

Some of the Big Names

Bulgari 27, av. Montaigne, 8e. Métro: Franklin D. Roosevelt. 47-23-89-89. Closed Saturday and Sunday. AE/V.

Cartier 13, rue de la Paix, 2e. Métro: Opéra. 42-61-58-56; 12, av. Montaigne, 8e. Métro: Alma-Marceau. 47-20-06-73; 23, rue du Faubourg-St.-Honoré, 8e. Métro: Madeleine. 42-65-79-81. All shops are closed Sunday.

Chaumet 12, pl. Vendôme, 1er. Métro: Tuileries. 42-60-32-82. Closed Sunday. AE/V.

Fred Joaillier 6, rue Royale, 8e. Métro: Concorde-Madeleine. 42-60-30-65. Fred is the designer of a jewelry line created for actress Catherine Deneuve. Closed Sunday. AE/DC/V.

Gérard 8, av. Montaigne, 8e. Métro: Alma-Marceau. 47-23-70-00. Closed Saturday and Sunday.

Mauboussin 20, pl. Vendôme, 1er. Métro: Tuileries. 42-60-44-93. Closed Sunday. AE/DC/V.

Van Cleef and Arpels 22, pl. Vendôme, 1er. Métro: Tuileries. 42-61-58-58. Closed Saturday and Sunday. AE/V.

Verney 8, pl. Vendôme, 1er. Métro: Tuileries. 42-60-33-55. Closed Sunday. AE/V.

Other Jewelers

Agatha 97, rue de Rennes, 6e. Métro: St.-Sulpice. 45-48-81-30; 84, av. des Champs-Elysées, 8e. Métro: George-V. 43-59-68-68; 8, rue de la Pompe, 16e. Métro: Muette. 42-88-22-15; Forum des Halles-niveau-2. Métro: Les Halles. 42-97-42-88. You can go crazy or classic in these shops that sell some gold pieces, some beads, some silver, and some plastic in necklaces, earrings, rings—you name it. There are a few watches, some coral, and some turquoise. All shops are closed Sunday. AE/DC/EC/V.

Aldebert 1, bd. de la Madeleine, 1er. Métro: Madeleine. 42-61-58-27. A huge variety of Swiss watches. Closed Sunday. AE/DC/V.

Allard et Autres 11, pl. des Vosges, 4e. Métro: Chemin-Vert. 42-71-69-10. This house crafts jewelry for the top jewelers, and beautiful pieces can sometimes be had here at a more advantageous price than elsewhere. Closed Saturday and Sunday. AE/DC.

Comptoir du Kit 42, Galerie Vivienne, 2e. Métro: Bourse. 42-60-81-81. You can buy just about everything here to make your own jewelry—real or costume. Closed Sunday. V.

Exactement Fauve 5, rue Princesse, 6e. Métro: Mabillon. No phone. Walking into this store is like stepping into a fantasy world of costume dress-up. Most of the necklaces, earrings, and hairpieces are handmade, imaginative combinations of glass beads, feathers, ribbons, and silk flowers—some antique. There are even wild and elegant masks. Closed Sunday.

Fabrice 33 and 33 bis, rue Bonaparte, 6e. Métro: St.-Germain-des-Prés. 43-26-57-95. There aren't many materials left untouched in these pieces of jewelry; you can find elephants' hair bracelets or ivory necklaces, pieces of shells and baubles of wood, all well designed. They also have a line of fine gold jewelry. Closed Saturday and Sunday at N.26; closed Sunday at the other stores. AE/DC/EC/V.

Fried Frères 13, rue du Caire, 2e. Métro: Réaumur-Sébastopol. 42-33-51-55. Lots of glitter and beads to create your own classics. Closed Saturday and Sunday.

Ilias Laiaounis 364, rue St.-Honoré, 1er. Métro: Concorde. 42-61-55-65. Rather heavy jewelry, inspired by Greek design and mostly wrought in gold. There are some smaller pieces as well. Closed Sunday. AE/DC/EC/V.

Jewelry

Jean Dinh Van 7, rue de la Paix, 2*e*. Métro: Opéra. 42-61-74-49. Pearls and precious stones, in unique and unusual settings, and signature gold chains. Jewelry for men and children as well. Closed Saturday and Sunday. AE/DC.

Jean Vendôme 352, rue St.-Honoré, 1*er*. Métro: Tuileries. 42-60-88-34. Almost more an art gallery than a jewelry store, this house was founded by Jean Vendôme, a gemologist and expert in the jewelry design field. He has a vast selection of precious stones which can be put in the setting of your choice. Closed Sunday. AE/V.

Oxeda 390, rue St.-Honoré, 1*er*. Métro: Madeleine. 42-60-27-57. This shop handles secondhand jewels, some of them with very well-known signatures. Closed Sunday. AE/DC/V.

Perlotte 12, rue Vavin, 6*e*. Métro: Vavin. 43-54-87-09. Another do-it-yourself jewelry shop, this one with sequins, beautiful glass pieces, and lots of ribbons. Closed Sunday and Monday.

Souche Lapparra 157, rue du Temple, 3*e*. Métro: Filles-du-Calvaire. 42-72-16-20. You will get wholesale prices on lengths of gold chain at this shop. You choose the length you want; they'll cut it, put a clasp on it, and it's yours. Closed Saturday and Sunday.

Técla 2, rue de la Paix, 2*e*. Métro: Opéra. 42-61-03-29. Pearls are this house's specialty, in any setting, design, or form you choose. Closed Sunday. AE/V.

Tiany Chambard 32, rue Jacob, 6*e*. Métro: St.-Germain-des-Prés. 43-29-73-15. Not quite antique jewelry but many pieces from the twenties, thirties, and even fifties that are in vogue now: earrings, geometric bracelets, necklaces, and more. Alongside the jewelry are many trinkets and treasures—inkwells, old-fashioned labels, frames for a sweetheart's picture. Closed Sunday and Monday.

Troc de Bijoux 3, rue Coëtlogon, 6*e*. Métro: St.-Sulpice. 45-48-93-54. You'll find the top names in secondhand jewelry at this shop, some sold by the piece, some by the pound. Closed Wednesday and Sunday. AE/DC.

KITCHEN EQUIPMENT

See SHOPPING.

Jewelry

LAUNDROMATS

Keeping clothes clean when you travel can be a problem. But armed with a few hints, you'll find it's really not very complicated in Paris. Modern technology has taken the city by storm, and there are laundromats in every *arrondissement*. They have many different names: **Lavomatique**, **Laverie Automatique**, **Laverie Libre-Service**.

These places are usually well equipped. They almost always have American-brand washing machines, so your clothes are washed rapidly—in about 25 minutes. They probably won't come out as clean as if they were washed in a small French machine, but you won't have to wait 2 hours either. Dryers are standard, too. Both machines usually operate with tokens, which you can buy in the laundromat.

If you don't want to waste time waiting for your clothes to get clean, you can take them to a **teinturerie** for *nettoyage-à-sec*, or dry cleaning. They will usually iron your clothes as well. If you have a quantity of laundry, you might want to take it to a **blanchisserie** (laundry), which will usually weigh your clothes and charge you by the kilo (*au poids*). They will be washed in water and ironed (*repassés*) if you request it. Be prepared to wait up to 4 days to get your clean laundry. A **laverie-pressing** will take individual items of clothing, wash them in water, and iron them if you request it.

LIBRARIES

Entrance to most of these libraries is free and unrestricted, unless otherwise stated. However, some libraries request a piece of identification with a photo on it before letting you in. A passport or student identification is usually sufficient.

English-Language Libraries

American Library in Paris 10, rue du Général Camou, 7e. Métro: Ecole Militaire. 45-51-46-82. A well-rounded library with books on American history, literature, periodicals, a children's selection, cassettes, and records. Anyone can borrow material if he or she pays an annual fee of about 325F. Otherwise, there is a minimal fee to use the library by the day, though there is no charge to stay and read the periodicals. Closed Sunday and Monday.

Benjamin Franklin Documentation Center 2, rue St.-Florentin, 1er. Métro: Concorde. 42-96-33-10. This library is open to university students and those who have a specific reason for using these historic, political, socio-economic, and current events books and documents. Closed Saturday and Sunday.

Bibliothèque du Centre Georges Pompidou 120, rue St.-Martin, 4e. Métro: Châtelet. 42-77-12-33. An incredibly diverse library with periodicals in just about every language, slides, films, videotapes, cassettes, records. They have rare and modern collections for use in the library. For language tapes, see FRENCH COURSES. Closed Tuesday.

British Council Library 9, rue de Constantine, 7e. Métro: Invalides. 45-55-95-95. Books on British civilization, literature, social sciences. Also, periodicals and cassettes. You can borrow material, provided you pay an annual fee of about 140F. Closed Saturday and Sunday.

Other Libraries

Bibliothèque des Arts Décoratifs 109, rue de Rivoli, 1er. Métro: Palais Royal. 42-60-32-14. This lovely library looks out into the Tuileries gardens, and it contains books on just about every aspect of architecture, art, decoration, interior design, and textiles, published throughout the world. There is also a well-known collection of books on the arts called the *Collection Maciet.* Closed Sunday.

Bibliothèque Forney 1, rue du Figuier, 4e. Métro: Pont-Marie. 42-78-14-60. Another art and design library with works on subjects from fine art to crafts like carpentry, plumbing, typography, stained glass, and more. There is an interior decorating section, posters, postcards, magazines, and slides. Some periodicals

Libraries

and books can be checked out. Closed Sunday and Monday.

Bibliothèque Historique de la Ville de Paris 24, rue Pavée, 4e. Métro: St.-Paul. 42-74-44-44. The reading room of this beautiful library is filled with long tables and comfortable chairs that overlook an inviting garden. There are all manner of books on the history of Paris from its politics to its food. Closed Sunday.

Bibliothèque Marguerite Durand 21, pl. du Panthéon, 5e. Métro: Luxembourg. 43-26-85-05. Works about women, including drawings, photos, letters. Closed Saturday and Sunday.

Bibliothèque Mazarine (Institut de France) 23, quai de Conti, 6e. Métro: St.-Michel. 43-54-89-48. Among other things, this library has a collection on the history of regional France. Closed Saturday and Sunday.

Bibliothèque du Musée Guimet 6, pl. d'Iéna, 16e. Métro: Iéna. 47-23-61-65. This is the library of the Musée Guimet, which concentrates on Asian civilizations, and includes works on art, history, and society. It is open by request, for research projects.

Bibliothèque du Musée de l'Homme Palais de Chaillot, 16e. Métro: Trocadéro. 47-04-53-94. This library is attached to the Musée de l'Homme, and it contains books on anthropology, ethnology, and works on prehistoric societies. Closed Tuesday, Saturday and Sunday.

Bibliothèque Nationale 58, rue de Richelieu, 2e. Métro: Bourse. 42-61-82-83. Only the intellectual greats get into this sacrosanct and renowned institution. Unless you have a documented research project you may not be included. It is rumored to be easier for foreigners to get into than for the French. Closed Sunday.

Bibliothéque de l'Opera pl. Charles Garnier, 2e. Métro: Opéra. 47-42-07-02. Every piece of music that has ever been played or sung in the Opéra is in this library. There is also a section on music, theater, and dance. Closed Sunday.

Bibliothèque Sainte-Geneviève 10, pl. du Panthéon, 5e. Métro: Cardinal-Lemoine. 43-29-61-00. There is a very old and important collection of theological and religious works as well as works on the history of Paris. The architecture of the library is worth a quick visit; it was rebuilt in the mid-1800s by Labrouste. Closed Sunday.

Libraries

LOST AND FOUND

For stolen items you must first report to the nearest police station (listed in the *Plan de Paris par Arrondissement*, or ask any policeman or meter maid that you see). You may be asked to fill out some forms. Try to be patient; there is likely someone who will understand a bit of English, but don't expect miracles.

Your next step is to go to the **Bureau des Objets Trouvés** (Lost and Found)—36, rue des Morillons, 15e. Métro: Convention. There is no one at the office who officially speaks English, but the staff will try their best to help you. They will not respond to any inquiries by telephone. And the office is closed on weekends.

If you lose your passport, again, report to the nearest police station first, then go directly to your consulate. A note of advice: write down the number of your passport and keep it in a secure place. It will help immensely in case it gets lost or stolen.

MAPS OF PARIS

See ARRIVAL IN PARIS.

MARKETS

If food is the quality of Paris, then markets are the texture—the warp and the weft of a society that thrives on lively commercial interchange. Going to the market in Paris is much more than just a shopping trip. It's a social visit—with your neighbor, your favorite merchant, the local restaurateur there to choose produce for the day's menu. You not only find out how everyone in the neighborhood is doing—either by chatting or by catching bits and pieces of the hundreds of conversations going on around you—but you get the lowdown on the day's current events, how people feel about politics, the weather, the state of the sports world, taxes, and the price of food. Merchants commiserate with customers when they're not loudly hawking their wares, brandishing a vivid green head of lettuce, or displaying a bunch of fresh-from-the-garden carrots.

Even if you don't buy anything, a trip to a market is a sensorial triumph. Piles of colorful fruits and vegetables are carefully arranged each morning, and often again each afternoon after the lunch break. Nothing is left to chance. Each stall is a monument to its proprietor's pride and artistic verve. Competition is stiff and customers wily, as they stop to look and visually savor plump red tomatoes, juicy white peaches, diminutive mirabelle plums, or dainty melons, before deciding where they'll buy. No one touches anything—it's not the market tradition. You look, you calculate, then you trust the merchant to give you what you want.

There are three kinds of food markets in Paris: the permanent street markets, the roving outdoor markets, and the covered indoor markets.

Street Markets

The character and quality of street markets is a direct reflection of the surrounding neighborhoods' personality. They are open from 9 AM to 12:30–1 PM, and from 4 PM to 7 PM, Tuesday through Saturday; from 9 AM to 1 PM on Sunday.

Rue des Belles Feuilles Begins at av. Victor-Hugo, 16e. Métro: Victor-Hugo. Very classy market with excellent-quality produce, meat, and fish.

Rue Cler Begins av. de la Motte-Picquet, 7e. Métro: École Militaire. This is a clean, uncrowded market street with good-quality produce and generally helpful merchants.

Rue de Lévis Begins bd. des Batignolles, 17e. Métro: Villiers. A real mixture of goods, from top-quality cheese to average-quality produce.

Rue Montorgueil Begins at rue Rambuteau, 1er. Métro: Les Halles. Going to rue Montorgueil is like stepping back in time, getting a little taste of Paris' former central market place, Les Halles, the *ventre de Paris* (belly of Paris). It's full of character with lots of tiny, jumbled stalls and shops, butcher stores with sawdust on the floor and good-looking produce.

Rue Mouffetard Begins rue de l'Epée-de-Bois, 5e. Métro: Monge. One of Paris' oldest markets, rue Mouffetard is loud, jostling, heavily touristed but nonetheless one of the city's best. The variety may be slightly limited, but the cafés are jumping, the merchants' goods picture-perfect, and the cacophony fulfills every expectation.

Rue Poncelet Begins at av. des Ternes, 17e. Métro: Ternes. A concentrated, lively market with an astounding choice of produce, from piles of wild mushrooms in the fall to myriad soft fruits in summer, and from fragrant white and yellow peaches to ambrosial nectarines, apricots, and just about every berry imaginable.

Rue du Poteau Begins pl. Jules Joffrin, 18e. Métro: Jules-Joffrin. Tucked away in the 18th *arrondissement*, this market is more relaxed and tidy than many others, with a real feel of yesteryear about it.

Rue de Seine/Rue de Buci Begins bd. St.-Germain, 6e. Métro: Odéon. Practically every tourist who visits Paris walks through this market, which doesn't detract an iota from its local character. The merchants are strident, the produce can be excellent, and if you're a regular it doesn't take long until you're swapping recipes with the fruit lady or joking with the man behind the lettuce. There's good cheese and *charcuterie* to be had here, too.

Roving Markets

Roving markets are just that—they move from neighborhood to neighborhood, appearing on fixed days with their farm-fresh produce and eagerness to please. Despite their peripatetic nature, the merchants still build up a rapport with customers whom they see on a regular basis, people who come for the fresher than average produce, variety, and diversity. You'll find not just produce, meat, fish, cheese and bread, but socks or buttons, dresses and towels, kitchen utensils and linens. Roving markets are open just in the mornings from 7 AM to 1:30 PM.

Alésia Rue d'Alésia, 14e. Métro: Alésia. Wednesday and Saturday.

Alibert Rue Alibert and rue Claude-Vellefaux, 10e. Métro: Goncourt. Thursday and Sunday.

Amiral-Bruix Bd. Bruix, between rue Weber and rue Marbeau, 16e. Métro: Porte Maillot. Wednesday and Saturday.

Auteuil Formed by rue d'Auteuil, rue Donizetti, and rue La Fontaine, 16*e*. Métro: Michel-Ange-Auteuil. Wednesday and Saturday.

Avenue de Versailles Rue Gros and rue La Fontaine, 16*e*. Métro: Jasmin. Tuesday and Friday; av. du Président-Wilson, between rue Debrousee and pl. d'Iéna, 16*e*. Métro: Alma-Marceau. Wednesday and Saturday.

Belgrand Rue Belgrand, rue de la Chine, and pl. de la Py. 20*e*. Métro: Gambetta. Wednesday and Saturday.

Belleville On the island of bd. de Belleville, 11*e*. Métro: Belleville. Tuesday and Friday.

Bercy Bd. de Reuilly, between rue de Charenton and pl. Félix-Eboué, 12*e*. Métro: Daumesnil. Tuesday and Friday.

Berthier Angle of av. de la Porte d'Asnière and bd. Berthier, 17*e*. Métro: Porte de Clichy. Wednesday and Saturday.

Bobillot Rue Bobillot, between pl. Rungis and rue de la Colonie, 13*e*. Métro: Maison Blanche. Tuesday and Friday.

Boulevard Brune Between passage des Suisses and N.49, bd. Brune, 14*e*. Métro: Porte de Vanves. Thursday and Sunday.

Bd. de Charonne Between rue de Charonne and rue Alexandre-Dumas, 11*e*. Métro: Alexandre-Dumas. Wednesday and Saturday.

Breteuil Av. de Saxe and av. de Ségur, toward pl. Breteuil, 7*e*. Métro: Ségur. Thursday and Saturday.

Carmes Pl. Maubert, 5*e*. Métro: Maubert-Mutualité. Tuesday, Thursday, and Saturday.

Cervantes Rue Bargue, 15*e*. Métro: Volontaires. Wednesday and Saturday.

Cité Berryer Begins rue Royale in the passage of the Cité Berryer, 8*e*. Métro: Madeleine. Tuesday and Friday.

Clignancourt Bd. d'Ornano, between rue du Mont-Cenis and rue Ordener, 18*e*. Métro: Ordener. Tuesday, Friday, and Sunday.

Convention Rue de la Convention, between rue Alain-Chartier and rue de l'Abbé-Groult, 15*e*. Métro: Convention. Tuesday, Thursday and Sunday.

Cours de Vincennes Between bd. de Picpus and av. du Dr. Arnold-Netter, 12*e*. Métro: Porte de Vincennes. Wednesday and Saturday.

Crimée 430, bd. Ney, 18e. Métro: Porte de Clignancourt. Wednesday and Saturday.

Davout Bd. Davout, between av. de la Porte de Montreuil and 94, bd. Davout, 20e. Métro: Porte de Montreuil. Tuesday and Friday.

Dupleix Bd. de Grenelle, between rue Lourmel and rue du Commerce, 15e. Métro: Dupleix. Wednesday and Sunday.

Edgar-Quinet On the island of bd. Edgar-Quinet, 14e. Métro: Raspail. Wednesday and Saturday.

Exelmans Along pl. de la Porte-Molitor, beginning av. du Général-Sarrail toward bd. Exelmans, 16e. Métro: Michel-Ange-Auteuil. Tuesday and Friday.

Gobelins Bd. Auguste-Blanqui, between pl. d'Italie and rue Barrault, 13e. Métro: Corvisart. Tuesday, Friday, and Sunday.

Javel Rue St.-Charles, between rue Javel and Rond-Point-St.-Charles, 15e. Métro: Charles-Michel. Tuesday and Friday.

Jean-Jaurès 145 to 185 av. Jean-Jaurès, 19e. Métro: Pantin. Tuesday, Thursday, and Sunday.

Joinville At the angle of rue de Joinville and rue Jomard, 19e. Métro: Crimée. Tuesday, Thursday and Sunday.

Lariboisière Bd. de la Chapelle, across from Lariboisière hospital, 18e. Métro: Barbès-Rochechouart. Wednesday and Saturday.

Lecourbe Rue Lecourbe, between rue Vasco-de-Gama and rue Leblanc, 15e. Métro: Place Balard. Wednesday and Saturday.

Ledru-Rollin Av. Ledru-Rollin, between rue de Lyon and rue de Bercy, 12e. Métro: Gare de Lyon. Thursday and Saturday.

Lefèbvre Bd. Lefèbvre, between rue Olivier de Serres and rue de Dantzig, 15e. Métro: Porte de Versailles. Wednesday and Saturday.

Maison-Blanche Av. d'Italie and rue Bourgon, 13e. Métro: Porte d'Italie. Thursday and Sunday.

Monge Pl. Monge. 5e. Métro: Monge. Wednesday, Friday, and Sunday.

Montrouge Among rue Brézin, rue Saillard, rue Mouton-Duvernet, and rue Boulard, 14e. Métro: Mouton-Duvernet. Tuesday and Friday.

Mortier Bd. Mortier, at av. de la Porte de Ménilmontant, 20e. Métro: St.-Fargeau. Wednesday and Saturday.

Markets

Navier Among rue Navier, rue Lantier, and rue des Epinettes, 17e. Métro: Guy-Moquet. Tuesday and Friday.

Ney Bd. Ney, between rue Jean-Varenne and rue Camille-Flammarion, 18e. Métro: Porte de Clignancourt. Thursday and Sunday.

Ordener Between rue Montcalm and rue Championnet, 18e. Métro: Guy-Moquet. Wednesday and Sunday.

Père-Lachaise Bd. de Ménilmontant, between rue des Panoyaux and rue de Tlemcen, 11e. Métro: Père-Lachaise. Tuesday and Friday.

Place des Fêtes Pl. des Fêtes, alongside rue Pré-St.-Gervais, rue Petitot, and rue des Fêtes, 19e. Métro: Place des Fêtes. Tuesday, Friday, and Sunday.

Point du Jour Av. de Versailles, between rue Le Marois and rue Gudin, 16e. Métro: Porte-de-St.-Cloud. Tuesday, Thursday, and Sunday.

Poniatowski Bd. Poniatowski, between av. Daumesnil and rue de Picpus, 12e. Métro: Porte Dorée. Thursday and Sunday.

Popincourt Bd. Richard-Lenoir, between rue Oberkampf and rue de Crussol, 11e. Métro: Oberkampf. Tuesday and Friday.

Porte Brunet Av. de la Porte Brunet, between bd. Sérurier and bd. d'Algérie, 19e. Métro: Danube. Wednesday and Saturday.

Port-Royal Bd. Port-Royal, alongside Hôpital du Val-de-Grâce, 5e. Métro: Port-Royal. Tuesday, Thursday, and Saturday.

Pyrénées Rue des Pyrénées, between rue de l'Ermitage and rue de Ménilmontant, 20e. Métro: Ménilmontant. Thursday and Sunday.

Raspail Bd. Raspail, between rue du Cherche-Midi and rue de Rennes, 6e. Métro: St.-Placide. Tuesday and Friday.

Réunion Pl. de la Réunion, between the place and rue Vitruve, 20e. Métro: Alexandre-Dumas. Thursday and Sunday.

Richard-Lenoir Bd. Richard-Lenoir and rue Amelot, 11e. Métro: Bastille. Thursday and Sunday.

Saint-Eloi 36–38, rue de Reuilly, 12e. Métro: Reuilly-Diderot. Thursday and Sunday.

Salpêtrière Pl. de la Salpêtrière, alongside bd. de l'Hôpital, 13e. Métro: St.-Marcel. Tuesday and Friday.

Télégraphe Rue du Télégraphe, to the right of Belle-

Markets

ville cemetery, 20e. Métro: Télégraphe. Wednesday and Saturday.

Tolbiac Pl. Jeanne-d'Arc, 13e. Métro: Nationale. Thursday and Sunday.

Villemain Av. Villemain, on the island between av. Villemain and rue d'Alésia, 14e. Métro: Plaisance. Wednesday and Sunday.

Villette 27-to-41, bd. de la Villette, 19e. Métro: Belleville. Wednesday and Saturday.

Covered Markets

Covered markets have come, have gone, and are back again in cavernous old market buildings, many of which have been spruced up, renovated into impeccable modernity while managing to retain some charm. Covered markets are quieter than their street or roving counterparts, but they have their own appeal, and they're great during inclement weather. They are open from 9 AM to 1 PM and from 4 PM to 7 PM, Tuesday through Saturday; from 9 AM to 1 PM on Sunday.

Batignolles 96, rue Lemercier, 17e. Métro: Brochant.

Beauvau-Saint-Antoine Between rue d'Aligre and rue Cotte, 12e. Métro: Ledru-Rollin.

Chapelle Rue de l'Olive, 18e. Métro: Max-Dormoy. Open until midnight on Friday and Saturday.

Enfants Rouges 39, rue de Bretagne, 3e. Métro: Filles-du-Calvaire.

Europe Rue Corvetto, between rue Maleville and rue Treihard, 8e. Métro: Villiers.

Passy Angle of rue Bois-le-vent and rue Duban, 16e. Métro: La Muette.

Porte Saint-Martin 31 and 33, rue du Château-d'Eau, 10e. Métro: St.-Martin.

Riquet 36–46, rue Riquet, 18e. Métro: Riquet. Open until 8 PM on Friday and Saturday.

Saint-Didier Angle of rue Mesnil and rue St.-Didier, 16e. Métro: Victor-Hugo.

Saint-Germain Among rue Lobineau, rue Clément, and rue Mabillon, 6e. Métro: Mabillon.

Saint-Honoré Pl. du Marché-St.-Honoré, 1er. Métro: Tuileries.

Saint-Quentin 85 bis, bd. de Magenta, 10e. Métro: Gare-de-l'Est.

Secrétan 46, rue Bouret, and 33, av. Secrétan, 19e. Métro: Bolivar.

Ternes Rue Lebon, rue Faraday, and rue Torricelli, 17*e*. Métro: Ternes.

Organic Markets (Marchés Biologiques)

The *biologique* (organic) movement in France is strong, and the produce sold at these markets is grown without *engrais chimiques* (pesticides). For more about organic markets or related information, call **Nature et Progrès**: 42-22-89-99.

Marché Biologique Pl. de Verdun, 94000 Joinville-le-Pont. Métro: RER line A2 to Joinville or suburban bus N.106 or 108. Takes place the third Saturday of each month.

Marché Nature et Progrès 140, route de la Reine, 92000 Boulogne-sur-Seine. Métro: Boulogne or Porte-de-St.-Cloud, or bus N.72 from Paris. Takes place the first Saturday of each month.

Rungis

Rungis, in the south suburbs of Paris, is the home of France's largest wholesale food market, the same market that used to occupy Les Halles, right in the center of Paris. Les Halles was the hub of the city, open in the wee hours of the morning when throngs—from chefs to housewives—came to buy their daily provisions. The crowd got too large and the conditions in the market too uncertain, and it was moved to Rungis—much to the sorrow of Paris' populace. Now the market is housed in sterile buildings on over 400 acres of tarmac, and it is open only to professionals who must show identification cards to get into the enormous complex.

There are 2 tours that give individuals the chance to look at the Rungis market area, which now includes several restaurants, cafés, and shops just for the needs of the personnel. The market itself offers a tour in French for groups. Prices range from 22F to 30F per person and reservations must be made two months in advance by calling 46-87-35-35. To get to Rungis from Paris, take bus RER line N.183, 185, 285, or 131.

Paris en Cuisine cooking school also offers tours of Rungis, in English, for groups of about 10. Call or write to Paris en Cuisine, 78, rue de la-Croix-Nivert, 75015 Paris. Métro: Cambronne. 42-50-04-23.

Flea Markets

For bargains, for treasures, for clothes, for furniture you've got to visit the *puces*.

Marché de Montreuil Av. de la Porte de Montreuil, 12e. Métro: Porte de Montreuil. Saturday and Sunday.

Marché de la Place d'Aligre Pl. d'Aligre, 12e. Métro: Ledru-Rollin. Daily from 9 AM to noon.

Marché de la Porte de Clignancourt Rue des Entrepots, 18e. Métro: Porte de Clignancourt. This is the biggest and best-known flea market in Paris.

Marché de la Porte des Lilas 19e. Métro: Porte des Lilas. Sunday and holidays.

Marché de la Porte de Vanves Av. Georges-Lafenestre, 15e. Métro: Porte de Vanves. Saturday and Sunday.

Flower Markets

These markets, with their profusion of colors and soft scents, immeasurably brighten up the neighborhood and the passersby. And most of the flower merchants will wrap your carefully chosen purchase in beautiful flowered paper and ribbon.

Monceau Fleurs 92, bd. Malesherbes, 8e. Métro: Villiers. 45-63-88-23. The choice here is vast and the prices some of the more reasonable in Paris.

Place Louis-Lépine And on adjacent quais, 4e. Métro: Cité. Closed Sunday.

Place de la Madeleine 8e. Métro: Madeleine. Closed Monday.

Place des Ternes 8e. Métro: Ternes. Open daily.

Stamp Market

Like little mushrooms, the tables, chairs, and booths for the stamp market pop up at the corner of the **av. des Champs-Elysées** and **av. Marigny**, 8e. Métro: Champs-Elysées-Clémenceau. There are old stamps, new stamps, cancelled stamps, and rare stamps. It's a wonderful scene as well. Saturday and Sunday.

MEN'S FASHIONS

Arny's 14, rue de Sèvres, 7e. Métro: Sèvres-Babylone. 45-48-76-99. Closed Sunday. AE/DC/EC/V.

Men's Fashions

Boutiques pour Lui 112, rue de Richelieu, 2e. Métro: Richelieu-Drouot. 42-96-66-12. Closed Sunday. AE/DC/V.

Cacharel 5, pl. des Victoires, 1er. Métro: Etienne-Marcel. 42-33-29-88. Closed Sunday. AE/DC/V.

Cerruti 1881 27, rue Royale, 8e. Métro: Madeleine. 42-65-68-72. Closed Sunday. AE/DC/V.

Christian Dior Boutique 13, rue François-1er, 8e. Métro: Franklin D. Roosevelt. 47-23-54-44. Closed Sunday. AE/DC/V.

Courrèges 40, rue François-1er, 8e. Métro: Franklin D. Roosevelt. 47-20-70-44. Closed Sunday. Also, 113 av. Victor-Hugo, 16e. AE/DC/V.

Daniel Crémieux 6, bd. Malesherbes, 8e. Métro: Madeleine. 42-65-96-15; 24, rue Marbeuf, 8e. Métro: Franklin D. Roosevelt. 42-25-45-91. Both shops closed Sunday and Monday morning. AE/DC/V.

Gillio 261, rue St.-Honoré, 1er. Métro: Concorde. 42-60-93-91; 2, bd. de la Madeleine, 9e. Métro: Madeleine. 47-42-69-41. AE/DC/EC/V.

Givenchy Gentleman 29–31, av. George-V. 8e. Métro: Alma-Marceau. 47-20-90-13. Closed Sunday. AE/DC/V.

Island 3, rue Montmartre, 1er. Métro: Châtelet-Les-Halles. 42-33-15-74. AE/V; 4, rue Vide-Gousset, pl. des Victoires, 2e. Métro: Bourse. 42-61-77-77. Both shops closed Sunday. AE/DC/V.

Pierre Cardin 59, rue du Faubourg-St.-Honoré, 8e. Métro: Miromesnil. 42-66-92-95. Closed Sunday. AE/DC.

Yves Saint Laurent 38, rue du Faubourg-St.-Honoré, 8e. Métro: Madeleine. 42-65-74-59. Closed Sunday. AE/DC/V.

For Big Sizes

Berdy 79, av. des Ternes, 17e. Métro: Ternes. 45-74-35-13; also 86, av. Ledru-Rollin, 12e. Métro: Ledru-Rollin. 46-28-18-24. Both shops closed Sunday and Monday.

METRO

See ARRIVAL IN PARIS.

Men's Fashions

MONEY EXCHANGE

See ARRIVAL IN PARIS.

MOVIES

Paris is a mecca for movie enthusiasts, with more than 500 movie theaters within the city limits. While they are sprinkled about town, the major *quartiers* for movies are the Champs-Elysées, the Latin Quarter, Montparnasse, and Les Halles. Invaluable movie guides are the *Pariscope* (available in almost all hotels in Paris and free to guests) and *L'Officiel des Spectacles*, which are published weekly and list every movie playing in Paris, giving a one-line synopsis, the theater where the film is playing, and either the showtime or the phone number of the theater. The letters *v.o.* after the movie's title mean it is being shown in its language of origin—*version originale*. The letters *v.f.* mean it has been dubbed into French—*version française.*

Monday is a discount day—and night—at the movies, and admission prices are lower by about a third. This does not apply to Mondays that happen to be holidays.

Remember when you enter the theater to have a franc ready to give to the usher, who may or may not show you to your seat. Tipping in this case is not a formality, but is expected—the tips the ushers get are their salaries.

If you're a movie history or old movie fan, go to the **Cinémathèque Française** in the Palais de Chaillot (east wing), pl. du Trocadéro, 16e. Métro: Trocadéro. 45-53-74-39. They show international classics every day but Monday, from 3 PM to 9 PM. Admission is about 16F. The Cinémathèque also offers a very informative guided tour of its movie museum, the Musée du Cinéma Henri Langlois (see MUSEUMS). There is another Cinémathèque Française on the 5th floor of the Centre National d'Art et de la Culture Georges-Pompidou, rue Rambuteau, 4e. Métro: Rambuteau. 42-78-35-57. This one shows films but has no museum, and is closed Tuesday. Entrance to films is about 12F. Call for information about what films are showing, or consult the *Pariscope* or *L'Officiel des Spectacles.*

Movies

If you're planning to be in Paris for any length of time, you might consider becoming a member of the Cinémathèque. For a small monthly or yearly fee you pay a reduced admission charge to all movies offered by the Cinémathèque as well as having opportunities to see first-run American films before they are released in France.

MUSEUMS

Paris has more than one hundred museums, some that can be visited in a short time, others that merit days, weeks, or months of study, observation, and enjoyment. And there are museums on just about every subject, from postage stamps to firearms, impressionism to dentistry. Not all museums or exhibits are in the most up-to-date condition, but in recent years more work has been done to expand and improve Paris museums.

State-owned museums are closed on Tuesdays, city-owned museums on Mondays, and private museums schedule their hours individually. Most museums are closed on legal holidays. On Sundays and Wednesdays admission to many museums is half-price or free. Students and senior citizens qualify for reduced admission in many museums on a regular basis. Always carry identification with you—a passport, student identification, or a *Carte Vermeille* (see SENIOR CITIZENS)—as proof of age is required.

The following is a selected list of Paris' museums and a general description of their permanent collections. For current expositions consult the *Pariscope* or *L'Officiel des Spectacles*.

Atelier Eugène Delacroix 3, rue de Furstemberg, 6e. Métro: St.-Germain-des-Prés. 43-54-04-87. This museum is Delacroix' former home and studio. It gives a vivid impression of his personality and life through an exhibit of his work and personal memorabilia. Closed Tuesday. Free admission Wednesday.

Bibliothèque-Musée de la Société de l'Histoire du Protestantisme Français 54, rue des Sts.-Pères, 7e. Métro: St.-Germain-des-Prés. 45-48-62-07. Closed Monday and holidays. A history of French Protestantism through paintings, engravings, medals, original manuscripts, and sculptures.

Museums

Cabinet des Médailles In the Bibliothèque Nationale, 58, rue de Richelieu, 2e. Métro: Bourse. 42-61-82-83. Open daily. More than 700,000 coins, medals, and artifacts are housed in this museum as well as a collection of royal treasures.

Centre Culturel du Marais 26, rue des Francs-Bourgeois, 3e. Métro: St.-Paul. 42-72-73-52. Hours variable. When this museum/gallery is open it has avant-garde and contemporary art and photography.

Centre National d'Art et de Culture Georges-Pompidou Rue Rambuteau, 1er. Métro: Rambuteau or Hôtel-de-Ville. 42-77-12-33. Closed Tuesday. Free admission to some permanent exhibits. Free admission to all exhibits for students and senior citizens, and to the general public Sundays and holidays. This huge steel-and-glass structure, which is consecrated to contemporary art of all kinds, was built in 1977. There is a re-creation of Brancusi's studio on the first floor with a collection of his works. On the third floor is an exhibit of works from the beginning of the 20th century until post-World War I: fauvism, cubism, and the beginning of abstract art. The fourth floor has a collection of modern art from post-World War I until the present, with works by Matisse, Picasso, Guéridon, Braque, Paul Klee, Fernand Léger, and Le Corbusier. In the central portion of the fourth floor are works by artists from the École de Paris: Bonnard, Modigliani, Soutine, Foujita. There are also pieces by Miró, Dali, and Brauner. There is a section given to "hyperrealism," with pieces by Giacometti, Mathieu, Kemeny, Soulages, and Calder as well as many temporary exhibits throughout the year. You can buy one ticket for all the exhibits for about 40F that is good all day, or pay for each exhibit separately.

Hôtel des Monnaies 11, quai Conti, 6e. Métro: Pont-Neuf. 43-29-12-48. Closed Sundays and holidays. This museum has a collection of coins and medals dating from the Middle Ages to the present. There are occasional temporary exhibits. The studio where commemorative coins and medals are made can also be visited.

Manufacture des Gobelins 42, av, des Gobelins, 13e. Métro: Gobelins. 45-70-12-60. Open Tuesday, Wednesday, and Thursday afternoons. You can visit the factory where Gobelins tapestries have been made for

Museums

centuries, and where they are still made painstakingly by hand and according to ancient methods. Apprentices train for 7 years before they are qualified to work here as weavers.

Musée de l'Affiche et de la Publicité 18, rue de Paradis, 10e. Métro: Château-d'Eau. 42-46-13-09. Closed Tuesday. This museum has a collection of posters throughout history to contemporary times as well as temporary exhibits on graphic publicity.

Musée Antoine-Bourdelle 16, rue Antoine-Bourdelle, 15e. Métro: Falguière. 45-48-67-27. Closed Mondays and holidays. Free admission Sunday. Works of Antoine Bourdelle, a student of Rodin, are housed in the artist's former studio including sculptures, paintings, watercolors, and pastels.

Musée de l'Arc de Triomphe Arc de Triomphe, pl. de l'Etoile, 8e. Métro: Charles-de-Gaulle-Etoile. 43-80-31-31. Closed Sundays and holidays. A small museum at the top of the Arc de Triomphe with documents and souvenirs on the construction of the Arc, ceremonies that have taken place there, a film that illustrates some of the Arc's grander moments, and various Napoleonic paraphernalia. There is also a wonderful view from this spot which is between the place de la Concorde and La Défense.

Musée de l'Armée Hôtel des Invalides, Esplanade des Invalides, 7e. Métro: Latour-Maubourg. 45-55-92-30. Permanent exhibit of military art, technique, and history throughout the world including arms, weapons, armor, and uniforms. Also houses the *Musée des Plans-Reliefs*; use the same entrance as for the Musée de l'Armée. This museum contains models of the city and its defenses in a collection begun under Louis XIV. There is also a museum showing fortifications throughout France's history, and the *Musée de l'Ordre de la Libération*, 51 bis, bd. de Latour-Maubourg, 7e. Métro: Latour-Maubourg. 47-05-04-10. The latter has trophies and relics from battles throughout French history. All museums at Les Invalides are closed Sundays and holidays.

Musée d'Art et d'Essai In the Palais de Tokyo, 13, av. du Président-Wilson, 16e. Métro: Alma-Marceau. 47-23-36-53. Closed Monday. Free admission Sunday. Several temporary thematic exhibits are shown here simultaneously which represent a style, a school, an artist, or a technique in art.

Musée d'Art Juif 42, rue des Saules, 18e. Métro: La-marck. 42-57-84-15. Closed Fridays, Saturdays, Jew-ish holy days, and the month of August. This museum was founded in 1949 and holds a collection of models of ancient synagogues, some traditional objects used in Jewish rituals, works by Chagall, and others by contemporary Jewish artists.

Musée d'Art Moderne de la Ville de Paris 11, av. du Président-Wilson, 16e. Métro: Alma-Marceau. 47-23-61-27. Closed Mondays and holidays. Free admission on Wednesday. Works by 20th-century artists includ-ing Picasso, Braque, Matisse, Derain, Modigliani, Dufy. The biggest painting in the world, *La Fée de l'Electricité* by Raoul Dufy, is housed there.

Musée des Arts Africains et Océaniens 293, av. Dau-mesnil, 12e. Métro: Porte Dorée. 43-43-14-54. Closed Tuesdays and holidays. In the Bois de Vincennes, on the east edge of Paris, this museum has art and ar-cheology from New Zealand and Australia, and a col-lection of art from black Africa, as well as represen-tative pieces showing their influence on French art with drawings by Gauguin, among others. Admission is half-price on Sundays, free on Wednesdays.

Musée des Arts Décoratifs 107, rue de Rivoli, 1er. Métro: Tuileries. 42-60-32-14. Closed Mondays and Tuesdays. The history and evolution of international art in all its form is illustrated in this museum through sculpture, painting, furniture, crystal and porcelain, weaving, and all aspects of interior design. On the second floor is a remarkable collection of works by Dubuffet including paintings, drawings, and sculp-tures. The museum also schedules major temporary exhibits, and offers a series of art classes. For infor-mation regarding classes call 42-60-32-14, ext. 933, on Wednesday, Thursday, and Friday afternoons.

Musée des Arts et Traditions Populaires 6, rue Ma-hatma Gandhi, 16e. Métro: Les Sablons, 47-47-69-80. Closed Tuesday. Admission half-price on Sunday, free on Wednesday. There are 2 galleries in this museum, located in the Bois de Boulogne, with exhibits that illustrate life in rural France before the Industrial Revolution. The *Galerie Culturelle* shows how French rural society evolved into organized social communi-ties by mastering the natural resources around them. The theme is continued in the *Galerie d'Etude*, which

Museums

shows specifically the function objects and discoveries had in daily rural life.

Musée de l'Assistance Publique 47, quai de la Tournelle, 5e. Métro: Maubert-Mutualité. 46-33-01-43. Closed Mondays, holidays, and August. This museum shows the history of hospitals and health services in Paris through photographs, engravings, art objects, furniture, and a collection of old pharmaceutical containers.

Musée Balzac 47, rue Raynouard, 16e. Métro: Passy or La Muette. 42-24-56-38. Closed Mondays and holidays. Admission free on Sundays. This museum, a rare example of an old Passy *quartier* residence, was the author's home and is filled with portraits, engravings, and all manner of personal memorabilia documenting his life, his times, and his works. There is a small library in the basement.

Musée Carnavalet 23, rue de Sévigné, 3e. Métro: St.-Paul. 42-72-21-13. Closed Mondays. Admission free on Sundays. The history of Paris is all here, from its grandest moments to the daily life of its populace in fascinating and sometimes macabre curios, furnishings, paintings, coins, and documents. Temporary exhibits are shown throughout the year.

Musée Cernuschi 7, av. Velasquez, 8e. Métro: Monceau. 45-63-50-75. Closed Mondays and holidays. Admission free on Sundays unless there is a special exhibit. This museum overlooks the beautiful Parc Monceau. It was owned by the banker Henri Cernuschi, who filled it with Chinese art—bronzes, ceramics, and pieces from the Tang Dynasty—then gave it to the city of Paris.

Musée de la Chasse et de la Nature 60, rue des Archives, 3e. Métro: Hôtel-de-Ville. 42-72-86-43. Closed Tuesdays and holidays. This museum presents hunting artifacts from prehistoric times to the 19th century, including weapons, trophies, and works of art related to hunting.

Musée du Cinéma Henri Langlois Palais de Chaillot, East Wing, 16e. Métro: Trocadéro. 45-53-74-39. Closed Monday. This museum has 60 rooms filled with cinema paraphernalia—costumes, cameras, film clips—all collected by Henri Langlois, venerable cinema historian. His collection tells the history of film from its pre-history of Chinese shadows to the *Théâtre Optique*

Museums

of Paris. Guided tours of the museum are given daily except Monday from 10 A.M. to noon and from 2 P.M. to 4 P.M. Tours in English can be arranged by special request. Group tours are discounted.

Musée Clémenceau 8, rue Franklin, 16e. Métro: Trocadéro. 45-20-53-41. This was the home of Georges Clémenceau, former French head of state who died in 1929. It is filled with memorabilia about his life as a journalist, writer, and political figure.

Musée Cognacq-Jay 25, bd. des Capucines, 9e. Métro: Opéra. 42-61-94-54. Closed Mondays and holidays. Admission free on Sundays. This museum portrays the elegant life of 18th-century France in a collection of art, furniture, sculptures, and other treasures, collected by the founders of La Samaritaine, one of Paris' biggest department stores. There are works by such artists as Rembrandt, Fragonard, Guardi, Boilly.

Musée de l'Ecole Supérieure des Beaux-Arts 14, rue Bonaparte, 6e. Métro: St.-Germain-des-Prés. 45-48-50-01. In the Petits-Augustins chapel and some of the classrooms of the Beaux-Arts, on quai Malaquais, one can see some of the best examples of work by students and professors of the Beaux-Arts.

Musée de l'Ecole Supérieure des Mines 60 bd. St.-Michel, 6e. Métro: Maubert-Mutualité. 43-29-21-05, ext. 339. One of the most extensive collections of precious stones, minerals, crystals, and geological finds. Closed Sundays, Mondays, and holidays. Hours are variable, so call first.

Musée d'Ennéry 59, av. Foch, 16e. Métro: Porte Dauphine. 45-53-57-96. Open Thursdays and Sundays in the afternoons. A collection of works by Adolphe Ennert, writer of melodramas and operas. Also, a collection of Asian art including bronzes, jades, and *netsukés* (small wood buttons that have been carved into miniature human forms, then painted). *The Musée Arménien*, at the same address (telephone: 45-53-57-96), is open Sunday afternoons and has a collection of Armenian jewels, ornaments, and religious objects and artifacts.

Musée Grévin Level 1, Centre National d'Art et de Culture Georges-Pompidou, 1er. Métro: Châtelet-Les-Halles. 42-61-28-50. Open daily. (The musée is part of the *Musée Grevin* on bd. du Montmartre.) A recreated Belle Epoque street showing the most important and elegant moments of Paris' history from 1885 to 1900.

Musée Grévin 10, bd. du Montmartre, 9e. Métro: Montmartre. 47-20-85-23. Open daily. A wax museum showing scenes and well-known figures—political, movie actors, singers, and many others from French history.

Musée Guimet in the Palais de Tokyo, 16e. Métro: Iéna. 47-23-61-65. Closed Tuesday. Admission half-price Sundays and holidays, free on Wednesdays. This museum has collections of Asian art from India, Central Asia, and the Far East.

Musée Gustave-Moreau 14, rue de la Rochefoucauld, 9e. Métro: Trinité. 48-74-38-50. Closed Mondays, Tuesdays, and holidays. Free admission on Wednesdays. This is the former home of painter Gustave Moreau, which is filled with more than 11,000 of his creations.

Musée Henner 43, av. de Villiers, 17e. Métro: Malesherbes. 47-63-42-73. Closed Monday. Admission free on Wednesday. Works by the Alsatian painter Jean-Jacques Henner (1829–1905) including an audio-visual program that shows the evolution of his work.

Musée de l'Histoire de France 60, rue des Francs-Bourgeois, 3e. Métro: Hôtel-de-Ville. 42-77-11-30. Closed Tuesdays and holidays. Admission free on Wednesdays. This museum, located in the magnificent Hôtel Soubise which was built in 1707, has souvenirs and important documents from French history including letters by Joan of Arc, by Jean Moulin, the Edict of Nantes, and the Declaration of the Rights of Man. When seen together, they illustrate the entire history of France.

Musée de l'Holographie Forum des Halles, niveau-1, 1er. Métro: Châtelet-Les-Halles. 42-96-96-83. Closed Monday. Holography—simply defined—is sculpting with light through a laser process invented by Dennis Gabor in 1947. The process has become an art form, and you'll see some semi-magical examples here.

Musée de l'Homme Palais de Chaillot, pl. du Trocadéro, 16e. Métro: Trocadéro. 45-53-70-60. Closed Tuesdays and holidays. A collection of artifacts showing different peoples, their physical attributes, and their ways of life, from prehistoric times.

Museums

Musée Instrumental du Conservatoire National de Musique 14, rue de Madrid, 8e. Métro: Europe. 42-93-15-20. Open Wednesday to Saturday afternoons. A collection of ancient and modern musical instruments, including the harp that belonged to Marie Antoinette, as well as famous musical scores are housed in this museum.

Musée Jacquemart-André 158, bd. Haussmann, 8e. Métro: St.-Philippe-du-Roule. 45-62-39-94. Closed Mondays, Tuesdays, and holidays. A collection of 18th-century furnishings and paintings in this lovely 19th-century home. There are also temporary exhibits staged throughout the year.

Musée du Jeu de Paume SEE Musée d'Orsay

Musée de la Légion d'Honneur 2, rue de Bellechasse, 7e. Métro: Solférino. 45-55-95-16. Closed Monday. Admission free on Sundays. The history of France's mounted corps, the creation of the Legion of Honor, and a collection of other French civil and military decorations.

Musée du Louvre Pl. du Carrousel, 1er. Métro: Louvre. 42-60-39-26, ext. 3588. Closed Tuesdays and holidays. Admission free Sundays and Wednesdays. The Louvre has collections from every school, every country, every aspect of painting throughout history and throughout the world. Until the present, the museum has occupied just one wing of the huge Palais du Louvre, the rest being occupied by the French Ministry of Finance. By recent decree, the Minister of Finance has been asked to leave the Louvre to make way for the expansion of art exhibits. There is much construction and renovation in progress, which may result in temporary closure of certain exhibits, so it is a good idea to check the *Pariscope* or *L'Officiel des Spectacles* for current information, or call before going.

Archeological work is under way in the central court of the Palais du Louvre exposing some fascinating artifacts from ancient Paris including huge portions of one of the city's first walls. A controversial, contemporary pyramidal structure is planned for the courtyard to house shops, restaurants, a public video room, and a large information office. For the present the museum is unchanged with its more than 6,000 paintings, 2,250 sculptures, 90,000 drawings, 46,000 engravings, and more. Works in the Louvre are constantly undergoing cleaning and restoration, and a recent policy provides for that work to be done on the premises so the public can observe the process when they visit the museum.

Musée du Luxembourg By the Senate building, 19, rue de Vaugirard, 6e. Métro: Luxembourg, 42-34-25-95. Open daily. Free admission. Has temporary exhibits on a variety of subjects from contemporary societies to arts and crafts.

Musée de la Marine Palais de Chaillot, pl. du Trocadéro, 16e. Métro: Trocadéro: 45-53-31-70. Closed Tuesdays and holidays. This museum was instituted in 1827, and has a unique collection of model ships, the history of naval forces, marine exploration and fishing since the 17th century, through paintings, artifacts, and sculptures.

Musée Marmottan 2, rue Louis-Boilly, 16e. Métro: La Muette. 42-24-07-02. Closed Monday. A former private home that now houses a lovely collection of Renaissance and impressionist works by artists such as Carmontelle, Vernet, Monet, Renoir, Sisley, Pissarro.

Musée de la Mode et du Costume Palais Galliéra, 10, av. Pierre-ler-de-Serbie, 16e. Métro: Iéna. 47-20-85-46. Closed Monday. Presents temporary exhibits on the evolution of fashion from 1735 to present.

Musée de Montmartre 12, rue Cortot, 18e. Métro: Caulaincourt. 46-06-61-11. Open afternoons only. Closed Monday. Paintings, engravings, and relics illustrating the history of Montmartre, from its cabarets to the lives of its artists. The museum is in the former country home of the actor Rosmond, who died in 1686.

Musée National d'Histoire Naturelle Jardin des Plantes, 57, rue Cuvier, 5e. Métro: Jussieu. 43-31-89-59. There are laboratories, a museum, a wonderful botanical garden, alpine garden, zoo, library, and winter garden collectively called Le Musée National d'Histoire Naturelle in the Jardin des Plantes. The winter garden is closed Tuesdays and holidays, the Jardin Alpin is closed on holidays; the zoo is open daily and the Botanical Garden is closed Saturdays, Sundays, and holidays.

Musée National des Monuments Français Palais de Chaillot, 16e. Métro: Trocadéro. 47-27-35-74. Closed Tuesday. Admission reduced on Sunday, free on Wednesday. This museum illustrates the development of the sculpture and painting of monuments throughout France, through models and copies.

Musée National des Techniques 270, rue St.-Martin, 3e. Métro: Arts-et-Métiers. 42-71-24-14. Closed Mondays and holidays. Free admission on Sundays. This museum shows the history of technology through a presentation of machines and machine prototypes.

Musée Nissim de Camondo 63, rue de Monceau, 8e, Métro: Villiers, 45-63-26-32. Closed Mondays, Tuesdays, and holidays. This museum is a re-creation of an 18th-century home with a remarkable art collection that includes tapestries, bronzes, porcelain pieces, and works by Vigée-Lebrun, Drouais, Huet, Guardi, Duplessi, and more.

Musée Notre Dame 10, rue du Cloître-Notre-Dame, 4e. Métro: Cité. 43-25-42-92. A history of the Cathedral through engravings, artifacts, and documents. Exhibits change and expand frequently in response to ongoing research. Open from October 1 to June 30 on Saturday and Sunday, except Easter, Pentecost, and Christmas.

Musée de l'Opéra 1, pl. Charles-Garnier, 2e. Métro: Opéra. 42-66-50-22. Closed Sundays and holidays. A collection of model stage sets and memorabilia of artists who have performed at the Opéra.

Musée de l'Orangerie des Tuileries Pl. de la Concorde, 8e. Métro: Concorde. 42-97-48-16. Closed Tuesdays. The recently reopened museum, which was built in 1853, now has a permanent collection of works by Jean Walter and Paul Guillaume as well as the *Nymphéas* by Claude Monet, which the artist gave to France in 1927.

Musée d'Orsay quai d'Orsay, 7e. Métro: Solférino 45-44-41-85. After many years of renovation, the Gare d'Orsay, formerly an important railroad station, was opened in 1986 as a huge, bright, extraordinary museum. The wonderful collection of Impressionists and Post-Impressionists (Cézanne, Monet, Renoir, Van Gogh, Lautrec, Degas, Seurat, Signat, etc.) was formerly housed in the famous Musée du Jeu de Paume in the Tuileries Gardens. It is now displayed to perfection in the new museum, which has received great acclaim for its architectural style. These works, plus a large collection of sculpture, furniture, photography, and decorative arts representing the last half of the 19th and beginning of the 20th centuries, are consid-

Museums

ered by many to be the most definitive in the world. Not to be missed is an outstanding collection of the pre-Impressionist painter, Gustave Courbet. The Musée d'Orsay is now considered the most important in France, after the Louvre.

Musée Pasteur 25, rue du Dr. Roux, 15e. Métro: Pasteur. 43-06-19-19. Closed Saturday, Sunday, and August. Open afternoons only. The apartment where Pasteur once lived is now filled with a collection of personal, historic, and scientific memorabilia.

Musée du Petit Palais av. Winston-Churchill, 8e. Métro: Champs-Elysées-Clémenceau. 42-65-12-73. Closed Mondays and holidays. Free admission Sundays. A permanent collection of art and antiques from the Middle Ages, and a collection of work by 19th-century artists including Géricault, Delacroix, Corot, Courbet, and others.

Musée Picasso (Hôtel Salé), 5, rue de Thorigny, 3e. Métro: St.-Sebastien. 42-71-25-21. An entire building devoted to Picasso. It's a truly remarkable collection and a remarkable building. Note the hand-carved door handles.

Musée de la Poste 34, bd. de Vaugirard, 6e, Métro: Luxembourg. 43-20-15-30. Closed Sundays and holidays. This museum contains a history of the French postal service with letters, papers, old mail coaches, and mailboxes as well as a complete collection of French stamps from 1849 to the present.

Musée de la Préfecture de Police 1 bis, rue des Carmes, 5e. Métro: Maubert-Mutualité. 43-29-21-57. Open Wednesday and Thursday afternoons. History of the police in Paris, with souvenirs and weapons from renowned prisoners, and documents on prisons and noteworthy executions.

Musée Radio France 116, av. du Président-Kennedy, 16e, Métro: Ranelagh, Passy or Mirabeau. 42-36-21-80 during the week, 42-30-33-84 on weekends. Closed Monday. Students half-price. This museum illustrates the evolution of radio and television technology. Guided tours are given of the 60 sound rooms and facilities of this building, where 5 major radio stations broadcast their programs.

Musée Rodin 77, rue de Varenne, 7e. Métro: Varenne. 47-05-01-34. Closed Tuesdays and holidays. Admission reduced Sunday, free Wednesday. This museum, housed in the Hôtel Byron which was built in 1728, contains a wonderful collection of Rodin's sculptures and drawings, as well as his personal collection of works by fellow-artists Monet, Carrière, Renoir, Van Gogh. There is a lovely sculpture garden that surrounds the museum as well.

Musée de Sculpture en Plein Air Quai St.-Bernard, 5e. Métro: Gare d'Austerlitz. Open daily. This lovely park along the Seine was created from 1974 to 1976, and was transformed into a striking, open-air museum in 1980. It is filled with contemporary sculptures by some of the best-known sculptors of the second half of the 20th century, including works by Cardénas, César, Di Teana, Féraud, Stahly, Arman, Ipoustéguy. There are occasional temporary exhibits.

Musée de la Sélita 12, rue Surcouf, 7e. Métro: Invalides. 45-55-91-50. Closed Sundays and holidays. A history of tobacco and its uses.

Musée des Thermes et de l'Hôtel de Cluny 6, pl. Paul-Pain-Levé, 5e. Métro: Maubert-Mutualité or St.-Michel. 43-25-62-00. Closed Tuesdays and holidays. Admission reduced Sundays, free Wednesdays. Partially restored public baths from the Middle Ages that contain the oldest sculpture in Paris, the *Pilier des Nautes*. The Museum has artifacts from daily life in the Middle Ages, as well as a collection of tapestries, including the famous *La Dame à La Licorne*, and a collection of calligraphy from the Middle Ages.

Musée des Transports Urbains 60, av. Ste.-Marie, Saint-Mande, 12e. Métro: Porte Dorée. 43-28-37-12. Open mid-April to the end of October on Saturdays, Sundays, and holidays, in the afternoons. Just on the edge of Paris, this former bus depot has a collection of vehicles used for urban transport throughout France in the 19th century.

Musée Victor Hugo 6, pl. des Vosges, 4e. Métro: Chemin-Vert. 42-72-16-65. Closed Mondays and holidays. Admission free on Sunday. Memorabilia of the famous author in his former home, including drawings, portraits of him and his family, documents about him and his political life. The museum overlooks the majestic Place des Vosges.

Musée Zadkine 100 bis, rue d'Assas, 6e. Métro: Notre-Dame-des-Champs. 43-26-91-90. Open Wednesday through Saturday. The former home and studio of the sculptor Zadkine. His sculptures are displayed both inside the house and in the tiny garden in front of it.

Museums

Palais de la Découverte Grand Palais, av. Franklin D. Roosevelt, 8e. Métro: Champs-Elysées-Clémenceau. 43-59-16-65. Closed Monday. The exhibits here show the history of scientific development, from the most ancient to the most recent discoveries. There is also a planetarium with 5 shows daily.

Trésors de Notre Dame In the Cathedral, 5e. Métro: Cité. Closed Sundays and religious holidays. A collection of ancient religious artifacts, in the former *Sacristie du Chapitre*.

NEWSPAPERS AND MAGAZINES

There are 2 English-language newspapers published in Paris. One is the highly respected *International Herald Tribune*, which is associated with the *Washington Post* and the *New York Times*. The "Trib" comes out 6 mornings a week, with news from all over the globe. It is available at kiosks, in English-language bookstores (see BOOKSTORES), and in many libraries. The other English-language newspaper published in Paris is *Passion*, a monthly newspaper with the ins and outs of Paris life from an American/Canadian/English point of view. *Passion* is also available at English-language bookstores and some kiosks and libraries.

There are several papers that are flown in daily from Britain, and these are available at the same places where you find the *International Herald Tribune* and *Passion*.

International Herald Tribune 181, av. du Général-de-Gaulle, 92200 Neuilly-sur-Seine. Métro: Argentine. 47-47-12-65.

Passion 18, rue du Pont-Neuf, 1er. Métro: Châtelet. 42-33-00-24.

Most of France's major newspapers are published in Paris, and the newspaper *quartier* is on the Right Bank. It includes rue de Richelieu (1er), rue Réaumur (3e), and rue des Italiens (9e). There are 2 newspapers that are published on Sundays: *France Dimanche* and *Humanité*. The others are published just 6 days a week.

Daily Newspapers

Croix 3, rue Bayard, 8*e*. Since 1883. Catholic-oriented with a leftist touch.

Echos 37, av. des Champs-Elysées, 8*e*. Financial news.

Equipe 10, rue du Faubourg-Montmartre, 9*e*. Sports newspaper founded in 1946.

Figaro 37, rue du Louvre, 2*e*. Founded in 1866, went out of circulation, and started up again in 1944. Fairly conservative.

France Soir 100, rue Réaumur, 2*e*. Evening paper, sensational news.

Humanité 5, rue du Faubourg-Poissonnière, 9*e*. Founded in 1904 by Jean-Jaurés. The communist newspaper.

Libération 27, rue de Lorraine, 19*e*. Sartre was one of the founders of this left-leaning newspaper.

Matin 21, rue Hérold, 1*er*. Left-leaning newspaper.

Monde 5, rue des Italiens, 9*e*. Always supportive of the left.

Nation 10, rue du Faubourg-Montmartre, 9*e*. Founded in 1962.

Nouveau Journal 108, rue de Richelieu, 1*er*, Budget policy newspaper.

Parisien Libéré 124, rue Réaumur, 1*er*. Emerged from the Résistance, started in 1944.

Le Quotidien de Paris 2, rue Ancelle, Neuilly-sur-Seine. 47-47-12-32. Right-leaning daily newspaper.

Magazines

Many English-language magazines, including the European editions of *Time, Newsweek*, and *Business Week International* are available at English-language bookstores, such as Brentano's, W. H. Smith, Galignani (see BOOKSTORES), from kiosks in the central *quartiers* of Paris, or from drugstores throughout the city.

French magazines include:
Le Canard Enchaîné—a satirical weekly.
Cuisine et Vins de France—a monthly magazine on the food and wine of France.

Elle—a woman's fashion magazine.

L'Express—weekly general news magazine.

Gault et Millau, Le Nouveau Guide—a monthly magazine primarily concerned with food, wine, and restaurants in France.

Jours de France—a classy, newsy fashion magazine.

Le Figaro Madame—a woman's magazine.

Le Figaro Magazine—general news; one of the most popular in France.

Magazine Hebdo—a weekly magazine with an important section on arts.

Marie-Claire—women's fashion magazine.

Le Nouvel Observateur—intellectual weekly.

Paris-Match—general news magazine with emphasis on celebrities.

Plaisirs de France—art and interiors magazine.

Le Point—weekly general news magazine.

Vogue—exclusive monthly fashion magazine. There is an issue devoted to women's fashion and one for men as well.

NIGHT CLUBS

See CABARETS

PAPER GOODS

See SHOPPING.

PARKING

When it comes to parking in Paris, it looks as if any place on or off the street, unless obviously marked *Stationnement Interdit* (no parking), is fair game, and many Parisian drivers treat it that way. But parking is rigidly controlled.

There are parking meters or *horodateurs* (which look like large parking meters) on the sidewalks of most streets in Paris. And there are armies of meter maids dressed in sky-blue uniforms who patrol the streets, issuing tickets. Parking meters are valid between 9 A.M. and 7 P.M. daily. Depending on the area, the rate is about 4F to 7F an hour, and there is no time limit. *Horodateurs* are another matter. Their use is also compulsory between 9 A.M. and 7 P.M. daily, and the cost is the same per hour as a parking meter. The difference is that parking time is strictly limited to 2 hours at a stretch.

Both parking meter and *horodateur* signs are large and white, with navy-blue lettering—a large *P*, and information about the type of metering system used. In rare instances there is free parking on weekends and holidays; the signs indicate when that is the case.

Should you come across a meter or *horodateur* that is out of order—*hors service*—you should get something called a *disque de contrôle*, which is available from your hotel, tourist offices, garages, even *librairies*, and put it in your car so it is easily seen.

If you're looking for a parking place, don't despair. There are more than 150 parking garages in Paris and its environs. Centrally located parking garages charge about 6,50F per hour, and those on the outskirts charge from about 4,50F to 12F for 6 hours. Just look for royal blue signs with a large *P*, or the words *Parking à . . . mètres* that indicate where the parking garages are located. The following is a selection of the larger parking garages listed by *arrondissement*:

1st Arrondissement

Saint-Honoré—pl. du Marché-St.-Honoré.
Samaritaine-Louvre—pl. and rue du Louvre.
Vendôme—pl. Vendôme.

2nd Arrondissement

Bourse—pl. de la Bourse.

3rd Arrondissement

Garage du Centre de Paris—11, rue Béranger.
Saint-Martin—rue St.-Martin.

4th Arrondissement

Bazar de l'Hôtel de Ville—15, rue de la Verrerie.
Parvis Notre Dame—pl. du Parvis Notre Dame.
Société Parisienne de Parking—15, rue St.-Antoine.

Parking

5th Arrondissement

Lagrange—rue Lagrange.
Parking des Patriarches—pl. du Marché des Patriarches.
Soufflot—rue Soufflot.

6th Arrondissement

Mazarine—27, rue Mazarine.
Saint-Sulpice—pl. St.-Sulpice.

7th Arrondissement

Bac-Montalembert—rue de Montalembert.
Invalides—rue de Constantine and rue Fabert.

8th Arrondissement

Concorde—pl. de la Concorde (Tuileries side).
FNAC-Diffusion-Parking Etoile-Wagram—22, av. de Wagram.
George V—101, av. des Champs-Elysées.
Haussmann—161–163, bd. Haussmann.
Malesherbes—20–35, bd. Malesherbes.
Parc Berri-Washington—5, rue de Berri.
Parking-Garages de Paris—25–27, pl. de la Madeleine.
Société d'Exploitation de Garage—60, rue de Ponthieu.

9th Arrondissement

Galeries Lafayette—54, bd. Haussmann and 91, rue de Provence.
Grand Garage Nord-Paris—71, rue de Dunkerque.
Groupement Commercial Automobile—8, rue Laferrière.

10th Arrondissement

Est-Parking—122, rue du Faubourg-St.-Martin.
Gare de l'Est (S.N.C.F.)—in front of the station (½-hour limit).
Gare du Nord (S.N.C.F.)—in front of the station (½-hour limit).

11th Arrondissement

Garage du Cirque d'Hiver—94–100, rue Amelot.
Grand Garage Charonnne—146, rue de Charonne.

12th Arrondissement

Parc Paris-Lyon—193, rue de Bercy and 58, quai de la Rapée.
Picpus—75–77, bd. de Picpus.

13th Arrondissement

Garage-Parking Auguste-Blanqui—111–117, bd. Auguste-Blanqui.
Porte d'Italie—av. de la Porte d'Italie.

14th Arrondissement

Montparnasse—bd. de Montparnasse (at the angle of rue de Chevreuse).
Porte d'Orléans—rue de la Légion-Etrangère and av. de la Porte d'Orléans.

15th Arrondissement

Bonvin-Lecourbe-Auto—28, rue Bonvin.
Gare Montparnasse (S.N.C.F.)—under the station.
Station Convention—159, rue Blomet.

16th Arrondissement

Foch—3, 6, and 50, av. Foch.
Victor-Hugo—av. Victor-Hugo, across from N.s 120–122, av. Victor-Hugo.

17th Arrondissement

Maillot—pl. de la Porte Maillot.
Ternes—av. des Ternes.

18th Arrondissement

Clichy-Montmartre—9, rue Caulaincourt.
Fiat Paris-Nord—50, rue Custine.
S.C.I.—N. 73-73, rue Riquet.

Parking

19th Arrondissement
Astel-Garage—138, av. Jean-Jaurès.
Grant Garage Belleville-Compans—221–243, rue de Belleville.

20th Arrondissement
Grand Garage des Gâtines—3–7, rue des Gâtines.

PARKS AND GARDENS

According to figures published by the city of Paris, if all the parks and gardens in the city were divided among the inhabitants, each person would have 30 square feet. Ever since Louis XIII decided, in 1636, to create the Jardin des Plantes (5e), parks and gardens have played an important part in Paris' history. First, only the grand residences and palaces had gardens: the Jardin du Luxembourg (5e), the Tuileries (8e). In the 17th century, trees were planted and a garden created for public use along the walls of the city, first near the Bastille (11e), then at the Cours de Vincennes (12e). In the 19th century, public parks were created, including the Parc de Monceau (8e), which had been an open space filled with wild game, the Palais Royal (1er), and many small gardens that were at that time attached to religious communities in Paris.

It wasn't until Baron Haussmann created the *Service des Promenades et Plantations de la Ville de Paris* in 1854 that the Bois de Boulogne (16e) and the Bois de Vincennes (12e) were designed, as well as parks for the working classes: the Parc Montsouris (13e) and the Parc des Buttes Chaumont (19e). It was at that time, too, that many of the squares in Paris were included in the city plan.

Since 1977 the city of Paris has created new gardens at Les Halles (1er), at the Bassin de la Villette (19e), at Bercy (12e), and at the former Abattoirs de Vaugirard (15e).

Whether they be formal or "wild," Paris' parks are impeccably maintained. Flowers and shrubs are regularly uprooted and replanted so that each park stays at its seasonal best. And unlike parks in many other parts of the world, those in Paris get constant use. Parents strolling with children, elderly people sunning themselves, men—and now some women—playing *boules*, runners, walkers, even roller skaters of all ages turn out. As long as it isn't raining, the parks are full—perfect spots to sit and observe some of the more relaxed aspects of Parisian life. The following is a selection of just some of Paris' parks.

Bois de Boulogne 16*e*. Métro: Porte d'Auteuil or Les Sablons. This rambling park goes on forever—2,000 acres of greenery right at the west edge of the city. Some of it is meticulously manicured, some of it wild and woodsy, and all of it carefully planned by Haussmann. On any given day it is filled with people playing football, riding horses or bicycles, paddling canoes (you can rent them at the edge of one of its 2 lakes), or taking a drive. There are 2 courses for horse racing, a football stadium, several elegant restaurants, and miles of pathways where you might stroll and hardly meet a soul. Many Parisians spend "a day in the country" at the Bois de Boulogne, arriving before noon and staying until nightfall—sunning themselves, eating, playing, or walking. A note of caution: it's best to steer clear of the Bois de Boulogne at night. The *Bagatelle* in the Bois de Boulogne was designed along English lines and donated to the city by Sir Richard Wallace, the Englishman also responsible for Paris' characteristic drinking fountains. The dainty Bagatelle is known for its exquisite flowers: iris in the spring, roses in the summer and fall.

Bois de Vincennes 12*e*. Métro: Porte de Charenton. The Bois de Vincennes has been a popular spot to take the country air since the 17th century, when it was filled with wild game. In 1860, Napoleon III gave the Bois de Vincennes to the city of Paris, and Baron Haussmann performed his magic on it, digging artificial lakes that are filled with water from the Marne River, and making a small course for horse races. The Bois de Vincennes has recently undergone a dramatic "remodeling," which won't come to full flower for another 20 years, but has already had a big effect. More than 13,000 trees—including oaks, sycamores, and cherry trees—have been planted in long double lines tracing the hunting paths of Louis XV. Look for the "Allée Royale," a grand alley of new trees planted perpendicular to the Château de Vincennes. It seems to go on forever. The Bois de Vincennes also has a zoo, the *Musée des Arts Africains et Océaniens* (see MUSEUMS), and a Buddhist temple built for the 1931 colonial "exposition" in Paris. On the east side of the Bois de Vincennes is a flower garden, the *Parc Floral de Paris*.

Jardin du Luxembourg 5e. Métro: Luxembourg. This is a mixed French- and English-style park filled with parents and their children, who take donkey rides or play at the fountain with rented sailboats. On the rue de Vaugirard side is a small glade surrounding the *Catherine de Médicis Fountain*, a magnet on a warm day for people taking a break from the sun; on the rue d'Assas side is the vestige of an ancient nursery where a few apple trees still produce fruit; farther into the garden, on the same side, is an apiculture school where one can sometimes buy honey made by bees that are kept in the garden.

Jardin des Plantes 5e. Métro: Jussieu or Gare d'Austerlitz. This lovely park has a beautiful, formal botanical garden; a wild, natural, hilly section called the *Labyrinthe*; a small zoo; and an alpine garden. During the siege of Paris, when no food was coming into the capital, the zoo animals were slaughtered and sold to restaurants. Elephant meat became almost common provender during that period. The *Natural History Museum* is also located here.

Jardin des Tuileries 1er. Métro: Tuileries. The Tuileries may be the most elegant gardens in Paris, or anywhere. The gardens were first established by Catherine de Médicis in 1563, though they didn't get their present design until 1664 when Le Nôtre—France's well-known park planner—was commissioned to design them. The Tuileries became almost instantly popular, and was nearly always filled with Parisians who would rent chairs for an afternoon outside. The Tuileries has been the sight of many famous and infamous historic events; one of the more amusing ones was the first lighter-than-air vehicle's successful launch in 1783.

The *Jeu de Paume* and the *Orangerie*, at the Place de la Concorde end of the Tuileries, are both part of

JARDIN DU LUXEMBOURG

the Louvre, and were transformed into museums at the beginning of the 20th century. More art is in the gardens, which are filled with statues—most of them by Maillol—and there is a café open in the summer; its chairs and tables are spread out under the cool shady trees.

Parc des Buttes Chaumont 19e. Métro: Buttes Chaumont. This was the first park planned by Baron Haussmann for the north part of Paris. It is 60 acres of lush greenery with little chalets and grottoes, miles of winding pathways, waterfalls, and a lake with a small butte in the middle of it. There are 2 bridges that go to the butte—one of brick called Suicide Bridge, the other a suspension bridge.

Parc Monceau 8e. Métro: Monceau. This park was modeled after English and German gardens and was intended by its designer, Carmontelle, to be a sort of fantasy world, which it still is today. Gone are the windmills and pagoda, but you can see a waterfall, picturesque flower gardens, and rolling hills. At one end are what looks like Roman ruins but are pillars from a mausoleum which Henri II intended to build but was never finished. There is a children's playground complete with a merry-go-round and always a throng of nannies and their charges, particularly on Wednesdays when there is no school.

Parc Montsouris 14e. Métro: Porte d'Orléans. RER: Cité Universitaire. This is a lovely park, tucked away in the 14th *arrondissement*, with green lawns, beautiful trees, and a man-made lake filled with ducks who clamor for bread proffered by visitors to the park. It is said that on the park's opening day the lake was still empty, and the engineer responsible committed suicide. There is a copy of a Tunisian temple on one side of the park, and a restaurant at the edge of the lake on the other. The streets—many of them brick—and neighborhood surrounding the park are quaint and charming, it's an oasis of old Paris.

Other Parks and Gardens Worth Visiting

Palais Royal 1er. Métro: Palais-Royal. This lovely garden, filled with flowers during spring and summer and a welcome respite from the crowded neighborhood even on a winter day, is surrounded by elegant shops, restaurants, and residences. Colette lived in an apartment overlooking the gardens, as did Jean Cocteau. Molière performed and died not far away, at N.40, rue de Richelieu. In the summer the garden at the Palais Royal is a perfect spot for a polite picnic on one of the several benches surrounding the flower garden. There is even a sandbox for children to play in.

Parc Georges Brassens 15e. Métro: Porte de Vanves. This park, named for a very popular French composer-singer who died a few years ago, was formerly the site of the Abattoirs de Vaugirard (slaughterhouses), which were long vacant and something of an eyesore. It is now a lovely park, created specially for the blind. All of the many species of flowers were chosen especially for their scent.

Ranelagh 16e. Métro: Ranelagh. This park goes back to 1774, when Parisians came here to dance under the night sky. A café was built which subsequently disappeared and later, Baron Haussmann designed the present green oasis, which has a playground for children, complete with donkeys. Ranelagh gardens are just a short walk from the Musée Marmottan.

See also CHILDREN'S PARIS.

PASTRIES AND PATISSERIES

See FOOD.

PHARMACIES

There seem to be almost as many pharmacies in Paris as there are pastry shops, and they can be identified by a green cross displayed outside, which is usually lit if the pharmacy is open. Pharmacies dispense anything from prescription drugs to herbal remedies, from homeopathic medicine (homéopathie) to shampoo, toothpaste, or dental floss. If you have a cold, a headache, or a toothache, take your pains to a pharmacy and while you won't get a prescription drug, the personnel will most likely be able to recommend an over-the-counter remedy, which is probably stronger than anything you would get over the counter at home. If your French is uncertain, sign language works well to indicate aches and pains; otherwise you can go to the following pharmacies:

British and American Pharmacy 1, rue Auber, 9e. Métro: Opéra. 47-42-49-40. Open from 8:30 A.M. to 7:45 P.M. Closed Saturday morning and Sunday.
Pharmacie Anglaise 62, av. des Champs-Elysées, 8e. Métro: Franklin D. Roosevelt. 43-59-22-52. Open from 8:30 A.M. until 10:30 P.M. Closed Sunday.
Pharmacie Anglo-Américaine 6, rue de Castiglione, 1er. Métro: Tuileries. 42-60-72-96. Open from 9 A.M. to 7:30 P.M. Closed Sunday.

The following pharmacy is open 24 hours, daily:
Pharmacie des Champs-Elysées 84, av. des Champs-Elysées, 8e. Métro: Franklin D. Roosevelt. 45-62-02-41. Some English spoken.

POSTAL AND TELEPHONE SERVICES

There are more than 160 post offices in Paris that handle both mail and telephone services. They are called *Bureaux des P.T.T. (Postes, Télégraphes,* and *Téléphone* offices) and they are open Monday through Friday from 8 A.M. to 7 P.M. and on Saturday from 8 A.M. to noon. Part of their service to the inhabitants of Paris is 7,000 public phone booths and 2,200 letter boxes.

Postal Service

You can buy stamps (*timbres*) at any *Bureau de tabac* or at the post office. At the post office, go to the window *Poste Aérienne* (air mail), and there you can get your letter stamped, by airmail—or regular—stamps, or *aérogrammes*. When you mail your letter in the post office, you'll see several slots marked "Paris," "*Banlieue*" (suburbs), "*Province*" (elsewhere in France), or "*Etranger-Par Avion*" (foreign countries—airmail).

Mail-boxes on the street are small, yellow boxes usually attached to buildings, particularly *tabacs*.

Telephone Services

Paris no longer has the public phones that require a token. If you want to make a long-distance call, you can do so from any post office at one of the booths with an ordinary black phone (rather than a pay phone). Tell a clerk that you want to make *un appel téléphonique*, write down and give him or her the number, go into one of the booths, and the clerk will put the call through for you. Talk for as long as you like, and pay afterwards.

If you want to dial a call yourself, get lots of 1- and 5-franc pieces and go into a phone booth. There's a panel that clearly explains how to dial a long-distance call, and lists country code numbers. Dial *19*, wait for the tone, dial the country code (*1* for the United States—*Etats-Unis*), then the area code, and finally the number you want. Add coins for as long as you want to talk. A round signal will flash white when you are about to be cut off; you have to be quick with your coins to catch it.

If you want to make a collect call—*un appel en P.C.V. (pay-say-vay)*—you can do so from a post office, private phone, or phone booth that has a blue-and-white decal with a bell on it and the words *cette cabine peut être appellée à ce numéro* . . . (this phone booth can be called at this number). Inside you'll find a number "*Ici, cabine N⁰* . . ." To make the call, dial the operator—*19*—then wait for the tone, dial *3344* for the United States, then give that operator the appropriate information. They will call you back when your call is put through. You may have to wait up to 2 hours, and no collect calls are put through on Sunday.

In Paris, telephone numbers now consist of eight digits. The number 4 was added to all Paris numbers, while other numbers were assigned to the suburbs. A local call in Paris is metered, so that after several minutes the indicator will flash white and you will need to put in more money. You can make local calls from some cafés; they usually cost a bit more than from a public phone booth. Ask at the cash register, and they will activate the phone for you and you pay after you've made the call.

The modern phones need a special card that can be purchased at any post office or tobacco store (including the airports) for thirty French francs (or more). It can be used for local, long distance, or international calls until the 30–franc credit is used up. The computer will automatically deduct the cost of the call from your card and tell you your remaining balance.

Telegrams

You can send a telegram from any post office. Just go to the window marked *"Télégrammes,"* or call 42-32-21-11 to send a telegram in English by phone.

PUBLIC SHOWERS

Some people in Paris live in rooms, studios, or apartments without baths or showers. Their rents are low, often even in very fashionable *quartiers*, and they get along very well using one of Paris' public shower facilities, *bains-douches municipaux*. If you should find yourself in need one day, don't hesitate to take advantage of a public shower; they are run by the city and kept impeccably clean (they're washed between each use).They generally cost less than 5F for 20 minutes of hot water and are usually open Thursdays from noon to 7 P.M., Fridays and Saturdays all day, and Sunday mornings until noon. You bring your own soap, shampoo, and towel, though in a pinch you will find all those available for a small fee.

Bains-Douches Municipaux Locations

18, rue du Renard, 4*e*. Métro: Rambuteau. 42-77-71-90.

34, rue Castagnary, 15*e*. Métro: Plaisance. 48-28-10-88.

188, rue Charenton, 12e. Métro: Reuilly-Diderot. 43-07-64-87.

8, rue des Deux-Ponts, 4e. Métro: Pont-Marie. 43-54-47-40.

34, rue des Bernardins, 5e. Métro: Maubert-Mutualité. 43-26-28-89.

42, rue Oberkampf, 11e. Métro: Oberkampf. 47-00-57-35.

38, rue du Rocher, 8e. Métro: St.-Lazare. 45-22-15-19.

RESTAURANTS

Trying to decide what restaurant to go to in Paris is like trying to choose which diamond to buy. Not all of Paris' nearly 5,000 restaurants are wonderful, but an extremely high proportion are worth visiting. From neighborhood bistros to grand restaurants, from contemporary-style cuisine to regional favorites, there are restaurants to suit every palate and every pocketbook. Use the following list as a reference guide but be adventuresome—there are always new discoveries to be made.

Unless you are planning to eat at the neighborhood café, reservations are always recommended. For the better-known, grand restaurants you may have to reserve up to 2 months in advance. If you're planning to eat out on a weekend, make a reservation as far ahead as possible. If you're planning lunch, often a reservation made in the morning is sufficient. Mealtimes in Paris aren't particularly flexible. The best time for lunch is usually 12:30; for dinner it is between 8 P.M. and 9 P.M. It is important to remember that not all restaurants take credit cards. Always check before going. If your plans change and you cannot keep your reservation, it is polite to call the restaurant and inform them.

Most restaurants offer a *menu* at a fixed price, which often represents the house specialties and includes a starter (*entrée*), main course (*plats*) and either cheese (*fromage*) or dessert (*dessert*). In *bistros*—small, neighborhood establishments that generally serve hearty, classic French dishes—wine is often included in the menu. *Menus* are a good course to follow. You won't have to guess about the amount of the bill, and you'll often get some of the best food in the restaurant. Another tip is to try the *plat du jour*—the daily special. It is usually reasonably priced and representative of whatever was fresh and abundant at the market. If you're not sure what to order, you can always ask the waiter for recommendations or if you see something on someone else's plate that looks good, don't be afraid to ask the waiter what it is. The interest you show will be appreciated.

The same goes for wine. If you aren't sure, trust the wine stewards. Wine is their specialty and their concern is that you get wine that goes with your meal.

A tip about coffee. In France, it is served after the meal. If you have a habit of drinking coffee with your meal, try to forego the habit while you are in Paris.

When you get the bill for your meal, the amount written at the bottom of the bill is what you owe. Don't calculate tips; they have already been included.

The following restaurants are arranged alphabetically, within *arrondissements*. Prices are indicated to give a general idea of what to expect, but they do fluctuate, so be prepared for some changes. If credit cards are not listed with a restaurant they are not accepted at that establishment. All restaurants marked with a (+) accept orders until at least midnight.

1st Arrondissement

Carré des Feuillants 14, rue de Castiglione, in the courtyard, 1e. Métro: Tuileries. 42-96-67-92. Closed Saturday evening and Sunday. V. Menus at 320F and 380F. This new restaurant, launched by Chef Alain Dutournier of Au Trou Gascon, has everyone whispering. Can a chef who already has a 2-star restaurant in

Paris manage another? Will he immediately be awarded Michelin star(s) based on his reputation? Thus far, he's taking the city by storm. The imaginative, fresh cuisine has hardly a hint of Dutournier's native Southwest. There's an emphasis on grilled meats and fish, sprightly combinations, and unusual offerings, such as a warm scallop salad with lentils.

Globe d'Or 158, rue St.-Honoré, 1er. Métro: Louvre. 42-60-23-37. Closed Saturday and Sunday. AE/V. Step off the tumultuous rue Saint-Honoré into this homey restaurant that at lunchtime is filled with businessmen there for the Southwest cuisine. There's a hearty *cassoulet* served in oven-hot individual baking dishes, *confit de canard* (duck preserved in duck fat), and liver with chunks of black peppercorns. Servings are copious and good.

Grand Véfour 17, rue de Beaujolais, 1er. Métro: Bourse. 42-96-56-27. Closed Saturday, Sunday, and August. AE/V/DC. This lovely, newly renovated, historic restaurant has been delighting personages with its classic cuisine and view over the Palais Royal gardens for centuries. In recent history, Colette and Jean Cocteau frequented the Grand Véfour, and it still has a cadre of regulars who come to enjoy the elegant bustle, subtly refurbished decor, and a menu that features both simple dishes, such as grilled steak and lamb chops, and sophisticated marvels, such as a frogs legs soufflé, *Sole Grand Véfour*, and chicken with saffron.

Louix XIV 1 bis, pl. des Victoires, 1er. Métro: Bourse. 42-61-39-44. Closed Saturday, Sunday, and August. This is a great neighborhood bistro where the action gets fast and furious around mealtimes and the waiters career about, serving plates of wonderful grilled fish, *boeuf bourguignon*, *escargots*, and *charcuterie*. Don't be alarmed when the waiter sets a plate with a huge chunk of butter on your table—you're not expected to use it all; take what you want and he'll whisk it away when the next table is ready.

(+) Main à la Pâte 35, rue St.-Honoré, 1er. Métro: Les Halles. 42-36-64-73. Closed Sunday. AE/DC. Walk upstairs into the Italian restaurant and you'll think you just entered a Hollywood set. It's green and lush, meant to give the impression of an Italian country garden. The pastas are homemade, the sauces rich and unctuous, the menu long and varied.

Pharamond 24, rue de la Grande Truanderie, 1er. Métro: Les Halles. 42-33-06-72. Closed Sunday, Monday, and July. AE/DC/V. This beautiful restaurant, with its turn-of-the-century mirrors and tile decor, is a classic. It offers specialties from Normandy, most notably *tripes à la mode de Caen* (tripe cooked in apple cider). But don't worry, they also have grilled lamb chops, *ris de veau à la crème* (sweetbreads in cream), *pieds de porc* (pigs feet), and delicious Normandy cider.

(+) Pied de Cochon 6, rue Coquillière, 1er. Métro: Châtelet-Les-Halles. 42-36-11-75. Open daily, 24 hours a day. AE/DC/V. This bistro is a landmark with a reputation that goes back to the heyday of Les Halles. It is best known for its all-night service and *soupe à l'oignon* (onion soup).

Ritz-Espadon 15, pl. Vendôme, 1er. Métro: Opéra. 42-60-38-30. AE/DC/EC/V. A visit to the Ritz, particularly for lunch, is truly part fantasy. The decor, the dining room overlooking a lovely, frivolous garden, the attentive service, and the whispered conversations all around provide an ambiance for food that is creatively—if not always perfectly—prepared. The presentations range from ingenious, as in the complicated layered seafood terrine to the simple yet elegant tomato and fennel side dish or the bass with flaming fennel stalks.

Vigne 30, rue de l'Arbre Sec, 1er. Métro: Louvre. 42-60-13-55. Closed Sunday. V. This long, narrow bistro is impeccable—simple decor, bursting with a lively crowd, amiable waiters and a good, solid classic bistro menu with changing daily specials of hearty stews and grilled meats. Order their *soufflé au grand marnier*—not only impressive, it is exceptionally good.

2nd Arrondissement

Drouant pl. Gaillon, 2e. Métro: Opéra. 47-42-56-61. Bistro-type Parisian institution. Popular with the literary world. The winner of the "Prix Goncourt," one of the highest literary awards in France, is chosen at this restaurant by the ten members of the Goncourt Academy.

Drouot 103, rue de Richelieu, 2e. Métro: Richelieu-Drouot. 42-96-68-23. Open daily. This is an inexpensive restaurant noted more for fun and filling up than for food—which includes *steak au poivre* (beef in a black peppercorn sauce), lamb, and a variety of *charcuterie*.

Pile ou Face 52 bis, rue Notre-Dame-des Victoires, 2e. Métro: Bourse. 42-33-64-33. Closed Saturday and Sunday. *Genteel* is the byword for this charming little restaurant right across from *La Bourse*, the stock exchange. The burgundy walls, the small, carefully arranged tables, and the impeccable service make it intimate and elegant without pretention. The food is inventive, light, and masterfully presented, each dish an artful composition of color, shape, and size. The combinations may sound startling but in almost every case they work: rabbit with rosemary, leeks with salmon eggs, red pepper mousse, beef with a tarragon cream sauce. Cheeses are carefully chosen and desserts, while complex, are light, lovely, and flavorful.

(+) Vaudeville 29, rue Vivienne, 2e. Métro: Bourse. 42-33-39-31. Open daily. AE/DC/V. If you're in the mood for a late meal come to this large, popular brasserie. Specialties are seafood, and your eyes will pop out at the sight of their *plateau de fruits de mer* (seafood platter), piled high with every imaginable shellfish and crustacean. They also have a large selection of hearty, meaty dishes. This isn't the spot for a languid meal. You can stay as long as you like of course, but the action is fast, the tempo furious, the noise level high.

Vishnou 11 bis, rue Volney, 2e. Métro: Opéra. 42-97-56-46. Closed Sunday and Monday. AE/DC/EC/V. Indian food, reputedly some of the best, most authentic in town, served in an Indian atmosphere.

3rd Arrondissement

(+) Chez Jenny 39, bd. du Temple, 3e. Métro: République. 42-74-75-75. Open daily. DC/V/AE. This is an enormous Alsatian *brasserie*, complete with waitresses who sport frilly uniforms, lively crowds there for the Alsatian fare, and Riesling that flows liberally. Their specialty is *choucroute* (sauerkraut with a multitude of sausages—bratwurst, frankfurters, grilled bacon, and pork), which manages to be light and delectable despite its proportions.

4th Arrondissement

Benoît 20, rue St.-Martin, 4e. Métro: Châtelet. 42-72-25-76. Closed Saturday and Sunday. This sparkling bistro has a classic decor and a menu that has changed with the times. You can still find hearty *boeuf à la mode* (braised beef with carrots), warm garlicky sausage, and lamb stew, but there is also light nouvelle cuisine with inspired fish dishes like the dainty and delicious filets of sole wrapped around a crisp-cooked bouquet of *haricots verts* (thin green beans) and carrots.

(+) Bofinger 3–7, rue de la Bastille, 4e. Métro: Bastille. 42-72-87-82. Open daily. V/AE/DC/EC. *Choucroute* is their specialty. The Mediterranean is represented, too, with *bouillabaisse* (fish soup) and garlicky *brandade de morue* (salt cod purée).

Jo Goldenberg 7, rue des Rosiers, 4e. Métro: St.-Paul. 48-87-20-16. Open daily. DC/V. This Jewish deli and restaurant in the heart of the Marais is authentic. The deli in front is stacked with breads and pastries, and filled with meats that hang from the ceiling, all in amiable disarray. The busy restaurant serves tasty chicken soup with an unending supply of matzoh and good, dark bread, *zatkouskis* (a selection of hors d'oeuvre that includes *tarama*—fish roe spread), *caviar d'aubergines* (eggplant spread), chopped, spiced chicken livers, and a variety of delicious salads—all great washed down with a chilled beer.

Montecristo 81, rue St.-Louis-en-l'Ile, 4e. Métro: Pont-Marie. 46-33-35-46. Closed Sunday and August. AE/DC/V. This small Italian restaurant right in the midst of the busy Ile Saint-Louis nonetheless manages to feel hidden and secluded. The food is fresh and simple, the pastas well-cooked, the flavors redolent of fresh herbs and tomatoes.

Quai des Ormes 72, quai de l'Hôtel-de-Ville, 4e. Métro: Hôtel-de-Ville. 42-74-72-22. Closed Saturday,

Sunday, and August. The food here is inventive; highly original, light, and usually successful, with a menu that includes exquisite wild mushroom ravioli, *canard de Challans à la pêche de vigne* (duck with peaches), *turbot étuvé aux morilles* (turbot steamed with morels), and refreshing fruit desserts.

5th Arrondissement

Ambroisie 65, quai de la Tournelle, 5e. Métro: Maubert. 46-33-18-65. AE/V. Tiny (12 tables), two-star restaurant, located in a newly-renovated 17th-century mansion. Chef Bernard Pacaud is known for his duck served with a foie gras that melts in your mouth, veal sweetbreads, and delicious pastries, especially the chocolate cake.

Chez René 14, bd. St.-Germain, 5e. Métro: Cardinal-Lemoine. 43-54-30-23. Closed Saturday, Sunday, and August. This is the quintessential neighborhood bistro with its stark and simple decor, bowls piled high with *charcuterie*, and waiters in crisp white aprons. The restaurant is so clean it sparkles, the food so fresh you don't want to stop. They have daily specialties as classic as French food can be: *pot-au-feu* (boiled beef), *mouton aux haricots* (lamb stew with white beans), *gras double* (tripe), *boeuf à la mode carottes* (braised beef with carrots), and *blanquette de veau* (veal in a white sauce).

Chez Toutoune 5, rue de Pontoise, 5e. Métro: Maubert-Mutualité. 43-26-56-81. Closed Sunday, Monday, and from August 15 to September 15. V. You hardly sit down at this friendly, crowded bistro before the waiter sweeps over with a huge tureen of hot soup, the start of everyone's menu. Through the course of an undoubtedly long evening—the service is friendly but not swift—you might sample a delectable pasta salad studded with seafood, a zucchini flan with a light garlic sauce, or the house terrine delivered right in its mold so you can help yourself. When you've had enough, the following course might be grilled lamb chops, steak with shallots, duck with garlicky potatoes, or fish fresh from the market.

(+) Dodin Bouffant 25, rue Frédéric-Sauton, 5e. Métro: Maubert-Mutualité. 43-25-25-14. Closed Saturday, Sunday, and August. DC/V. Seafood is among the specialties at this restaurant, which caters

Restaurants

as easily to families as to trendy young couples, and has a feel of established good will about it. It's always crowded with those who come for the fresh oysters, *foie gras*, and the substantial offerings of game, lamb, or pork dishes. The restaurant serves good, classic dishes which are executed with a light hand and creative touch.

Estrapade 15, rue de l'Estrapade, 5e. Métro: Luxembourg. 43-25-72-58. Closed Sunday. AE/DC/V. This minuscule restaurant is tucked away in a side street off the Place de la Contrescarpe. It exudes charm with its trio of tables on the sidewalk and its little lace curtains. You can sample a broiled *crottin de Chavignol* (goat cheese on a bed of curly endive), turbot in a light butter sauce, *steak de canard* (duck breast), calf's liver with seasonal vegetables, and game when in season. It's not haute cuisine but the atmosphere is comfortable, the clientele jovial.

Gueuze 19, rue Soufflot, 5e. Métro: Luxembourg. 43-54-63-00. Closed Sunday. More a beer bar than a restaurant, La Gueuze nonetheless serves some of the best mussels and French fries in town. You'll get a huge platter of *frites* and a steaming bowl of *moules* (mussels) that have been quickly steamed in wine. So choose a sidewalk table, order a beer, and enjoy the view of the nearby Jardin du Luxembourg.

Le Pactole 44, bd. St-Germain, 5e. Métro: Maubert. 46-33-31-31. AE/V. Popular bistro with a nearby parking lot. Delicious food and reasonable prices.

Raccard 19, rue Laplace, 5e. Métro: Cardinal-Lemoine. 43-25-27-27. Open daily. Raclette—the creamy, slightly tangy Swiss cheese that is broiled crispy under a special broiler and served with potatoes in their skins, *cornichons*, and tiny pickled onions—is the specialty of the house, served in a rustic ambiance.

Savoyards 14, rue des Boulangers, 5e. Métro: Jussieu. 46-33-53-78. Closed Saturday night, Sunday, and August. Rue des Boulangers used to be thick with *boulangeries* (bread bakeries), thus its name. Now it hosts, among others, this minute, crowded neighborhood bistro where people sit at paper-covered tables to enjoy simple bistro food: sparkling fresh *côtes de porc* (thick, golden pork chops) beef tongue in an aromatic sauce, or a plate of *crudités* piled high with crispy fresh vegetables.

CATHEDRAL OF NOTRE DAME

Tour d'Argent 15, quai de la Tournelle, 5e. Métro: Cardinal-Lemoine. 43-54-23-31. Closed Monday. AE/V/DC. It's probably safe to say that everyone has heard of this grand old restaurant, in existence in some form since the 16th century. It remains one of Paris' best-known restaurants with a spectacular view of Notre-Dame Cathedral. The specialty here is *caneton Tour d'Argent* (duckling served in 2 courses, the breast meat in a rich sauce thickened with duckling liver and juices extracted from pressing the carcass, and the legs, which are grilled golden and crispy). The first duck prepared in this way was served to the Prince of Wales, then Edward VII, in 1890. Since then, the birds are all numbered and each guest is given a card bearing his or her duck number.

Villars Palace 8, rue Descartes, 5e. Métro: Cardinal-Lemoine. 43-26-39-08. Closed Saturday at lunchtime. AE/DC/EC/V. Don't let the façade of this restaurant put you off. Inside it is all soothing blue, white, and gray contemporary decor. The specialty is fish, and it is given utmost respect—lightly cooked so it retains its character and exudes its natural, subtle flavor.

6th Arrondissement

Allard 41, rue St.-André-des-Arts, 6e. Métro: St.-Michel. 43-26-48-23. DC/V. A rendezvous of gastronomes, this crowded, well-known bistro has a charming atmosphere and wonderful food. The *boudin aux pommes* (blood sausage served with apples), *escargots de Bourgogne* (snails), *fromage de tête* (head cheese) and *gigot aux flageolets* (leg of lamb with beans) are all superb.

Charpentiers 10, rue Mabillon, 6e. Métro: Mabillon. 43-26-30-05. Closed Sunday. 125F. As simple and unpretentious as they come, this bistro is filled with the neighborhood crowd who come for the hearty, classic, home cooking. Try *lapin à la moutarde de Meaux* (rabbit with mustard), the *chou farci campagnard* (stuffed cabbage), *boeuf à la ficelle* (stewed beef).

Chez Maître Paul 12, rue Monsieur-Le-Prince, 6e. Métro: Odéon or Luxembourg. 43-54-74-59. Closed Sunday, Monday, and August. AE/DC/V. 125F. Walking into this restaurant is like walking into a private home; everything is clean, polished, comfortable, and comforting. The specialties are from the mountainous Jura region—characterized by dishes cooked in the regional Arbois wine, including a homey *coq au vin de paille* (chicken simmered in vegetables) or *escargots au vin d'Arbois* (snails in the white wine of Arbois).

Lipp 151, bd. St-Germain, 6e. Métro: Maubert. 45-48-53-91. Like Maxim's, Lipp welcomes the Parisian Jet Set. If you are a celebrity—or hope to be one—you have to be seen there! For the "habitués," the food is secondary. In fact, it is very well accepted to show some disregard for such a material thing. However, for those who want to satisfy their palate before their fame, *choucroute* (sauerkraut) is more than acceptable, as well as its *cassoulet* (beans with pork, beef and lamb), and its fruit tartes are always tempting. If you are not an habitué or a friend of the "patron" it is very hard to get a table.

Lozère 4, rue Hautefeuille, 6e. Métro: St.-Michel. 43-54-26-64. Closed Sunday, Monday, and August. This restaurant was opened at the initiative of the Tourist Office in Lozère, which explains why the specialties are from that region in South-central France. There are big crusty loaves of bread on the paper-covered tables. Try the pork with lentils—so fresh it glistens—or the *tripoux* (tidy, tasty little packages of stuffed tripe served with a fresh tomato sauce and sprinkled with bright chopped parsley), followed by a simple *clafoutis* (fruit flan), or a tangy Cantal cheese.

Polidor 41, rue Monsieur-Le-Prince, 6e. Métro: Odéon. 43-26-95-34. Closed Sunday, Monday, and August. 50F–100F. One of the joys in life is finding a restaurant like Polidor, which has catered to students and intellectuals, including Paul Valéry and Ernest Hemingway, since time immemorial.

Relais Louis XIII 1, rue Pont de Lodi, 6e. Métro: Odéon. 43-26-75-96. AC/DC/EC/V. This 2-star restaurant, with beautiful and rare pieces of furniture and old paintings, is located in a very old section of Paris. It is known for its *millefeuille de rognons et ris de veau* (kidneys and sweetbreads in a flaky pastry and served with a light sauce) and green cabbage stuffed with a delicious *foie gras*.

7th Arrondissement

Divellec 107, rue de l'Université, 7e. Métro: Invalides. 45-51-91-96. Closed Sunday, Monday, and August. AE/DC/V. 300F. This restaurant makes no attempt to hide its intentions to be the best, showiest fish restaurant in Paris. The fish comes direct from the coast, and the preparations are ingenious but not bizarre, showing a solid, knowledgeable background so that everything arrives perfectly cooked, as good to eat as it is lovely to look at: whole trout served carefully twisted around so the tail just touches the mouth, glistening black (squid) pasta, pungently sweet mint-and-chocolate soufflé.

Fontaine de Mars 129, rue St.-Dominique, 7e. Métro: Ecole-Militaire. 47-05-46-44. Closed Saturday night, Sunday, and August. This restaurant is so cute it almost makes your eyes hurt with its little checked curtains, crowded tables, tile floor, and feeling of yesteryear. The food is fresh and simple: country soups, fresh *foie gras* (fattened duck or goose liver), grilled or poached fish. The waitresses are capable and kind, the crowd a gamut from neighborhood worker to comfortable *bourgeois* couples.

Glenans 54, rue de Bourgogne, 7e. Métro: Varenne. 45-51-61-09. Closed Saturday, Sunday, and August. 200F. Imaginative fish preparations are the specialty here, from grilled salmon to gently spiced *pétoncles* (tiny scallops with artichokes). You might want to try a dessert fruit tart or the white chocolate charlotte with a bitter chocolate sauce.

Jules Verne Tour Eiffel, 2nd floor, 7e. Métro: Ecole-Militaire. 45-55-61-44. Open daily. This new restaurant with a view of the city has been an astonishing success. Contemporary decor in grays, blacks, metal, and plastic is softened by the incomparable skies of Paris. The menu changes often, and according to the seasons. You might find sweetbreads cooked in white wine, *fricassée* of crayfish perfumed with curry, or kidneys prepared with crispy chunks of fried, smoked bacon. If you want to splurge, make a reservation, take the private elevator to the second floor, and enjoy one of the rare spots in Paris where the food comes close to doing justice to the view.

La Flamberge 12, av. Rapp, 7e. Métro: Ecole-Militaire. 47-05-91-37. AE/DC/EC/V. This one-star restaurant offers a menu that is truly an adventure all by itself. Who could forget the salad of oak leaves, artichokes, and fennel, with warm langoustines and a touch of raspberry? Or the *magret de canard* (duck filets served with foie gras)? Many more unusual dishes are available and all are delicious.

Quai d'Orsay 49, quai d'Orsay, 7e. Métro: Invalides. 45-51-58-58. Closed Sunday and August. AE/DC/EC/V. This is the businessman's restaurant. The crowd rushes though they still spend well over an hour eating the copious portions (which can be ordered by the half portion). In the fall, you'll find wild mushrooms, dandelion greens in a salad, many game offerings. There are interesting fish dishes, and some of the best breads in town.

8th Arrondissement

Ambassadeurs 10, pl. de la Concorde, 8e. Métro: Concorde. A new 2-star restaurant decorated by fashion designer Sonia Rykiel in dramatic colors. Black dominates everything. A superb flower arrangement welcomes guests at the entrance, located in the grandiose hall of the Hôtel de Crillon. The dining room is large and very bright, with windows overlooking the Place de la Concorde. The service is not always perfect though, like the wine, it has a tendency to improve with the years. You will taste, of course, the *St. Jacques* (scallops) Sonia Rykiel and you might never forget the large selection of desserts, supposed to be the best in Paris.

Androuët 41, rue d'Amsterdam, 8e. Métro: Liège. 48-74-26-93. Closed Sundays and holidays. AE/DC/V. Upstairs from the cheese shop (see FOOD) is a rustic, old-fashioned restaurant with wooden booths, arched doorways, and a menu based on cheese: Camembert fritters, heavy meat dishes with cheese-based sauces, and savory pastries flavored with cheese, all served up with hurried, flambéed flair. But what one goes to Androuët for—or used to (on a recent visit neither cheese nor service was up to par)—is their 6- or 7-course cheese tasting that takes you through the entire range of French—and some Italian—cheeses.

Boutique à Sandwiches 12, rue du Colisée, 8e. Métro: Franklin D. Roosevelt. 43-59-56-69. Closed Sunday and August. 80F. This "sandwich shop" offers a filling and good raclette: a dish of broiled raclette cheese, small potatoes with their skin on, pickled onions, and *cornichons*.

Le Bristol 112, rue du Faubourg-St.-Honoré, 8e. Métro: St.-Philippe-du-Roule. 42-66-91-45. Open daily. AE/DC/V/EC. Menu 360F. F. The dining room in this newly remodeled and very sumptuous hotel is large and oval, and is the epitome of elegance. Waiters rush about attending to the needs of an international clientele, and the dishes are nouvelle style and generally exquisite. Worth trying, if it's on the menu, is a wonderful oyster and salmon tartar. Stay away from the truffles—they were less than top quality.

Caviar Kaspia 17, pl. de la Madeleine, 8e. Métro: Madeleine. 42-65-33-52. Closed Sunday. AE/DC/V. This is the place to sample a thimbleful (30 grams) of delicate caviar perched atop a blini, the whole washed down with chilled vodka. They serve it with cream, but try it plain to get the full effect of the caviar in all its purity.

Chiberta 3, rue Arsène-Houssaye, 8e. Métro: Charles-de-Gaulle-Etoile. 45-63-77-90. Closed Saturday, Sunday, holidays, and August. AE/DC/V. This restaurant is a temple to nouvelle cuisine, with its artfully prepared, diminutive presentations and slightly exotic combinations. There's rabbit and fish *terrine, fricassée* of lobster, *lapereau au gingembre* (young rabbit with ginger), all served graciously in a dramatic 1930s decor.

La Marée 1, rue Daru, 8e. Métro: Courcelles. 47-63-77-90. AE/DC. 2-star restaurant. Do not mind the decor, which is that of an old and small bistro, nothing else. Here the emphasis is on food and wine. Everything is carefully prepared, from the *Belons* (oysters from Brittany) *au champagne*, the *petits rougets grillés* (little grilled fish), *la petite marmite marseillaise* (fish soup), to the runny Camembert (the best in Paris) and the specialty of the house, a gigantic *millefeuille (Napoleon)*. Closed Saturday and Sunday.

Lamazère 23, rue de Ponthieu, 8*e*. Métro: Franklin-Roosevelt. 43-59-66-66. AE/DC/EC/V. One of the best ambassadors from the Southwest of France. Menu is devoted to the specialties of Gascogne. The *truffles "a la croque," truffles Lamazère*, an unforgettable *cassoulet* (beans and pork), a *foie gras* out of this world, an unusual goose tripe as you would eat it in the Landes region, have earned Roger Lamazère one star. Closed Sunday.

Lasserre 17, av. Franklin-Roosevelt, 8*e*. Métro: Franklin-Roosevelt. 43-59-53-43. An "old" 2-star restaurant. One of the best tables in Paris that has maintained its quality and reputation and has emerged undamaged from the Nouvelle Cuisine era. If you go there during the summer you will be able to dine *al fresco*. You will enjoy the *sole marinière*, as well as the chocolate charlotte with caramelized pears. Closed Sunday and Monday.

Lucas-Carton 9, pl. de la Madeleine, 8*e*. Métro: Madeleine. 42-65-22-90. Thanks to Alain Senderens (former owner of l'Archestrate), Lucas-Carton has recovered its three stars. In a 1900's authentic décor, Senderens works for the glory of the *gastronomie française*. His *foie gras de canard aux choux* (duck with cabbage and goose liver) is absolutely perfect and the roasted and poached duck with honey is a delight. Closed Saturday and Sunday.

Pavillon-Elysée (owned by Lenôtre) 10, av. des Champs-Elysées, 8*e*. Métro: Etoile. 42-65-85-10. AE/DC/V. Michelin gave two stars to this restaurant, located on the first floor of the building, while the *rez-de-chaussée*" (main floor) is devoted to a more modest restaurant (one Michelin star). As usual, the *charette des desserts* (dessert cart) is something no one should to miss. Here you will be served the best chocolate cake (among other treats) in Paris. Closed Saturday and Sunday.

Petit Montmorency 5, rue Rabelais, 8*e*. Métro: St.-Philippe-du-Roule. 42-25-11-19. Closed Saturday and Sunday. V. One is immediately at ease in this sophisticated yet homey bistro, which offers hearty and inventive twists on classic cuisine. There's fresh *foie* *gras maison* (prepared by the chef), really fresh, fragrant truffle and potato salad; warmed oysters stuffed with spinach and a fish-and-vegetable medley served in a quaint, silver-covered dish; fresh game in season; and light, imaginative desserts.

Taillevent 15, rue Lamennais, 8e. Métro: George-V. 45-63-39-94. Closed Saturday, Sunday, holidays, Easter, and the end of July to the end of August. Dining at Taillevent is like being transported to a dream world where the sauces are always rich but never heavy, the turbot always grilled to perfection, the truffle-and-pistachio nut seafood *boudin* (sausage) always a sensation, the *marquise au chocolat* (light chocolate cake) like a taste of heaven, and the service gracious, attentive to the smallest detail. Taillevent has the best wine cellar in Paris. Here you will find unbelievable wines at a price that will not make your hair stand on end!

9th Arrondissement

Café de la Paix pl. de l'Opéra, 9e. Métro: Opéra. 47-42-97-02. AE/DC/EC/V. After many years, this restaurant was finally awarded one star by Michelin. In a Second Empire decor, sometimes a little too heavy, you will enjoy watching the people strolling in the Place de l'Opéra, while sampling a *noisette* of lamb or a *canette* (filet of young duck), fresh fruit amandine or a *millefeuille praliné* (a type of flaky Napoleon).

Chartier 7, rue du Faubourg-Montmartre, 9e. Métro: Montmartre. 47-70-86-29. Open daily, The phenomenon and the price make this 1920s-style restaurant a landmark. There are 25 choices for a main course, 40 possibilities for cheese and dessert; it is rumored the waiters all have photographic memories, for they don't write anything down.

Petit Riche 25, rue Le Peletier, 9e. Métro: Le Peletier. 47-70-68-68. Closed Sunday and August. AE/V. This restaurant doesn't look as if it has changed much since it was first established 100 years ago: the stark, simple authentic decor is old Paris and very well kept; the businesslike lunchtime crowd is serious about their eating. The food is classic with modern inspiration—you can still find *andouillette* (tripe sausage), but you can also order a filet of haddock, an octopus salad, sautéed veal with leeks, and a truly fine light, individual apple tart made to order—seemingly the most popular dessert in the house.

Roi du Pot-au-Feu 34, rue Vignon, 9e. Métro: Madeleine. 47-42-37-10. Closed Sunday, holidays, and July. V. The specialty here—as the name indicates—is heartwarming beef stew served traditionally in 2 courses, beginning with the hearty broth, then followed by a platter of beef and vegetables topped with marrow.

10th Arrondissement

(+) Brasserie Flo 7, cour des Petites-Ecuries, 10e. Métro: Château-d'Eau. 47-70-13-59. Open daily until 1:30 A.M. AE/DC/V. Reputedly crowded, hectic, and noisy but a very popular place that caters to late-night eaters who go for Alsatian specialties and the authentic 1900 decor.

Chateaubriant 23, rue de Chabrol, 10e. Métro: Gare-de-l'Est. 48-24-58-94. Closed Sunday, Monday, and August. AE/V. While it may not be 100 percent authentic, the food at this Italian restaurant is superb. The pastas are unctuous, the asparagus in season sublime—a perfect foil for the veal dishes, ravioli Piemontese, Spaghetti Napoletana, and a good selection of Italian wines.

(+) Julien 16, rue du Faubourg-St.-Denis, 10e. Métro: Strasbourg-St.-Denis. 47-70-12-06. Open daily; closed July. AE/DC/V. Specialties here are *cassoulet d'oie* (goose with white beans), *foie gras* (fattened duck or goose liver), fish and seafood specialties—all served up in a large, beautifully decorated Belle Epoque dining room.

(+) Terminus Nord 23, rue de Dunkerque, 10e. Métro: Gare-du-Nord. 42-85-05-15. Open daily. AE/V/DC. Reputedly exquisite fresh oysters, shellfish, *choucroute*, grilled fish, and inexpensive wines at this boisterous brasserie—all served in a flamboyant 1925-era decor.

Restaurants

11th Arrondissement

A Sousceyrac 35, rue Faidherbe, 11e. Métro: Faidherbe. 43-71-65-30. AE/V. This provincial one-star bistro has been run by the same family for years. The *foie gras en terrine* (duck liver tureen) is always a delight, as well as the *Coquilles St-Jacques* (scallops) *au champagne*. But nothing beats the *cassoulet* (meat and beans) served every Wednesday and Friday. Closed Saturday and Sunday.

Chardenoux 1, rue Jules-Vallès, 11e. Métro: Charonne. 43-71-49-52. Closed Saturday, Sunday, holidays, and August. As soon as you walk into this corner bistro you know you've found something good. Try the spicy duck *tourte* (savory double-crust pie), a serving of tiny, delicate wild mushrooms, and the fruit desserts.

Chez Michel 10, rue Belzunce, 10e. Métro: Gare du Nord. 48-78-44-14. AE/DC/V. Small, two-star restaurant. Reservations necessary. Some traditional dishes and some in the Nouvelle Cuisine style. The *foie gras de canard* (duck liver) is superb (not served during the summer). The *Belons* (oysters) are second to none and the veal *Vallée d'Auge* always perfect. Closed Friday and Saturday.

Chez Philippe (Auberge Pyrénées-Cévennes) 106, rue de la Folie-Méricourt, 11e. Métro: République. 43-57-33-78. Closed Saturday, Sunday, holidays, and August. It's hard to decide what's best at this tucked-away enclave filled with Parisians who come for the impeccable Southwest food and the amiable, intimate atmosphere. The goose is queen here. You can choose from meltingly rich, nutty *foie gras, cassoulet d'oie toulousain* (truly a winter dish of goose and white beans), *confit d'oie Auberge* (goose preserved in goose fat, then roasted), or a whole *bar au four* (baked fish similar to striped bass), salmon, or grilled lobster.

12th Arrondissement

Au Pressoir 257, av. Daumesnil, 12e. Métro: Porte-Dorée. 43-44-38-21. V . One star. Spacious dining-room with a provincial ambiance. The menu is innovative enough to satisfy every gourmet palate. A *damier de foie gras en chaud et froid* (hot and cold goose liver) is always a sure bet, as is the filet of duck and the rabbit with oysters. Closed Saturday and Sunday.

Au Trou Gascon 40, rue Taine, 12e. Métro: Daumesnil. 43-44-34-26. V. Old Parisian bistro renovated a few years ago, with limited seats. Reservations advisable. Here the *foie gras des Landes* (goose liver) and the *poulet* (chicken) *des Landes sautéed with cèpes* (mushrooms) are succulent, as well as the *raviolis au foie gras truffé* or the leg of lamb. Closed Saturday and Sunday.

Train Bleu 20, bd. Diderot, on the 1st floor, Gare-de-Lyon, 12e. Métro: Gare-de-Lyon. 43-43-09-06. Open daily. AE/DC/V. Even if you're not embarking on an exciting voyage, you can pretend you are in this breathtaking, expensive Belle Epoque restaurant just above the hustle-bustle of the Gare de Lyon. You can enjoy a very adequate—even good—meal of fish dumplings in butter sauce, grilled salmon or steak, or fresh raw vegetables with a garlicky sauce as you watch your fellow diners sop up the last bit from their plates before they descend to board a train. Or notice the waiters who, like the decor, seem to be from another, more refined era.

14th Arrondissement

Cagouille 89, rue Daguerre, 14e. Métro: Denfort-Rochereau. 43-22-09-01. Closed Sunday, Monday, and August. Some of the best fish in Paris is offered at this small, homey bistro, right near the Montparnasse cemetery. Go and enjoy a rare occasion to eat truly fresh seafood.

Coupole 102, bd. du Montparnasse, 14e. Métro: Vavin or Montparnasse. 43-20-14-20. Open daily; closed August. V. This is the place for Sunday lunch. It's a bit like a huge old food hall.

Le Duc 243, bd. Raspail, 14e. Métro: Raspail. 43-22-59-59. Very good one-star fish restaurant—a place known by Parisians. The owners are sure that no one else knows how to prepare fish. Even if they are exaggerating, no one is going to hold it against them—their cuisine is delicious. Closed Saturday, Sunday and Monday.

Le Dôme 108, bd. du Montparnasse, 14e. Métro: Vavin. 43-35-25-81. AE/DC/V. Beautiful brasserie (one star) that serves fresh fish and shellfish. Simple but refined cuisine like the *fricassée de langoustines à l'estragon* (prawn fricassee with taragon), *bar poché à la citronnelle* (poached bass with herbs), *oursins* (sea urchins), etc. Closed Monday.

15th Arrondissement

Aquitaine 54, rue de Dantzig, 15e. Métro: Convention. 48-28-67-38. Closed Sunday and Monday. AE/DC/V/EC. This restaurant is a surprise way out in the 15th arrondissement. The food here, too, is a pleasant discovery. Southwestern specialties made with a light touch: duck *confit*, new potatoes and *foie gras*, filet of beef with *cèpes* (meaty, wild mushrooms). The meat dishes are nicely paired with light fish dishes: *fricassée de poissons aux champignons sauvages* (a fish stew with wild mushrooms), steamed turbot with Roquefort sauce, or roast lobster.

Le Western 18, av. de Suffren, 15e. Métro: Bir-Hakeim. 42-73-92-00. AE/DC/EC/V. A truly American restaurant in the Hotel Hilton near the Eiffel Tower. They serve corn bread, rye and buckwheat bread with butter, ribs, T-bones that come directly from the U.S.A, chili, cheesecake, strawbery shortcake, muffins, American wine, and American coffee. If you are homesick, go to Le Western—the ambiance is not all that is American. The customers are too!

Also in this section, of Paris, **Les Célébrités**, 61, quai de Grenelle. Métro: Bir-Hakeim. 45-75-62-62 (one star); **Morot-Gaudry** 6, rue Cavalerie. Métro: Motte-Picquet. 45-67-06-85 (one star); **Olympe** 8, rue Nicolas Charlet. Métro: Pasteur. 47-34-86-08; Le Toit de Paris, 18, av. de Suffren. (on the 11th floor). Métro: Bir-Hakeim. 42-73-92-00 You can eat, dance, and enjoy the view, all at the same time.

16th Arrondissement

Faugeron 52, rue de Longchamp, 16e. Métro: Bois-sière. 47-04-24-53. For its prawns with cucumber mousse, its rabbit with salad of artichokes, its lamb sautéed with herb mint and many other delicious "cré-ations," Faugeron was awarded two stars by Michelin. Closed Saturday and Sunday.

Guy Savoy 28, rue Duret, 16e. Métro: Argentine. 45-00-17-67. V. A two star restaurant with a warm atmosphere that makes one feel at home. Savoy is one of the most talented and creative chefs in France today. Who could resist his *aspic de foie gras au riz sauvage*,(wild rice), his *huîtres* (oysters)*en nage glacée*, or his *chaussons* (turnover) *de pommes-de-terre* (po-tatoes) *truffés*? And don't forget the raspberry *mille-feuille*. Closed Saturday and Sunday.

Jamin/Joël Robuchon 32, rue de Longchamp, 16e. Métro: Trocadéro. 47-27-12-27. Closed Saturday, Sunday, and July. AE/DC/EC/V. The food in this restaurant is inspired from the diminutive appetizers that melt in your mouth and gently demand the presence of every taste bud, to the delicate though sometimes dramatically exciting dishes that supersede each other in a crescendo of fulfillment and satisfaction. Bright red egg-shaped scoops of light to-mato mousse are set in a pool of slightly more red tomato sauce punctuated with green dots of fresh herb sauce; small *rosettes* of trout are offered with a slightly sour sauce.

Pré Catelan Route de Suresnes, Bois de Boulogne, 16e. Not accessible by métro. 45-24-55-58. Closed Sunday night, Monday, and February. AE/DC/V. 350F–500F. You can enjoy an elegant meal in grand style at this restaurant under the trees of the Bois de Boulogne. It merits 2 stars in Michelin for its game, its inventive sea-food dishes, and its reliable desserts (owned by Lenôtre).

Vivarois 192, av. Victor Hugo. Métro: Pompe. 45-04-04-31. AE/DC/V. Elegant two-star restaurant with a garden. The cuisine is excellent as well as the service. We have only good things to say about the *soufflé d'oursins* (sea urchins soufflé) or the *feuilleté aux truffes*, or *le canard* (duck) *au miel* (with honey). Don't pass up the desserts; you will regret it. Closed Sat-urday and Sunday.

17th Arrondissement

Bernardin 18, rue Troyon, 17e. Métro: Charles-de-Gaulle-Etoile. 43-80-40-61. Closed Sunday, Monday, and August. AE/V. The decor in this seafood restaurant is reminiscent of the sea—soothing tones, space, and light. Fish and seafood are served here exclusively, and everything is done to honor their inherent flavors, textures, and appearances.

Coquille 6, rue du Débarcadère, 17e. Métro: Porte Maillot. 45-74-25-95. Closed Sunday, Monday, holidays, and August. V. Simple, satisfying, seasonal dishes characterize this friendly, bistro. Try their *coquille Saint-Jacques* (scallops served with their orange-hued *corail*, or coral), meaty frogs legs, or game in season.

La Lorraine pl. des Ternes, 17e. Métro: Ternes. AE/DC/VI. A huge brasserie where fresh oysters (Belons, Marennes etc.), shellfish, and a delicious *boudin* (blood sausage), a spicy *choucroute* (sauerkraut), little shrimps called *crevettes grises et crevettes roses* are served day and night. Order their a Kir (white wine and cassis) or a Kir Royal (champagne and raspberry). The restaurant is always crowded, even the big terrace looking out on the Place de Ternes and flanked on one side by several "écaillers" (oyster men) who work nonstop. La Lorraine might not be what it was, but it is still a great place to go at three o'clock in the morning.

Michel Rostang 20, rue Rennequin, 17e. Métro: Ternes. 47-63-40-77. Closed Saturday lunch and October to March; all day Saturday, April to September; Sunday, and holidays. V. This restaurant is right up with the stars—it merits 2 in the Michelin guide. Sophisticated, country-style cuisine. The poached quail eggs served perched atop a just-cooked sea urchin are ambrosial, the perfectly roasted pigeon in its rich but light sauce is a dream, the cheese tray is laden with seasonal splendors.

Other "centres de la gastronomie" include, **L'Etoile d'Or** 3, pl. du Géneral Koenig. Métro: Porte Maillot. AE/DC/V. 47-58-12-84. **Michel Comby** 116, bd. Pereire Métro: Porte Maillot. AE/DC/V. 43-80-88-68. **TIMGAD** 21, rue Brunel. Métro: Argentine. AE/DC/V. 45-74-23-

70. **Manoir de Paris**, 6 rue Pierre-Demours. Métro: Wagram. AE/DC/V. 45-72-25-25. **Sormani** 4, rue du Général Lanrezac. Métro: Etoile. V. 43-80-13-91. **Le Petit Colombier** rue des Acacias. Métro: Argentine. Visa. 43-80-28-54. **La Petite Auberge** 38, rue Laugier. Métro: Ternes. DC/V. 47-63-85-51. **La Mère Michel** 5, rue Rennequin. Métro: Ternes. V. 45-63-59-80.

Outside City

If you want to have a lunch or dinner outside of Paris you could go to one of the following. **Le Coq Hardy** in Bougival, 18 kilometers from Paris, 16, quai Rennequin-Sualem. 36-69-01-43 AE/DC/V. **Au Comte de Gascogne** at Boulogne-Billancourt (10 kilometers from Paris). 89, av. J. B Clement. 46-03-47-27. AE/DC/V. **Le Tastevin** at Maisons-Laffitte (21 kilometers from Paris), 9, av. d'Egle. 39-62-11-67. AE/DC/V. **Le Relais des Gardes** at Meudon (12 kilometers from Paris), 42, av. Gallieni. 45-34-11-79. AE/DC/EC/V. Maxim's at Roissy-Charles de Gaulle Airport. 48-62-16-16. AE/DC/V.

RUNNING

Running in Paris? It hasn't quite hit the fever pitch, but parks and gardens are becoming increasingly filled with runners. Running has a special tone to it in Paris, where women dress in color-coordinated outfits complete with scarves, makeup, and perfume to do their daily kilometers. It's almost the opposite with men, who can often be seen in ordinary tennis shoes, white dress shirts and jeans. There's a fashion to running, a certain effortlessness, an inherent elegance and sophistication so typical to Parisians one doesn't even notice if they're sweating.

The *Mairie de Paris* has a fitness program called *Allosport*. They sponsor running get-togethers for women, men, and children, called "Sport-Nature," in many of the city's parks on Sunday mornings at 9:30 and again at 10:45. They are free of charge, and anyone can participate. Just look for the sign "*SPORT-NATURE*" at the following parks and join in:

Bois de Vincennes pl. du Cardinal La Vigerie. 12*e*. Métro: Porte Dorée.

Jardin du Luxembourg The bd. St.-Michel entrance, 5*e*. Métro: Luxembourg.

Parc des Buttes Chaumont The entrance across from the Marie du XIXème Arrondissement. 19*e*. Métro: Laumière.

Plaine de Vaugirard Entrance at the Stade Suzanne Lenglen, 2, rue Louis-Armand, 15*e*. Métro: Place Balard.

Porte d'Ivry The entrance at the Stade Georges Carpentier, 81, bd. Masséna, 13*e*. Métro: Porte d'Ivry.

Square René Legall At the rue Croulebarbe, 13*e*. Métro: Gobelins.

Stade Emile-Anthoine 9, rue Jean-Rey, 15*e*. Métro: Bir-Hakeim.

Stade Lucien Godin Quai Saint Bernard, 5*e*. Métro: Gare d'Austerlitz.

For more information on running and races in Paris call *Allosport*, 42-76-54-54, Monday through Friday.

For specific runs or information about running or sporting events, check *L'Equipe*, the daily French sports magazine, which often publishes announcements of upcoming races. It is available at all kiosks. If organized running isn't your style, the following is a short list of parks that make ideal running spots.

Bois de Boulogne, 16e.
Bois de Vincennes, 12e.
Champ de Mars (7e)
Jardin du Luxembourg, 5e.
Jardin des Plantes, 5e.
Jardin des Tuileries, 8e.
Parc Monceau, 8e.
Parc Montsouris, 14e.
Also, along the quais of the Seine, particularly dramatic at sunset or sunrise (5e, 4e).

SALONS DE THE (TEA SALONS)

The first heyday for tea salons in Paris was at the turn of the century, when it was fashionable for women who didn't want to receive guests at home to invite them out instead. They would pass the afternoon sipping tea, tasting pastries, and discussing the day's events, with a background of gentle classical music.

In the past 7 or 8 years Paris has experienced a renaissance in *salons de thé*. Neither restaurants nor cafés, *salons de thé* fall somewhere in between. They offer a haven from the daily rush, a place to have a light lunch, then linger over dessert and a pot of scented tea, a cup of frothy chocolate, or coffee. *Salons de thé* are as different in style as they are numerous,

PONT NEUF

yet they are another dimension of the Parisian flare for enjoying spare hours in comfort and style. The following is a selected list of *salons de thé*—you'll surely find your own.

Angelina 226, rue de Rivoli, 1*er*. Métro: Tuileries. 42-60-82-00. Open daily; closed August. Slightly faded elegance marks this *salon de thé* across from the Tuileries, where *le Tout Paris* once gathered to sip tea and chocolate. It is still a lovely spot with its tiny, marble-topped tables and funny little armchairs. Their hot chocolate is some of the best in Paris. It's made with a melted bar of chocolate and comes steaming, with a little pot of cream and a glass of iced water.

A Priori Thé 35–37, Galerie Vivienne, 2*e*. Métro: Bourse. 42-97-48-75. Closed Sunday. This *salon de thé* feels like a direct import—the furnishings are British, the atmosphere American, the clientele decidedly French. It was started by 3 American women, and their backgrounds are reflected in the menu, which includes brownies, muffins, and a selection of classic black and scented teas.

Carette 4, pl. du Trocadéro, 16*e*. Métro: Trocadéro. 47-27-88-56. Closed Tuesday and August. For a real treat on a sunny day come here and sit outside for a cup of *café au lait*, a *pain au chocolat*, and a lazy morning enjoying the trees of the Place du Trocadéro, the slice of view through the Palais de Chaillot, and the general 16th *arrondissement* activity.

Clichy 5, bd. Beaumarchais, 3*e*. Métro: Bastille. 48-87-89-88. Closed Monday. This is a simple, classic *salon de thé*, right at the back of this pristeen neighborhood *pâtisserie*. They serve traditional pastries, homemade ice creams and sorbets, and hot chocolate and tea, all in a comfortable neighborhood atmosphere.

Dalloyau 2, pl. Edmond-Rostand, 5*e*. Métro: Luxembourg. 43-29-31-10. Open daily. You'd never know there was a light, airy little *salon de thé* upstairs from the vaguely snooty pastry shop. Overcome the chill and climb the stairs; you'll get a view of the Place Edmond-Rostand, the bustling traffic, and the comings and goings into the beautiful, lush Jardin du Luxembourg. Their croissants and *pains du chocolat* are best in the morning, the tea and coffee warming.

Eurydice 10, pl. des Vosges, 4*e*. Métro: Chemin Vert. 42-77-77-99. Closed Monday and Tuesday. It's the location that makes this *salon de thé* special. In fine weather there are tables and chairs outside under the colonnade of the Place des Vosges, and you can sit and enjoy the soothing, calm atmosphere while tasting a rich chocolate cake, fruit tart, or a plate of blinis and Scandinavian-style pickled fish.

Flore en l'Ile 42, quai d'Orléans, 4*e*. Métro: Pont-Marie. 43-29-88-27. Open daily. This is a very Parisian establishment, far from quaint, always bustling with a trendy young crowd who come for the Berthillon ice cream, light meals, teas, and a view of the river and its traffic. It's most enjoyable at night when the Bateaux-Mouches go by, their bright lights illuminating the quais as they pass.

Fourmi Ailée 8, rue du Fouarre, 5*e*. Métro: Maubert-Mutualité. 43-29-40-99. Closed Tuesdays. This is a *salon de thé* bookstore with a literary emphasis on women's works. The few tables at the back are charming, the natural light soft and comforting, ideal for an afternoon pot of tea and one of the British-style pastries—scones, muffins, or perhaps a warming vegetable tart.

Jardin de Thé 81, rue St.-Louis-en-l'Ile. 4*e*. Métro: Pont-Marie. 43-29-81-52. Closed Tuesdays. A *salon de thé* reminiscent of grandmother's living room. More than 65 varieties of teas, English-style pastries, and light meals.

Ladurée 16, rue Royale, 8*e*. Métro: Madeleine. 42-60-21-79. Closed Sunday and August. This is the quintessential *salon de thé* with its shining wood tables and dainty chairs. Customers are generally seated looking into the room—the best vantage point for seeing and being seen. The bustling, rather solemn waitresses are businesslike, and the place is usually filled with a preponderance of well-dressed and very elegant elderly women, and couples who are most likely taking a break from a rigorous look up and down the rue du Faubourg-Saint-Honoré. The *café au lait* is superb, the croissants and *pains au chocolat* glistening and feather-light.

Loir dans la Theière 3, rue des Rosiers, 4e. Métro: St.-Paul. 42-72-90-61. Closed Mondays and August. This *salon de thé* is a bit like a comfortable old shoe—with deep easy chairs, round tables, simple, refreshing salads, and wonderful pastries that vary from day to day. It is also a gallery with temporary art and photography exhibits. Order up a cup of tea and a homemade pastry and be careful—you might end up spending the entire day there.

Mosquée de Paris 39, rue Geoffroy-St.-Hilaire, 5e. Métro: Censier-Daubenton. 43-31-18-14. Open daily. You'll be transported to another world when you walk into this exotic *salon de thé*, part of Paris' first mosque. People are perched like butterflies on the low soft seats; the air is filled with their hushed and hurried conversations and the scent of the sweet mint tea that is brought to your table. You don't order; someone will come around with a plate of Middle-Eastern cookielike pastries and if you want one, make a sign. This is a cool, quiet place for a break after a visit to the nearby Jardin des Plantes, or the rue Mouffetard market.

Salon Belusa 86, rue du Cherche-Midi, 6e. Métro: Sèvres-Babylone. 42-22-52-58. Closed Sunday. This antique-filled *salon de thé* has a comfortable atmosphere and is filled with well-dressed regulars from the neighborhood. The desserts are appealing, the hot chocolate some of the best, the location right for a pause after a visit to Au Bon Marché.

Stubli 11, rue Poncelet, 17e. Métro: Ternes. This is a touch of Vienna in the bustle of the rue Poncelet market. Neat, tidy, and so quaint it hardly seems real, the *salon de thé* is up a narrow, winding staircase from the Patisserie Stubli. You can enjoy everything here from a warm slice of quiche to almond-rich turnovers, poppy-seed cake, brioche loaded with walnuts, and more, all made with the best ingredients.

Verlet 256, rue St.-Honoré, 1er. Métro: Louvre. 42-60-67-39. Closed Monday and August. This shope ostensibly sells freshly roasted coffee beans, teas, and exotic

Salons de Thé

dried fruits and nuts, all carefully displayed in the crowded window. Once inside past the jumble you'll notice the few tables that just beg to be used. Settle in and order a cup of one of their own roasts or a pot of tea and try one of their ultra-fresh pastries or a satisfying and dainty *croque-monsieur*.

SECRETARIAL SERVICES

See BUSINESS SERVICES.

SENIOR CITIZENS

Senior citizens in France—women over 60 years of age and men over 62 years of age—are referred to as people of the *Troisième Age* (third age) or *Personnes Agées* (older people). If you fit into those categories you can qualify for certain travel and entertainment privileges. You will need to buy a *Carte Vermeil*, which is available at any train station and costs about 61F. With this card you can travel half-price on the train during the *périodes bleues*—mostly during the week, though at certain times on weekends, too—and you can get reduced admission to many movies and museums. To find out about *périodes bleues*, just ask for a *Carte Vermeil* brochure when you get your card. It is clearly and graphically explained inside. When going to a movie, check in the *Pariscope* or *L'Officiel des Spectacles*, and under individual theaters, with the movie listing you'll see "*Etu. et Cartes Vermeil . . .*" or "*C.V.*," then a price. That means students and holders of the *Carte Vermeil* get in for that price. For museums, show your card before paying and you'll be told whether or not you qualify for a discount.

Senior Citizens

Hospitals

The American Hospital is the only 100% participant in the Empire Blue-Cross/Blue Shield program. (see HOSPITALS)

Hotels

We have selected several small hotels, quiet, well located and yet reasonable in prices:

Esmeralda 4, rue St-Julien Le Pauvre, 5e. Métro: St-Michel. 43-54-19-20. Near Quais de la Seine (Quai des Grands Augustins, Quai de la Tournelle). In the center of La Cité. 19 rooms with bathrooms. Prices range from 80F (for a single room without bath) to 300F.

Family Hotel 35, rue Cambon, 1e. Métro Concorde. 42-61-54-84. In the center of Paris, near Place de la Concorde and church of La Madeleine. 22 rooms with bathrooms and 3 with just a sink. Prices range from 95F (single room, no bath) to 300F.

Hôtel des Deux Continents 25, rue Jacob, 6e. Métro: St-Germain des-Prés. 43-26-72-46. Also located in the center of Paris, on the left bank. A very animated "quartier." 40 rooms, all with bathrooms. Prices range from 200F (single room) to 400F.

Hôtel du College de France, 7, rue Thenard, 5e. Métro: Maubert. 43-26-78-36. Near the Pantheon and the Sorbonne. No restaurant. 29 rooms with bathrooms. Prices range from 250F to 300F.

Les Marronniers 21, rue Jacob, 6e. Métro: St-Michel. 43-25-30-60. No restaurant. Charming little hotel with a "jardinet" (small garden) where breakfast is served when the weather permits. Tables are graciously set under a veranda. 37 rooms (with baths). Prices range from 200F to 350F.

Résidence d'Orsay 93, rue de Lille, 7e. Métro:Chambre des Députés. 47-05-05-27. No restaurant. Very quiet street in this select section of the Left Bank. Not far from les Quais de la Seine and from "Assemblée Nationale" where the French representatives (the "Députés") meet . . . and fight. 32 rooms with baths. Prices range from 150F to 300F.

SHOES

Boot Shop 25, rue du Four, 6e. Métro: Mabillon. 43-54-12-82. Shoes and boots with flair. Closed Sunday. AE/DC/V.

Carel 22, rue Royale, 8e. Métro: Madeleine. 42-60-23-05. Both classic and trendy. Many other addresses in Paris. Closed Sunday, Monday. AE/DC/EC/V.

Charles Jourdan 5, bd. de la Madeleine, 1er. Métro: Madeleine. 42-61-15-89; 12, rue du Faubourg-St.-Honoré, 8e. Métro: Concorde. 42-65-35-22; 86, av. des Champs-Elysées, 8e. Métro: George-V. 45-62-29-33. Many other addresses in Paris. The penultimate French shoe—styles and colors for everyone. Closed Sunday. AE/DC/EC/V.

Christian Dior 28, av. Montaigne, 8e. Métro: Alma-Marceau. 47-23-54-44. Excellent quality shoes made by Charles Jourdan for Dior. Closed Sunday. AE/DC/V.

France Faver 81, rue des Sts.-Pères, 6e. Métro: Sèvres-Babylone. 42-22-04-29. Elegant shoes, most of them Italian made. Closed Sunday and August. AE/V/EC.

Free Lance 22, rue Mondétour, 1er. Métro: Etienne-Marcel. 42-21-30-96. Fun, trendy shoes—rainbow rubber boots, ballerina-style shoes, etc. Closed Sunday.

Mancini 20, rue du Boccador, 8e. Métro: Alma-Marceau. 47-23-35-05. These elegant shoes are made right in Paris. You can get shoes made specially to order if you have 2 to 3 weeks. Closed Sunday. AE/DC/EC/V.

Maud Frizon 83, rue des Sts.-Pères, 6e. Métro: Sèvres-Babylone. 42-22-06-93; 12, av. Montaigne, 8e. Métro: Alma-Marceau; 47-20-92-22. Sophisticated, chic, expensive shoes of top quality. Closed Sunday. AE/V/DC.

Sacha 15, rue de Turbigo, 2e. Métro: Etienne-Marcel. 42-33-48-08; 24, rue de Buci, 6e. Métro: Mabillon. 43-54-43-50. Trendy shoes at reasonable prices. Both shops close Sundays. AE/DC/V.

Tilbury 23, rue du Four, 6e. Métro: Mabillon. 43-26-03-84. Luxuriously elegant, subtle styles, often in narrow sizes. Closed Sunday. AE/V/DC.

Tokio Kumagai 52, rue Croix-des-Petits-Champs, 1er. Métro: Bourse. 42-36-08-01. Wild and wonderful designer shoes. There are several other shops in Paris. Closed Sunday. AE/DC/V.

Designer Discounts

These shops are discount stores where you can find last year's designer shoes at very reduced prices. Sometimes the inventory is small and they don't always have all the designers, but if you're willing to look a bit you can find some good bargains.

Childerène 262, rue de Charenton, 12e. Métro: Daumesnil. 23-41-40-89. Closed Sunday and Monday morning. Shoes by Cardin, Dior, Xavier Danaud, and Bally for women. Bally and other Italian brands for men.

Gianni 104, rue du Bac, 7e. Métro: Rue-du-Bac. 25-44-29-53. Classic and trendy shoes for men and women. Closed Sunday.

Gigis Soldes 30, pl. du Marché-St.-Honoré, 1er. Métro: Pyramides. 42-60-08-98. Valentinos, Ungaros, and others. Closed Saturday afternoon and Sunday.

Marc Soldes 1, rue Ordener, 18e. Métro: Max-Dormoy. 42-45-00-50. Saint Laurents' for women, some shoes for men. Closed Sunday. V.

Mi-Prix 27, bd. Victor, 15e. Métro: Porte de Versailles. 48-28-42-48. Top-designer shoes from Maud Frizon to Tokio Kumaki and France Favier. Ballys for men. Some children's shoes. Closed Sunday.

Royal Solde 137, bd. de Magenta, 10e. Métro: Gare-du-Nord. 42-80-12-01. Shoes by Cardin, Xavier Danaud, Jourdan for men and women. Purses also. Closed Sunday and Monday morning.

Sabotine 35, rue de la Roquette, 11e. Métro: Bastille. 43-55-10-04. Last year's Carels for women only. Closed Sunday and Monday.

Children's Shoes

Bonpoint 86, rue de l'Université, 7e. Métro: Solférino. 45-55-63-70. Closed Sunday. AE/DC/V.

Cendrine 3, rue Vavin, 6*e*. Métro: Vavin. 43-54-81-20. Closed Sunday. V.

Josia 9, rue Emile-Landrin, 20*e*. Métro: Gambetta. 47-97-98-71. Closed Sunday and August.

Neut 9, rue Lépold-Bellan, 2*e*. Métro: Sentier. 42-33-83-46. Closed Saturday, Sunday, and August.

Pascal 55, av. de La Bourdonnais, 7*e*. Métro: Ecole-Militaire. 45-51-90-55. Closed Sunday and Monday. V.

Sidonie Larizzi 8, rue Marignan, 8*e*. Métro: Franklin D. Roosevelt. 43-59-38-87. Closed Sunday. AE/DC/V.

SHOPPING

There are 2 major sales in Paris—in January and July—when stores of every kind, from fashion to kitchenware, substantially reduce their prices.

Antiques

You'll find antiques stores throughout the city to poke around in. The following are some of the most important:

Cour aux Antiquaires 54, rue du Faubourg-St.-Honoré, 8*e*. Métro: Concorde. 47-42-43-99. Closed Sunday, Monday, and August. There are 18 stands assembled in this courtyard; some sell paintings, others engravings, icons, vases, trinkets, and all manner of things. Certain credit cards are accepted at some stands.

Hôtel Drouot 9, rue Drouot, 9*e*. Métro: Richelieu-Drouot. 42-46-17-11. Closed Saturday and Sunday in July and September. Closed in August. You look at items to be auctioned—including antique and sometimes very valuable paintings, jewelry, and furniture—any time the auction house is open. Auctions, open to everyone, are held Mondays, Wednesdays, and Fridays starting at 2 P.M.

Louvre des Antiquaires 2, pl. du Palais-Royal, 1*er*. Métro: Palais-Royal. 42-97-27-00. Closed Mondays. There are more than 200 elegant, luxurious shops in this complex that sell everything from valuable paintings to tiepins. Even if you're not planning to buy, it is a wonderful place to wander. There is a department for mailing your purchase home.

Village Saint-Paul Between rue St.-Paul and rue Charlemagne, 4e. Métro: St.-Paul. Closed Tuesday and Wednesday. Here you'll find *objets* and artifacts from the Napoleon III epoch (end of the 18th century) to the 1920s.

Village Suisse At the angle of av. de Suffren and av. de la Motte-Picquet; 15e. Métro: La Motte-Picquet. Closed Tuesday and Wednesday. A cluster of dealers who sell mostly furniture, but also some art and *objets*.

Note: Other good spots for antiquing are the city's flea markets (see MARKETS).

For the Home and Table

You'll find it all in a 4-block-long stretch of the rue de Paradis: crystal from Baccarat, Saint-Louis, and Daum; Porcelaine de Paris, de Sèvres, de Limoges; Christofle silver; china from Pillivuyt; and designer pieces from all over Europe.

Shop after shop lines both sides of the street, offering an almost unparalleled selection and many unparalleled prices. The shops are generally open from 9:30 A.M. to 6:30 P.M. and are closed Sunday and Monday. The following are just a few of what you'll find.

Boutique Paradis 1 bis, rue de Paradis, 10e. Métro: Château-d'Eau. 48-24-45-96. Closed Sunday and August. AE/DC/EC/V. Hundreds of pieces of crystal and china, some silver.

Limoges Unic 12, rue de Paradis, 10e. Métro: Château-d'Eau. 47-70-54-49 and 45-23-31-44. Closed Sunday. AE/V. Primarily Limoges china but silver, crystal and porcelain by the best names too.

Tisanerie 35, rue de Paradis, 10e. Métro: Château-d'Eau. 47-70-40-49. Closed Sunday and Monday. V. White porcelain that you can have personalized right in the store.

Others for the Home and Table

Au Bain Marie 20, rue Hérold, 1er. Métro: Bourse. 42-60-94-55. Closed Sunday. AE/V. This shop is filled with an awesome and lovely collection of china, copper, glass and crystal antique and often rare pieces. Upstairs are linens—some old, some new, all in the finest fabrics, from silk to the purest cotton.

Papeterie Moderne 12, rue de la Ferronerie, 1er. Métro: Châtelet-Les-Halles. Closed Sunday and 2 weeks in August. 42-36-21-72. If you've always wanted a French street sign to hang on your wall, this is the place to get it, as well as just about any other sign you've ever seen in France. They are all new, but authentic, and you can even get them personalized.

Kitchen Equipment

Bazar de l'Hôtel-de-Ville (B.H.V.-bay-ash-vay) 52, rue de Rivoli, 4e. Métro: Hôtel-de-Ville. 42-74-90-00. V. Everyday kitchen utensils, gadgets, and machines are available on the third floor of this huge department store. They also have linens, baskets, and lots of knickknacks for the home kitchen.

Bovida 36, rue Montmartre, 1er. Métro: Les Halles. 42-36-09-99. Closed Saturday afternoon and Sunday. AE/DC/V. This shop has professional-quality stainless steel and copper, some serving dishes and platters, and a whole range of paper doilies.

Culinarion 99, rue de Rennes, 6e. Métro: St.-Placide. 45-48-94-76. Closed Sunday. V. Utensils, serving and baking dishes, and a variety of kitchen trifles.

Dehllerin 18–20, rue Coquillière, 1er. Métro: Les Halles. 42-36-53-13. Closed lunchtimes and Sunday. Everything for the professional and the passionate cook here; copper pots by the dozen, serving dishes, utensils, from pastry tips to whisks to knives, strainers, pastry molds of every size and shape. Some English spoken. They will mail your purchases home.

Kitchen Bazaar 17, bd. de Courcelles, 8e. Métro: Villiers. 45-63-79-66. Closed Sunday and August; also 11, av. du Maine, 15e. Métro: Montparnasse. 42-22-91-17. Closed Sunday, Monday, and August. V. Wonderful kitchen utensils—some decorative, many useful—also kitchen linens and some cookbooks.

Lescene-Dura 63, rue de la Verrerie, 4e. Métro: Hôtel-de-Ville. 42-72-08-74. Closed Sunday. V. Everything for the wine enthusiast in this funny old shop.

Mora 13, rue Montmartre, 1*er*. Métro: Les Halles. 45-08-19-24 or 45-08-11-47. Closed lunchtimes, Saturday afternoon, and Sunday. V. A good selection of professional equipment, from copper pots to stainless-steel sieves. Lots of knives, bread pans, some serving dishes, and cookbooks.

Simon 36, rue Etienne-Marcel, 2*e*. Métro: Les Halles. 42-33-71-65. Closed Sundays. Their strength here is serving dishes. They have porcelain, crystal, and china, doilies, basketry, and more. Their annex at 33, rue Montmartre, just across the street and through the courtyard, has professional-quality cookware—bread pans, tart molds, some copper.

Paper Products

Au Bon Marché 38, rue de Sèvres, 7*e*. Métro: Sèvres-Babylone. 42-60-33-45. Closed Sunday. AE/DC/V. On the ground floor of this department store you'll find an art office supplies department with a wonderful choice of notebooks, portfolios with ribbon ties in bright, exotic colors, diaries, pocket calendars, blank books, plastic and paper folders as well as a whole range of writing implements.

Papeterie Joseph Gibert 30, bd. St.-Michel, 6*e*. Métro: St.-Michel. 43-29-67-50. Closed Sunday. Nirvana for people who love French-style office and school supplies—folders, portfolios, notebooks of every size in beautiful colors, and lots of pens, pencils, and related odds and ends.

Papier + 9, rue du Pont-Louis-Philippe, 4*e*. Métro: Pont-Marie. 42-77-70-49. Closed Sunday and Monday. Absolutely lovely paper by the pound, empty books, photo albums—a joy to behold. V.

Papiers Paris 54, bd. Pasteur, 15*e*. Métro: Pasteur. 43-22-93-60. Closed lunchtimes, Sundays, and Mondays. Every kind of paper you could want—for drawing, calligraphy, painting. There's French paper, Japanese paper, paper from throughout the world.

Sennelier 4 bis, rue de la Grande-Chaumière, 6*e*. Métro: Vavin. 46-33-72-39. Closed Sunday and Monday; also 3, quai Voltaire, 7*e*. Métro: Rue-du-Bac. 42-60-72-39. Closed Sunday. AE/DC/V. High-quality drawing and watercolor paper.

Specialty Foods

A dab of caviar, a slice of *foie gras* to eat on hot toast, an earthy truffle, a tour of France through its regional *bonbons*, you can find all these specialty foods and more in Paris' food shops.

Izraeël 30, rue François-Miron, 4e. Métro: St.-Paul. 42-72-66-23. Closed Sunday and Monday. V. Everything is stacked everywhere in this spicy, delightful, exotic shop. You'll find delicious marinated olives, baskets, baubles, and every imaginable condiment, sauce, or ingredient from the world over.

Maison de la Truffe 19, pl. de la Madeleine, 8e. Métro: Madeleine. 42-65-53-22. Closed Sunday. This is the place to buy fresh truffles—black diamonds—fresh from November to March, preserved truffles year-round.

Olivier 77, rue St.-Louis-en-l'Ile, 4e. Métro: Pont-Marie. 43-29-58-32. Closed Sunday and Monday. V. This shop has every kind of oil. For cooking there's olive oil, hazelnut oil, walnut oil. There's oil for the hair, for the skin, even sheeps-foot oil for the mechanic. They also have fresh olives and vinegars.

Soleil de Provence 6, rue du Cherche-Midi, 6e. Métro: Sèvres-Babylone. 45-48-15-02. Closed Sunday, Monday, and August. Huge crocks of olive oil, olive oil soap, lavender, spices—all fresh from the Provence region of France.

Spécialités de France 44, av. Montaigne, 8e. Métro: Franklin D. Roosevelt. 47-20-99-63. Closed Sunday. AE/DC/V. Here you'll find the sweet regional specialties of France, from chocolates to sugar-coated, cocoa-dusted almonds. Many of them come in beautiful tins or boxes.

Sports Equipment

F.N.A.C. Sport Forum des Halles, 1–7, rue Pierre-Lescot, 1er. Métro: Châtelet-Les-Halles. 42-61-81-18. Closed Sunday and Monday. A large selection of reasonably priced sports equipment and clothing.

Sparty 68–80 av. du Maine, 14e. Métro: Reuilly-Diderot. 43-27-50-50. Closed Sunday. Two floors in this huge store filled with sports clothing and some equipment, including ski clothes, wonderful karate outfits, sets of balls for playing *boules*, and more.

Shopping

Vieux Campeur 48, rue des Ecoles, 5e. Métro: Maubert-Mutualité. 43-29-12-32. Closed Sunday. V. This is "sports-central," particularly for hiking, climbing, skiing, horseback riding, and other hearty activities. You'll find brand-name equipment, clothes, books, maps, and a general outdoorsy atmosphere. If you want to try out their climbing equipment there is an indoor climbing rock that is visible from the street and seemingly always in use. This store has spread into buildings throughout the neighborhood. If you don't find what you're looking for, just ask and the personnel will direct you to the appropriate place.

Toys

Boutique DAC 10, rue du Cardinal-Lemoine, 5e. Métro: Cardinal-Lemoine. 43-54-99-51. Closed Sunday and Monday. Hand-crafted toys: string puppets, porcelain dolls, wooden trains of excellent quality.

Nain Bleu 406–410, rue St.-Honoré, 8e. Métro: Madeleine. 42-60-39-01. Closed Sunday. AE/V. This elegant toy shop has been at the same spot since 1909, and is filled with wondrous toys—romantic porcelain-and-lace dolls, china doll dishes, doll furniture, cars, even electronic toys—all of the best quality.

Pain d'Epices 29, passage Jouffroy, 9e. Métro: Montmartre. 47-70-82-65. Closed Sunday. V. This store is a jumble of froth-and-frills things, wonderful toys, miniatures, baskets, ribbons, buttons, bows, labels, and some children's clothes.

SIGHTS AND TOURS

Paris is a walker's city, full of sights both monumental and banal. Use this guide as a start for your wanderings through Paris. You'll find some of the best sights on your own in a courtyard, down an alley, across a bridge. Keep one thing in mind. When you are visiting churches, remember they are used on a daily basis as places of worship. Pay attention to the service schedule, usually posted outside the church, and time your visit accordingly.

Sights

Churches

Basilique du Sacré Coeur 18e. Métro: Anvers. This church was built by public subscription after the Franco-Prussian War, as a measure of public faith in the destiny of the Church of France. Construction of the Roman-Byzantine structure began in 1876 and was completed in 1910. The church was consecrated in 1919. The glistening white Basilique du Sacré Coeur sits majestically on a hill in Montmartre. One of the biggest bells in the world, the *Savoyard*, is in the bell tower. You can climb to the dome and get a wonderful, panoramic view of the city.

Cathédrale Notre-Dame de Paris Ile de la Cité, 4e. Métro: Cité. You can climb the tower—it's 225 feet high—and get a fabulous view of the entire city, or take a tour of this cathedral which dates from 1163. Notre Dame has been the scene of many historic events: Henry IV of England was crowned there; during the Revolution Robespierre dedicated the cathedral to the "Cult of Reason" and all the bells, except the large *Bourdon*, were melted. The cathedral went into a gradual decline and it was thanks in part to Victor Hugo and his novel *Notre-Dame de Paris* that renovation work was begun by Viollet-le-Duc in 1841 and finished in 1863 and its illustrious history continued. The end of the Second World War was celebrated in Notre Dame by the ringing of the *Te Deum*; de Gaulle's funeral took place there; and Pope John-Paul II celebrated mass on the "parvis" in 1980.

Eglise de la Madeleine Pl. de la Madeleine, 8e. Métro: Madeleine. Construction was first started on this Greek-style church in 1764. Its destiny was changed several times. It was first intended to be a church, then a library, a bank, a variety of financial institutions; then Napoléon wanted it as a temple to the glory of his army. It was finally consecrated as a church in 1842.

Eglise Saint-Etienne-du-Mont Pl. Ste.-Geneviève. 5e. Métro: Cardinal-Lemoine. This church was the chapel of the Abbey of Sainte Geneviève, and dates back to the 12th century. It is a most unusual church with a mixture of architectural styles, some impressive stained glass windows, and a pulpit dating from the 15th and 16th centuries that is unique in Paris.

Sights

MONTMARTRE SCENE

Eglise Saint-Eustache Rue du Jour, 1er. Métro: Les Halles. This church is a mixture of Gothic and Renaissance architecture. Construction was first begun in 1532, but wasn't finished until 1637. In 1754 the main façade was demolished and replaced with the present Gothic façade. This was the parish church for the Les Halles marketplace. Inside is a contemporary sculpture commemorating the merchants and the lively life of Les Halles.

Eglise Saint-Germain-l'Auxerrois 2, pl. du Louvre, 1er. Métro: Louvre. Many artists who used to work at the Louvre are buried in this church, which was restored by Baltard from 1838 to 1855. On the first Sunday of the Easter season artists still come to this church to pray for those among them who will die during the year.

Eglise Saint-Germain-des-Prés Pl. St.-Germain-des-Prés, 6e. Métro: St.-Germain-des-Prés. This is the oldest church in Paris, first built to shelter relics that Childebert, son of Clovis, brought back from Spain in 542. The church was destroyed 4 times between then and 990, when construction of the present structure was begun.

Eglise Saint-Gervais–Saint-Protais Pl. St.-Gervais, 4e. Métro: Hôtel-de-Ville. Closed Mondays. This Gothic work of art was completed in 1657. It was dedicated to Saint Gervase and Saint Protase, 2 brothers who were Roman soldiers martyred under Nero. In 1918 one of the vaults was destroyed by a bomb and subsequently rebuilt.

Eglise Saint-Merri 76, rue de la Verrerie, 4e. Métro: Hôtel-de-Ville. Built between 1520 and 1612, this was the parish church of the Lombardian moneylenders. It now has homes built right up against it, and even a hotel that has incorporated some of the vaulting into one of its rooms. The oldest bell of Paris is here, and the interior is most notable for its woodwork—in the sacristy, at the back of the choir, and in the pulpit.

Eglise Saint-Nicolas-des-Champs 254, rue St.-Martin, 3e. Métro: Arts-et-Métiers. This church was built to honor the patron saint of young boys, sailors, and travelers in the 12th century. It was rebuilt in the 15th and 16th centuries and again in the 17th century. It is a mixture of Gothic and Renaissance styles. One of its most notable characteristics is a Renaissance door built in 1581, inside on the right when facing the church.

Eglise Saint-Paul–Saint-Louis 99, rue St.-Antoine, 4e. Métro: St.-Paul. This is one of the most ancient examples of Jesuit architecture in Paris. Built from 1627 to 1641, it was modeled after a Baroque church in Rome.

Eglise Saint-Pierre 2, rue du Mont-Cenis, 18e. Métro: Abbesses. This is the only vestige of the Montmartre Abbey, and the third oldest church in Paris. It was built in the 12th century and rebuilt several times until the 18th century. It continues to undergo changes—the 3 bronze doors on the front of the church are contemporary works by the Italian sculptor Gismondi and were installed in 1980. There is also a group of contemporary stained glass windows by Max Ingrand that were installed in 1952.

Eglise Saint-Roch 24, rue Saint-Roch, 1er. Métro: Tuileries. The cornerstone of this church was laid in 1653. Because of a slight hill, the nave points toward the north instead of to the east. Funds ran out during construction, and donations and money raised from a lottery helped finish the building in 1736. Many well-known figures in French history are buried in the church, including Diderot, Le Nôtre, l'Abbé de l'Epée, and Pierre Corneille.

Eglise Saint-Severin 1, pl. des Prêtres-St.-Severin, 5e. Métro: St.-Michel. Toward the end of the 11th century this was the Paris church for the whole of the Left Bank. Work on the present structure began in the 13th century, though its style was changed many times until the end of the 17th century. The front door dates from the 13th century and came from a church that was demolished in 1839 to make way for the rue d'Arcole (4e). Some of the higher windows in the church date to the 15th century; others are contemporary works by Bazaine, installed in 1966.

Eglise Saint-Sulpice Pl. St.-Sulpice, 6e. Métro: St.-Sulpice. This church was founded by Saint Germain-des-Prés for his parishioners. It was enlarged in the 16th and 17th centuries and went through many changes—and many architects—before being completed. There is a beautiful mural by Delacroix inside the church, in the first chapel of the nave.

Sights

Eglise du Val-de-Grâce 277 bis, rue St.-Jacques, 5e.
Métro: Port-Royal. This is one of the oldest Roman
churches in France. The dome was inspired by the
Saint Peter's Church in Rome. Like many churches it
has a somewhat macabre history. From 1662 the
hearts of the royal families were kept here, in the
Chapel of Sainte Anne, a practice that continued until
1792, when there were 45 of them collected as relics.

Sainte Chapelle Palais de Justice, Ile de la Cité, 4e.
Métro: Cité. Closed Sundays and holidays. The true
splendor of this lovely Gothic chapel is its stained glass
windows, the oldest in Paris. This church, consecrated
in 1248, was built in 33 months.

Other Sights of Interest

Bourse Pl. de la Bourse, 2e. Métro: Bourse. Tours Monday through Friday from 11 A.M. and 1 P.M. From July
1 to September 30 there is 1 visit daily at noon. Closed
Saturdays, Sundays, and holidays. Housed in a former
convent this is now the Stock Exchange, at its busiest
between 12:30 P.M. and 2:30 P.M. during the week,
when trading is lively and spirited. The tour includes
a look at the trading and an audio-visual program that
explains the furious action.

Conciergerie 1, quai de l'Horloge, 4e. Métro: Cité. The
3 rooms that make up the Conciergerie are beautiful
examples of Gothic architecture. Once a palace built
by Philippe-the-Fair, it was used as a prison for up to
200 prisoners at a time, many of whom lost their heads
under the blade of the guillotine during one of France's
more gruesome periods. Some of the Conciergerie's
more famous inmates included Marie Antoinette,
Madame Elisabeth (sister of Louis XVI), Charlotte
Corday (Marat's murderer), Madame du Barry (Louis
XV's mistress), General Hoche, and many more. More
than 2,600 prisoners made their way through the Conciergerie to the guillotine between 1793 and 1794.

Grand Palais Av. Alexandre III, 8e. Métro: Champs-
Elysées-Clémenceau. This beautiful, ornate structure
was built for the *Exposition Universelle* in Paris at the
turn of the century. Formerly used as an exposition
hall, it now houses a library, conference rooms, and
important temporary art exhibits including the yearly
Salon d'Automne.

PONT ALEXANDRE AND GRAND PALAIS

Hôtel de Rohan 67, rue Vieille-du-Temple, 4e. Métro: Hôtel-de-Ville. Open only during temporary exhibits or for special conferences. This building, officially called the Hôtel de Strasbourg, was built in 1705. There is a beautiful frieze in the courtyard, to the right—*Chevaux d'Apollon* by Robert Le Lorrain. Upstairs inside are the Cardinal's apartments, which are filled with tapestries from the Gobelins manufacturers in Paris and Beauvais. Included in these apartments is the *Salon Doré* (gold room), a small room called the *Cabinet des Singes* (Monkey Office) done by Christopher Huet, and smaller rooms decorated in delicate colors with wood carvings of fable creatures called the *Cabinet des Fables* (Fable Office).

Hôtel de Ville Pl. de l'Hôtel-de-Ville, 4e. Métro: Hôtel-de-Ville. Guided visits take place Mondays at 10:30 A.M. Go to the *Bureau d'Acceuil*, 29, rue de Rivoli, 4e. Métro: St.-Paul. 42-76-40-40. This is Paris' City Hall, where official guests are entertained by the city government. This neo-Renaissance building dates from 1882, built after the former Hôtel de Ville was burned by the French Federalists. Its 46 statues represent famous figures in French history.

Opéra 1, pl. de l'Opéra, 9e. Métro: Opéra. 42-66-50-22. Open from 11 A.M. to 5 P.M. daily. Guided tours can be arranged; for specific hours consult the *Pariscope* or *L'Officiel des Spectacles*. It was Haussmann who provided for this sumptuous opera house in his plans for Paris. A contest was held in 1860 and 171 designs were submitted. Charles Garnier, a relative unknown, was chosen as the architect and, after many delays, the Opéra was inaugurated in 1875. It is the largest theater building in the world, though it seats only 2,200 spectators.

Palais Bourbon Pl. du Palais Bourbon, 7e. Métro: Chambre-des-Députés. Built in 1722 as a private residence, it was given its present façade under Napoleon so it would match the Madeleine Church, which it faces across from the Place de la Concorde. It now houses the Assemblée Nationale and can be visited by request from the Service des Affaires Administratives Générales, 126, rue de l'Université, 7e. 42-97-64-08. There is much artwork inside; particularly notable is the library, which has a series by Delacroix that represents the history of Creation.

Sights

cent soixante-sept (*san̲-swah-ssahn̲t-seht*) **167**

Palais de l'Elysée 55, rue du Faubourg-St.-Honoré, 8e. Métro: Champs-Elysées-Clémenceau. This historic palace was built in 1718 and was home to illustrious personages, including Joséphine and Louis-Napoléon Bonaparte. It serves as the official residence of the presidents of France—though President Francçis Mitterand lives elsewhere—and as government offices.

Palais de l'Institut de France 23, quai de Conti, 6e. Métro: Odéon. The Collège des Quatre Nations de France, representing 4 regions in France, opened here in 1688 and closed in 1790. It then became the home to the Cinq Académies, which include l'Académie Française, *Inscriptions des Belles Lettres, Sciences, Beaux-Arts,* and *Sciences Morales et Politiques.* The Académie Française, responsible for keeping the French language pure and the most notable of the 5 academies, still meets in this building.

✗ **Palais de Justice** Bd. du Palais, 6e. Métro: Cité. Open Monday through Friday from 9 A.M. to 6 P.M. After the Révolution, the judicial arm of the government took up residence in this edifice, which was thereafter called the Palais de Justice, and judicial affairs are still carried out here. The public is welcome to sit in on court hearings.

Palais du Luxembourg 15–19, rue de Vaugirard, 6e. Métro: Luxembourg. 42-34-20-60. The Palais du Luxembourg can be visited on Sundays between 10 A.M. and 11 A.M. and between 2:30 P.M. and 3:30 P.M. Group visits can also be arranged. This palace, surrounded by the lovely Jardin du Luxembourg, was first built in 1615 under the direction of Marie de Médicis. It now houses the French *Sénat*, whose leader takes over for the president when he is out of the country. The *Sénat* is a law-making body of representatives from throughout the country and, among other things, acts as an arbiter between the *Assemblée Nationale* and the government.

Panthéon Pl. du Panthéon, 5e. Métro: Cardinal-Lemoine or Luxembourg. Closed Tuesday. Reduced admission Sundays and holidays. Designed by Soufflot, the Panthéon was commissioned by Louis XV to replace the decrepit Abbaye de Sainte Geneviève, and in thanks for surviving a serious illness. It was first a church, then in 1791 it was transformed into a *Panthéon* to house the ashes of great personages. It was

Sights

given back to the church by Napoleon once again, in 1885, returned to its status as *Panthéon*, and it received the ashes of Victor Hugo. His ashes rest in good company with those of Voltaire, Rousseau, Mirabeau, Jean Moulin, Emile Zola, Jean Jaurès, Félix Eboué, and many more. There are frescoes, sculptures, and paintings in the Panthéon; the most noteworthy are paintings which show the life of Sainte Geneviève.

Sorbonne 1, rue Victor-Cousin, 5*e*. Métro: Luxembourg. This is one of the world's oldest universities, begun in 1253 by the confessor to Saint Louis, Robert de Sorbonne, for 16 impoverished theology students. The Sorbonne is now the major institute of higher learning in France, with colleges throughout the city.

Tour Eiffel Champ de Mars, 7*e*. Métro: Ecole-Militaire. This controversial structure, designed by Gustave Eiffel in 1884, was built for the 1889 *Exposition Universelle* (World's Fair). It was nearly demolished after the event, but proved its utility by being used as a communications tower. The first transoceanic telephone communication was transmitted from the Eiffel Tower. It is built of cast iron, weighs approximately 7,000 tons, and is repainted every 7 years with 52 tons of paint. There are several restaurants and a museum with films showing the *Tour's* history (the museum can be reached by elevators or stairs), as well as an observatory deck on the third floor (accessible only by elevator).

Tour Saint-Jacques Square St.-Jacques, 4*e*. Métro: Hôtel-de-Ville or Châtelet. This tower, standing alone in a small, parklike place, was the steeple to the former Eglise Saint-Jacques-de-la-Boucherie and is known as the butchers' tower. It was the major meeting point in Europe for religious pilgrims on their way to the holy city of Saint-Jacques-de-Compostelle, in Spain.

Tours

Catacombes 2, pl. Denfert-Rochereau, 14*e*. Métro: Denfert-Rochereau. 43-22-47-63. Tours Tuesday through Friday from 2 P.M. to 4 P.M. On weekends from 9 A.M. to 11 A.M. and from 2 P.M. to 4 P.M. Closed Monday. Formerly Roman quarries, these underground vaults were first used as catacombs in the late 18th century. Bones from other cemeteries in Paris—most notably from the Cimetière des Innocents where the *Fontaine des Innocents* is now, in the midst of Les Halles—are now stacked against the walls of the catacombs, making for a macabre, though interesting scene. Flashlight and heavy sweater are recommended.

Egouts de Paris (Paris' Sewers) Pl. de la Résistance, on the Left Bank and right by the Seine River. Entrance across 93, quai d'Orsay. Métro: Alma-Marceau. 43-20-14-40. Open Monday, Wednesday, and the last Saturday of each month from 2 P.M. to 5 P.M. You can take a walk through parts of the sewers of Paris to get a feeling of how the system is organized. The walking tour includes an audio-visual program and a historic presentation. Rubber-soled shoes are recommended, and visits may be cancelled during heavy rains or if the Seine is particularly high.

Tours of Paris by Air

Chainair 43-59-20-20. You can see Paris, the Mont Saint-Michel, châteaux in the Loire Valley, even Corsica—or just about anywhere you want to go. Call for information.

Hélicap 4, av. de la Porte de Sèvres, 15*e*. Call for an appointment: 45-57-75-51. Offers tours of La Défense, Paris, Paris and Versailles. 1080F–1100F.

Héliport de Paris 4, av. de la Porte de Sèvres, 15*e*. Métro: Place Balard. 45-54-04-44. Call for information and reservations. Offers trips over Paris, "Paris in the year 2,000," Paris and Versailles, châteaux of the Loire Valley. From 180F.

SPORTING GOODS
See SHOPPING.

STAMP MARKET
See MARKETS.

Sights

STATIONERY

See SHOPPING.

STREET ADDRESSES

See ARRIVAL IN PARIS.

STUDENTS' PARIS

Paris is an ideal student city, one that has been catering to the student population for centuries. There are more movies in Paris than you can imagine, inexpensive places to get good meals, flea markets, bookstores, and of course, excellent institutes of higher learning.

As a student you can qualify for discounts at movies, theaters, museums, concerts, and for train travel. All you need is an *International Student Identity Card.* To get a card, take proof that you are enrolled in a high school or university and about 20F and go to: C.I.E.E., 16, rue de Vaugirard, 6e. Métro: Luxembourg; or to C.I.E.E., 51, rue Dauphine, 6e. Métro: Odéon.

The C.I.E.E. (Council on International Educational Exchange) also organizes get-togethers for foreign and French students twice a month, from mid-October to the end of April at their office at 1, pl. de l'Odéon, 6e. Métro: Odéon. 46-34-16-10. Call or stop by for details.

As a student you can qualify for temporary working papers in France for up to 3 months. You need proof of registration in a high school or university and a French person or company who is willing to hire you on a temporary basis. Go to the C.I.E.E. on the Place de l'Odéon, and they will help you get the necessary papers.

Permanent working papers are a different matter. It is increasingly difficult for foreigners to get working papers in France. If you are thinking about trying to stay in France and work, you must find a French employer willing to go through the considerable red tape to prove to the French government that you are the

Students' Paris

only person who can do the job, then be prepared to spend hours and days going into offices trying to get the necessary papers filled out and fees paid. Before you even start, however, you must have a visa, and you must get that before you leave home. Once you're in France you cannot get a visa of any kind.

Carte de Séjour

Once in France, you must validate your visa by obtaining a *Carte de Séjour*. You will need:
Your passport
A copy of the page in your passport with your name, address, and vital statistics
A copy of the page in your passport that has your visa stamped on it
Proof of your address in France (a rent receipt is best)
Your school registration papers
4 black-and-white photographs of yourself
2 stamped, self-addressed envelopes

Take these items to the Préfecture de Police in the *arrondissement* where you live (ask for the "*Services Etrangers*"). They will process the paper work and notify you by mail when you can pick up your *Carte de Séjour*. To do so, go to the central Préfecture de Police, 1, rue de Lutèce, 4e. Métro: Cité (it's a huge building, you can't miss it). Go to the *Services Etrangers* office.

Lodging

There are alternatives to Paris' inflated housing prices, and one of the more interesting ones is through *au pair* work. To apply for an *au pair* position you must be a student, have a valid student visa, and be under 30 years of age. As an *au pair* you live with a French family, are required to work for them 30 hours a week, and are expected to be enrolled in school and attend classes. You will be paid 1.000F a month plus room and board.

The following organizations arrange *au pair* situations:

Acceuil Familial des Jeunes Etrangères 23, rue du Cherche-Midi, 6e. Métro: Sèvres-Babylone. 42-22-50-34. Open Monday through Friday from 10 A.M. to 4 P.M. and Saturday from 10 A.M. to noon except July and August.

L'Arche 7, rue de Bargue, 15e. Métro: Volontaires. 42-73-34-39. Open Monday through Friday from 9 A.M. to 5 P.M. Closed weekends and August.

Goelangues 15, rue de Bruxelles, 9e. Métro: Place Clichy. 45-26-14-53. Open Monday through Friday from 10 A.M. to 7 P.M. Closed weekends.

Inter Sejours 4, rue de Parme, 9e. Métro: Liège. 42-80-09-38 or 48-74-04-98. Open Monday through Friday from 9:30 A.M. to 5:30 P.M., Saturday from 9:30 A.M.–12:30 P.M. Closed Sunday.

Relations Internationales 20, rue de l'Exposition, 7e. Métro: Ecole-Militaire. 45-51-85-50. Open Monday through Friday from 9 A.M. to 12:30 P.M. and from 2 P.M. to 6:30 P.M. Closed weekends.

Another great possibility for lodging is in a *chambre de bonne*, or maid's room. Most apartments in Paris have maids' rooms that are located on the top floor of the building, completely independent from the apartment. They range from minuscule quarters, barely or not furnished, with no running water, to large, comfortably furnished rooms, with hot and cold running water. The toilets are always down the hall, there is usually one at each end of the building. Shower or bath arrangements can often be worked out with the family so you can use their facilities. As for cooking, getting a *plaque chauffante* (hot plate) is usually the best solution. Depending on the *quartier*, you may find a room that has an elevator going up to the top floor. More often than not, you'll have to go up the service stairs; *chambres* aren't accessible from the main entrance. *Chambres de bonnes* in Paris are filled with foreigners and even some French people. Whole families live in *chambres* that have been converted into studios or larger apartments. They offer many advantages: they're inexpensive, completely independent, and they often afford some wonderful views. The disadvantages are the lack of bathing and kitchen facilities, the stairs, and usually no telephones. Nonetheless, if you're short of funds and even the least bit romantic, *chambres de bonne* are one of the best things about Paris. There are no agencies who handle *chambres de bonnes* rentals. Ask around, or go to the ad-boards of the *American College*, 31 av. Bosquet, 7e. Métro: Ecole-Militaire. Or try the American Church, 65 quai d'Orsay, 7e. Métro: Invalides. Also try the Canadian

Cultural Center, 5 rue de Constantine, 7e. Métro: Invalides. Lastly, the C.I.D.J. (Centre d'Information et de Documentation Jeunesse), 101 quai Branly, 15e. Métro: Alma-Marceau.

If you're set on renting an apartment, the best place to look is a weekly paper called *De Particulier: à Particulier*, which comes out every Thursday morning. It is filled with apartments and objects for rent or for sale by individuals. If you find something in this paper, you can avoid paying a steep rental agency fee. Get to a kiosk early—by 7:30 A.M.—and buy the paper, then rush to a phone booth so you can start making calls immediately. Competition is stiff.

If you are visiting Paris, there are several reasonable alternatives to hotels. The following are operated either by the M.I.J.E. (Maison Internationale des Jeunes et des Etudiants) or C.I.S.P. (Centre International de Séjour de Paris). These organizations operate facilities that are neither hotels nor hostels, but somewhat of a cross between the two. They run from 51F to about 75F a night, breakfast and shower usually included. Some of them offer individual rooms; others, rooms with several beds. They are limited to people between 18 and 30–35 years of age. There is also a 5-night maximum stay, though arrangements can sometimes be made to extend that limit. They are all open year-round.

Centre International de Paris 20, rue Jean-Jacques-Rousseau, 1er. Métro: Les Halles. 42-36-88-18. Groups a priority. Rate is 55F a night, breakfast included. 18 to 35 years only.

C.I.S.P. Kellerman 17, bd. Kellerman, 13e. Métro: Porte d'Italie. 45-80-70-76. Groups a priority. Rates are 58F–78F a night, breakfast not included. There is no age limit.

C.I.S.P. Maurice Ravel 6, av. Maurice-Ravel, 12e. Métro: Porte de Vincennes. 43-43-19-01. Groups a priority. Rates are 70,50F–90,50F a night, breakfast included. There is no age limit.

M.I.J.E. Centre Fauconnier 11, rue du Fauconnier, 4e. Métro: St.-Paul. 42-74-23-45. 51F a night, breakfast extra. 18 to 30 years only.

M.I.J.E. Centre François Miron 6, rue François-Miron, 4e. Métro: Hôtel-de-Ville. 42-72-72-09. 51F a night, breakfast extra, or 59F a night, breakfast included. 18 to 34 years only.

M.I.J.E. Centre Maubuisson 12, rue des Barres, 4e. Métro: Hôtel-de-Ville. 42-72-72-09. 51F a night, breakfast extra, or 59F a night, breakfast included. 18 to 34 years only.

Résidence Bastille 151, av. Ledru-Rollin, 11e. Métro: Voltaire. 43-79-53-86. 52F–62F a night, breakfast included. 18 to 34 years only.

Another alternative is the **Auberges de Jeunesse** (French hotels for young people), which are in the same price range and serve breakfast for an additional fee. A stay cannot exceed three days. There are branches all over Europe, but only some accept reservations. They require sleeping bags (that they will rent or sell you). You can obtain all necessary information before your departure by calling the American Youth Hostels Council or, when in Paris, **La Ligue Française pour les Auberges de Jeunesse,** 38 boulevard Raspail, 75007, Paris 7e. 45-48-69-84.

If you can't find a room in Paris, try the following place, which is accessible by RER:

Foyer International d'Acceuil à Paris (F.I.A.P.A.D.) 19, rue Salvador-Allende, 92600 Nanterre. 47-25-91-34. RER Line A1, stop Nanterre-Préfecture. Restricted age limit. Open year-round.

Restaurants

Students with a valid college ID card or with an international student ID card can eat in "Resto-U," university restaurants for less than 15F.

To have detailed information and addresses, please call the Association des Jeunes de France, 119, rue St-Martin, 4e. 42-77-87-80, Métro: Rambuteau.

Syndicat d'Initiatives et Accueil de France, 127 av, champs Elysees, 8e. 47-23-61-72. Information and hotel reservations: 47-20-77-19.

American Embassy. American Consulate (see under "EMBASSY"), page 35.

Camping

If you're equipped, there are 2 possibilities for camping: one in Paris, the other one just east of the city.

Bois de Boulogne Allée du Bord de l'Eau, 16e. Métro:

Porte Maillot or Porte d'Auteuil. 45-06-14-98. From April 1 to September 15 there is a shuttle from both métro stops to the campground. The camping site has telephones, grocery stores, a restaurant that is open daily, and free showers. Prices are about 12F per person per night, plus about 6F for a double tent or about 12F for a car. Children up to 7 years of age are half-price. Reservations are necessary during the season. The facility is open year-round.

Camping de Champigny bd. des Alliés, 94500 Champigny-sur-Marne. 42-83-38-24. Owned by the same people who own Camping Bois de Boulogne, and provides the same services for the same fees.

Travel

You don't have to be a student but you must be under 26 years of age to qualify for the S.N.C.F.'s travel reductions. You can purchase the following cards at any train station:

Carte Carré Jeune Costs 145F and entitles the user to half-price fares on 4 trips—2 round trips—in France only.

Carte Inter-rail Costs 1.320F, is good for 1 month, and entitles the user to half-price fares throughout France and most of Europe.

Travel Agencies

The following travel agency offers reductions on train, boat, and air travel to anyone younger than 26 years of age. You do not have to be a student to qualify but you must show proof of your age when buying a ticket.

Transalpino 16, rue La Fayette, 9e. Métro: Chaussée-d'Antin. 42-47-12-40. Closed Sunday; 36 bis, rue de Dunkerque, 9e. Métro: Gare-du-Nord. 42-81-26-11. Closed Monday: 137, rue de Rennes, 6e. Métro: Montparnasse. 45-48-67-56. Closed Monday.

SWIMMING POOLS

If you like to swim for exercise or for fun there are 29 swimming pools in Paris to accommodate you. Three of them are privately owned pools that are open to the public; the others are run by the city of Paris.

Hours That City-Run Pools Are Open to the Public

Tuesdays, Thursdays, and Fridays—all pools from 7 A.M. to 8:30 A.M. and from 11:30 A.M. to 1:30 P.M.

Wednesdays—all pools except Butte-aux-Cailles, Porte-de-la-Plaine, Ilot Riquet, Aspirant-Dunand from 7 A.M. to 8:30 A.M. and from 11:30 A.M. to 6 or 6:30 P.M.

Saturdays—all pools except Blomet, Butte-aux-Cailles, Château-Landon, and Aspirant-Dunand, from 7 A.M. to 6 or 6:30 P.M.

Sundays—all pools except Blomet from 8 A.M. to 6 P.M.

Certain swimming pools are open to the public at other times during the week. Check at the individual pools.

City Pools (By Arrondissement)

Saint-Merri—18, rue du Renard, 4e. Métro: Hôtel-de-Ville. 42-72-29-45.

Jean-Taris—16, rue Thouin, 5e. Métro: Cardinal-Lemoine. 43-25-54-03.

Georges-Drigny—18, rue Bochard-de-Saron, 9e. Métro: Anvers. 45-26-86-93.

Valeyre—22–24, rue de Rochechouart, 9e. Métro: Cadet. 42-85-27-61.

Cour des Lions—11, rue Alphonse-Baudin, 11e. Métro: Richard-Lenoir. 43-55-09-23.

Georges-Rigal—115, bd. de Charonne, 11e. Métro: Alexandre-Dumas. 43-70-64-22.

Ledru-Rollin—10, av. Ledru-Rollin, 12e. Métro: Quai-de-la-Rapée. 43-43-67-69.

Didot—22, av. Georges-Lafenestre, 14e. Métro: Porte de Vanves 45-39-89-29.

Armand-Massard—66, bd. du Montparnasse, 15e. Métro: Montparnasse. 45-38-65-19.

Blomet—17, rue Blomet, 15e. Métro: Volontaires. 47-83-35-05.

Emile-Anthoine—9, rue Jean-Rey, 15e. Métro: Bir-Hakeim. 45-67-10-20.

Porte de la Plaine—13, rue du Général-Guillaumat, 15e. Métro: Porte de Versailles. 45-32-34-00.

René-et-André-Mourlon—19, rue Gaston-de-Cavaillet, 15e. Métro: Charles-Michels. 45-75-40-02.

Auteuil—route des Lacs, Porte de Passy, 16e. Métro: Auteuil. 42-24-07-59.

Henry-de-Montherlant—32, bd. Lannes, 16e. Métro:
Porte Dauphine. 45-03-03-28.
Bernard-Lafay—79, rue de la Jonquière, 17e. Métro:
Porte de Clichy. 42-26-11-05.

Privately Owned Pools

Deligny 22, quai Anatole-France, 7e. Métro: Solférino.
45-51-72-15 (uncovered in summer).
Keller 14, rue de l'Ingénieur Robert Keller, 15e. Métro:
Javel. 45-77-12-12.
Oberkampf 160, rue Oberkampf, 11e. Métro: Ménil-
montant. 43-57-56-19.

TAKE-OUT FOOD
See FOOD.

TAXIS
See ARRIVAL IN PARIS.

TEA SALONS
See SALONS DE THE

TELEPHONES, TELEGRAMS
See POSTAL AND TELEPHONE SERVICES.

THEATERS AND PERFORMANCE HALLS

Paris has some extremely beautiful theaters and
world-renowned acting, dance, and music companies,
as well as a strong community of experimental theaters. International theater and dance companies visit
Paris frequently as well. There is always much theater
and dance in Paris, but particularly during the **Festival du Marais** in early summer and the **Festival
Estival** from mid-July to mid-September.

Theaters

Consult the *Pariscope* or *L'Officiel des Spectacles* for specific shows, theaters, and showtimes. Under each theater and show listing you will see *"location"* and the times, for example "14h–19h30." That indicates you should go to the theater between 2 P.M. and 7:30 P.M. to buy tickets. *"Relâche"* indicates which nights the theaters are closed. You may want to call the theater before going to get tickets to be sure there are seats available.

You can get half-price tickets for some performances by going to **Places de Théâtre**, 15, pl. de la Madeleine, 8e. Metro: Madeleine. Booth is open from 12:30 P.M. to 8 P.M. the day of the performance.

This information on theater in Paris was prepared with the help of M. Jean Gaudrat.

Opera and Dance

Théâtre National de l'Opéra 1, pl. de l'Opéra, 9e. Métro: Opéra. 42-66-50-22. Opera and ballet. Rudolf Nureyev is currently the ballet director of the Opéra.
Théâtre National de l'Opéra Comique 5, rue Favart, 2e. Métro: Richelieu-Drouot. 42-96-12-20. *Opéra comique* (opera with a spoken dialogue).

Theater and Dance

Cartoucherie de Vincennes Route de la Pyramide, 12e. Métro: Château de Vincennes. Next to the Château de Vincennes, this is a group of 5 theaters, reconstructed in the buildings of a former ink-cartridge factory (*cartoucherie*). Both classical theater—French and International—and original intellectual pieces are performed at these theaters. They are the Théâtre de l'Aquarium, 43-74-72-74; Théâtre de Soleil, 43-74-88-15; Théâtre de la Temple, 43-74-94-07; Théâtre de l'Epée du Bois, 48-08-39-74; Théâtre du Chaudron, 43-28-97-04.
Comédie des Champs-Elysées 15, av. Montaigne, 8e. Métro: Alma-Marceau. 47-23-37-21. Dramatic theater by well-known contemporary authors.
Comédie Française 2, rue de Richelieu, 1er. Métro: Palais-Royal. 42-96-10-20. Very classical theater—Molière, Racine—as well as occasional contemporary French pieces.
Lucernaire Centre National d'Art et d'Essai 53, rue Notre-Dame-des-Champs, 6e. Métro: Vavin. 45-44-57-34. Highly regarded experimental theater.

Theaters

Petit Odéon Pl. de l'Odéon, 6e. Métro: Odéon. 43-25-70-32. Highly regarded contemporary theater. Plays are often written by the actors.

Théâtre Antoine et Simone Berriau 14, bd. de Strasbourg-St.-Denis, 10e. Métro: Strasbourg-St.-Denis. 42-08-77-71. Theater in Paris was reborn here, at the end of the 19th century. It is considered a *théâtre de divertissement* (light drama of excellent quality).

Théâtre du Gymnase Marie Bell 38, bd. Bonne-Nouvelle, 10e. Métro: Strasbourg-St.-Denis. 42-46-79-79. Dramatic theater and popular musical performances.

Théâtre de la Huchette 23, rue de la Huchette, 5e. Métro: St.-Michel. 43-26-38-99. This tiny theater, a *théâtre de poche* (so small it would fit in your pocket), is where Ionesco got his start. Still stages work by Ionesco as it has for 30 years.

Théâtre Michel 38, rue des Mathurins, 8e. Métro: Havre-Caumartin. 42-65-35-02. Another good-quality *théâtre de divertissement* (light drama).

Théâtre National de Chaillot Pl. du Trocadéro, 16e, Métro: Trocadéro. 47-27-81-15. Stages very well-known, intellectual, often political theater.

Théâtre de l'Odéon Pl. de l'Odéon, 6e. Métro: Odéon. 43-25-70-32. This is where major foreign companies perform, in their own languages. The company from the Comédie Française also performs here.

Théâtre Palais-Royal 38, rue Montpensier, 1er. Métro: Bourse. 42-97-59-81. This historic, beautiful, well-restored and well-cared-for theater hosts very popular, expensively produced, "chic" theater.

Théâtre de Poche Montparnasse 75, bd. du Montparnasse, 6e. Métro: Montparnasse. 45-44-50-21. Another *théâtre de poche* (so small it would fit in your pocket) that has launched some very well-known French playwrights, and continues the tradition of giving young playwrights a place to start.

Théâtre des Variétés 7, bd. Montmartre, 2e. Métro: Montmartre or Bourse. 42-33-09-92. Under the same direction as the Théâtre Palais-Royal, this theater hosts large, popular productions.

Théâtre de la Ville Pl. du Châtelet, 4e. Métro: Châtelet. 42-74-22-77. This theater has its own company that produces large, internationally known plays both classic and contemporary. Well-known music and dance performances are also staged here.

Theaters

Performance Halls

These performance halls may have one or two theater performances a year as well as large ballet productions, concerts, and variety shows.

Bobino 20, rue de la Gaîté, 14e. Métro: Gaîté. 43-22-74-84.

Olympia 28, bd. des Capucines, 9e. Métro: Opéra. 47-42-52-86.

Palais des Congrès 2, pl. de la Porte Maillot, 17e. Métro: Porte Maillot. 47-28-27-08.

Palais Omnisports de Bercy 8, bd. Diderot, 12e. Métro: Bercy. 43-42-01-23 or 43-46-12-21.

Palais des Sports Pl. de la Porte de Versailles, 15e. Métro: Porte de Versailles. 48-28-41-79.

TIME, FRENCH CLOCKS

See ARRIVAL IN PARIS.

TOURIST OFFICES

See ARRIVAL IN PARIS.

TOURS

See SIGHTS AND TOURS.

TOYS

See SHOPPING.

TRAINS, TRAIN STATIONS

See ARRIVAL IN PARIS.

USEFUL NUMBERS

Police—17 or 42-60-33-22.
Ambulance—18 or 43-78-26-26.

Fire (*Sapeurs-Pompiers*)—18.

Information (*Renseignements*)—12.

S.O.S. Médecins (for medical emergencies)—47-07-77-77.

S.O.S. Help (crisis line in English daily after 7 P.M.)—
47-23-80-80.

S.O.S. Dentiste (emergency dental service)—43-37-51-00.

S.O.S. Infirmiers (emergency nurse service 24 hours
a day, including Sunday)—48-87-77-77.

American Embassy and Consulate—42-96-12-02. (See
page 35).

Road conditions (*Etat des routes*)—48-58-33-33.

Time of day (*Horloge parlante*)—3699 or 46-99-84-00.

Day's headlines (*Informations Telephonées*)—36-36-
11-11 or 44-63-1.

Telephone wake-up service (*Réveil par téléphone*)—
dial 3688 or 42-71-13-13 if you wish to have automatic
daily service. A recording will tell you to dial your
phone number. After you have done so, a recording
will tell you to dial in the time you want to be awoken.
Remember to dial in the time according to the 24-hour
clock—i.e., 3 P.M. is 1500 hours. The recording will
tell you to hold on until the service is activated, then
to hang up.

International Herald Tribune—47-47-12-65.

Suggested daily menu and recipes (*Allo menu*)—42-
55-66-77.

Alcoholics Anonymous (in English)—46-34-59-65.

Syndicat d'Initiatives (See page 175).

WINE

See FOOD.

WINE BARS

Wine bars are neighborhood spots often open during
working hours, from early in the morning for that first
coup de rouge to early evening for the *ballon* on the
way home. They are also very personal affairs, reflect-
ing the proprietor's interest in and dedication to
searching out quality wines from a particular region
or of a particular style.

Wine bars used to cater to the working class but
now they're for everyone, and they're increasingly pop-

ular. They not only afford a chance to taste a variety of usually very good—sometimes little-known—wines, but are also jolly kinds of places. You won't always find a hot meal, but you can get at least a *tartine* (open-faced sandwich) or a plate of *charcuterie* to accompany the wine specialties of the house.

Blue Fox Bar 25, rue Royale, Cité Berryer, 8*e*. Métro: Madeleine. 42-65-08-47. Closed Saturday night and Sunday. There are 15 different French wines offered by the glass here each day in this British-run wine bar, and light salads and desserts to accompany them. Try going on a Tuesday or Friday when the lively Cité Berryer market is in progress. It's bound to be crowded, so get there early.

Bons Crus 7, rue des Petits-Champs, 1*er*. Métro: Bourse. 42-60-06-45. No matter the hour, this wine bar and mini-wine shop is always a-bustle. Wine is for sale by the glass or bottle for sipping inside, or by the bottle to take along. If you're headed to Palais Royal for a picnic, this is the place to get your bottle of wine. The jolly madame behind the bar will happily recommend wines to suit any budget.

Café de la Nouvelle Mairie 19, rue des Fossés-St.-Bernard, 5*e*. Métro: Luxembourg. 43-26-80-18. Closed Saturday and Sunday. There's something Old World and intellectual about this wine bar, which has a unique character and charm. It's always packed with a crowd who's there for fun but is also seriously interested in wine. When the *patron* isn't filling glasses with Saint-Nicolas de Bourgueil, Beaujolais, or perhaps Gamay, he's engaged in thoughtful discussion with his loyal clientele, most of whom seem to prefer crowding around the bar instead of sitting at the tables that spill out onto the sidewalk in summer.

Cloche des Halles 28, rue Coquillière, 1*er*. 42-36-93-89. Métro: Les Halles. Closed Sunday. It's most fun to come here and stand at the bar after a tour of the hectic Les Halles neighborhood, and sip a glass of Morgon or full-bodied Brouilly. If you go in the morning you'll have a bit of tranquility to savor the flavor—otherwise watch out, the neighborhood descends on this popular spot at lunchtime or right after work.

Coude Fou 12, rue du Bourg-Tibourg, 4*e*. Métro: Hôtel-de-Ville. 42-77-15-16. Open daily. 150F. V. This wine bar caters to a very Parisian, young, and rowdy crowd, who go for the vast selection of regional wines and good, hearty, and inexpensive meals like broiled goat cheese on a salad of curly endive, grilled duck breast with vegetables, and garlicky sausage with steamed potatoes and mustard.

Ecluse 15, quai des Grands-Augustins, 6e. Métro: St.-Michel. 46-33-58-74. Closed Sunday; 15, pl. de la Madeleine, 8e. Métro: Madeleine. 42-65-34-69. Closed Sunday. Also 64, rue François-1er. 8e. Métro: Franklin D. Roosevelt. 47-20-77-09. Open daily. These wine bars are more substantial than most, offering fairly sophisticated meals—*foie gras tartines* or a nice Roquefort or *chèvre tartine*—to an elegant after-theater crowd. Go early in the evening and you won't have any trouble finding a seat at one of the minuscule, charming tables. Around 10 P.M. it'll start filling up, the *foie gras* starts coming out, and the red and white Bordeaux really start to flow. These charming wine bars are ideal for a romantic interlude or a relaxed, late afternoon snack and drink, though they can be a bit stingy when filling up your glass.

Franc Pinot 1, quai de Bourbon, 4e. Métro: Pont-Marie. 43-29-46-98. Closed Sunday and Monday. This wine bar isn't very inviting from the outside, and it may even be a bit deserted inside, but the location on the Ile-Saint-Louis is great for a pause. The light salads and cheese plates are good and the Beaujolais, Sancerre, and Côtes du Jura worth tasting.

Jacques Melac 42, rue Léon-Frot, 11e. Métro: Charonne. 43-70-59-27. Closed Sunday, Monday, and July. If you ever happen to walk by this funny little wine bar you won't miss it; it has grapevines growing up the front and sides of the building, which the proprietors and whoever wants to join them harvest each year about the middle of September, amidst much merriment. This is a casual, neighborhood spot that serves hearty lunchtime fare and cheeses from the mountainous Auvergne region in central France. Wine specialties are Beaujolais, Gigondas, Cahors, Sauternes, and Côtes du Jura.

Petit Bacchus 13, rue du Cherche-Midi, 6e. Métro: Sèvres-Babylone. 45-44-01-07. This cozy wine bar is owned by Briton Steven Spurrier, and it offers the same selection of wines that are available at his Caves de la Madeleine. Weekly wine tastings feature 8 regional wines served with *charcuterie* from Auvergne or Italy. English spoken.

Wine Bars

Rubis 10, rue du Marché-St.-Honoré, 1er. Métro: Tuileries. 42-61-03-34. Closed Saturday, Sunday, and August. This wine bar is popular with regulars from the neighborhood—the local policeman, or the staff from the Chédeville *charcuterie* up the street who go for a quick coffee in the morning and are right back there for lunch. There are omelettes, a hot *plat du jour* (changing daily special), or *charcuterie* to eat with a glass of Brouilly, Morgon, Chiroubles, or Côtes-du-Rhône.

Willi's Wine Bar 13, rue des Petits-Champs, 1er. Métro: Pyramides. 42-61-05-09. Closed Saturday and Sunday; 18, rue des Halles, 1er. Métro: Châtelet. 42-36-81-80. Closed Saturday and Sunday. Willi's on rue des Petits-Champs feels more like a restaurant than a bar, and it is definitely the place to come see, be seen, and nibble at the salads, or hot *plat du jour* (daily special). If you want a look at a rarified aspect of Paris, come to this wine bar, run by an Englishman, and at the same time enjoy the good selection of Côtes-du-Rhône.

WORK CLOTHES

French workers' clothes including chefs' jackets, laborers' pants or hats, jewelers' smocks, butchers' aprons, bright and sturdy overalls, and black corduroy suits can make great fashion.

Adolphe Lafont 69, av. du Maine, 14e. Métro: Gaîté. 43-22-68-79. This shop specializes in overalls and chefs' clothes. Closed Sunday and Monday. V.

Bazar de l'Hôtel de Ville (BHV) 52, rue de Rivoli, ground floor, 4e. Métro: Hôtel-de-Ville. 42-74-90-00. Closed Sunday. AE/V.

Duthilleul et Minart 13 and 15, rue de Turbigo, 1er. 42-33-44-36. Métro: Les Halles. Closed Saturday and Sunday. This shop has a large and varied stock of work clothes and artisans' uniforms.

Samaritaine 19, rue de la Monnaie, Magasin 2, 1er. Métro: Pont-Neuf. 45-08-33-33. Closed Sunday. AE/DC/V.

ZOOS

See CHILDREN'S PARIS.

VOCABULARY

Pronunciation Key*

a, à, â, ah = AH / ai, ais, ay = EH
an, am, en, em, an, ent = AH<u>N</u>
é, er, ef, et, ez = AY
ẽ, ê, eh, ei, es = EH
e, eu, eux = UH / eune = UH<u>N</u>
eil, eille = EHY / euil, euille = UHY
i, ie, = EE / ia = YAH
ieu = YUH / (i)lleur = YUHR
ie, ier, illé = YAY / (i)lle = YUH
ière, iers = YEHR / ièce = YEHSS
iène = YEHN / ième = YEHM / iette = YEHT
ian, iant = YAN / ien, ient = YEN
in, im, ain, aim, int, aint = AN / aine, eine = EHN
io = YOH / ion = YOH<u>N</u> / iom = YOHM
iun = YUH<u>N</u> / ium = YUHM
o, oh, au, eau, aux = OH / ou, hou = oo
oy, oi, oie, oix = WAH
oin, oint = WA<u>N</u>
on, ont, om = OH<u>N</u>
u, ue = EW / ui, uïe, oui = WEE
un = UH<u>N</u> / um = UHM
y = EE / yé, yer = YAY / yen = YAH<u>N</u>
ç, c = S / ca, co, cu = KA, KO, KU
g = ZH / ga, go, gu = GA, GO, GE / gn = NY
j = ZH / qu = K
s (between vowels) = Z / ss (between vowels) = SS
th = T
x (between vowels) = SS
(All other consonants are pronounced the same as in English.)
*NOTE: N = a nasalized pronunciation of the "N" sound.

A

à at; to; in; with
accident *(m)* accident
acheter to buy
acteur *(m)* actor
activité *(f)* activity
adieu farewell
adresse *(f)* address
agent *(m)* policeman
agreáble pleasant

aide *(f)* help
aimer to like, love
aller to go
alors well
ami *(m)* friend
an *(m)* year
ancien old, ancient
anglais English
appareil *(m)* machine

Vocabulary

appartement *(m)* apartment
appétit *(m)* appetite
après after
après-midi *(m)* afternoon
argent *(m)* money
armée *(f)* army
arrêter to stop
arriver to arrive; to come
ascenseur *(m)* lift
assez quite
attaque *(f)* attack
attendre to wait
attention! careful!
au *(pl* **aux)** at the
au revoir goodbye
aucun none
aujourd'hui today
aussi as well; too
autobus *(m)* bus
autoroute *(f)* highway
autre other
avec with

B

baguette *(f)* French loaf
banque *(f)* bank
bâtiment *(m)* building
beaucoup very much
beurre *(m)* butter
bien well
bien sûr of course
bientôt soon
bière *(f)* beer
billet *(m)* ticket
blanc white
blessé hurt
bleu blue
boire to drink
bon good
bonjour hello
bonsoir good evening
bouteille *(f)* bottle

C

ça va? all right?
cabine *(f)* booth

café *(m)* **crème** white coffee
calme quiet
campagne *(f)* countryside
car as; because
carte *(f)* map
carte postale *(f)* post card
cathédrale *(f)* cathedral
ce it; **c'est** it is
cela that
ceci this
cent hundred
centre *(m)* center
ces these; those
cet *(f* **cette)** this; that
chambre *(f)* (bed)room
chanson *(f)* song
charmant charming
château *(m)* castle
chaussette *(f)* sock
chaussure *(f)* shoe
chemise *(f)* shirt
chèque *(m)* check
cher expensive
cinq five
circuler to move
citron *(m)* lemon
classe *(f)* class
clé *(f)* key
climat *(m)* climate
combien? how much?
comme like; as
commencer to begin
commerce *(m)* business
complet full
compris included
confiture *(f)* jam
content happy
côté (à) next to; beside
couleur *(f)* color
couteau *(m)* knife
couturier *(m)* fashion designer
cravate *(f)* tie
crème *(f)* cream

Vocabulary

D

d'abord first of all
d'accord all right, O.K.
dans in
danser to dance
de of; from
dehors out; outside
déjeuner (m) lunch
demain tomorrow
demi half
déranger to disturb
dernier last
descendre to go down
désolé sorry
dessert (m) dessert
deux two
deuxième second
devant in front of
dimanche Sunday
directeur (m) manager
dix ten
dizaine (f) about ten
docteur (m) doctor
donc therefore; so; then
donner to give
dormir to sleep
douche (f) shower
douzaine (f) dozen
droit straight
droite right
du of the; some
du tout at all

E

eau (f) water
également also; as well
église (f) church
élégant elegant
elle she
émission (f) broadcast
encore still; yet
endroit (m) place
enfant (m or f) child
enfin at last
ensemble together
ensuite next
entre between

entrer to come in
escargot (m) snail
et and
étage (m) floor
été (m) summer
être to be
étudiant (m) student
excusez-moi excuse me
exercice (m) exercise
exposition (f) exhibition
extérieur outside

F

face opposite
facile easy
faire to make; to do
fatigué tired
femme (f) woman; wife
fermé closed
feux (m) **rouges** traffic
  lights
février February
fille (f) girl
fils (m) son
fin (f) end
finir to finish
fois (f) time
forêt (f) forest
foule (f) crowd
frais fresh
fraise (f) strawberry
framboise (f) raspberry
français French
frère (m) brother
frites (f) chips
froid cold
fromage (m) cheese
fruit (m) fruit
fumer to smoke

G

garçon (m) waiter
gare (f) station
gâteau (m) cake
gauche left
gendarme (m) policeman
gentil nice; kind
grand big; great

Vocabulary

gratuit free
grenouille *(f)* frog
grillé grilled
gros big; large

H

habiter to live
haut high
heure *(f)* hour
homme *(m)* man
honnête honest
hôpital *(m)* hospital
hôtesse *(f)* receptionist
huile *(f)* oil
huit eight
huître *(f)* oyster

I

ici here
il he
il y a there is; there are
industrie *(f)* industry
infirmière *(f)* nurse
informations *(f)* news
interdit forbidden
intéressant interesting

J

jardin *(m)* garden; park
jeudi Thursday
jeune young
joli pretty
jour *(m)*, **journeé** *(f)* day
jus *(m)* juice
jusqu'à as far as; until
juste just; exactly

K

kilomètre *(m)* kilometer
klaxon *(m)* horn

L

la *(f)* the
là there; here
laisser to leave
lait *(m)* milk
lapin *(m)* rabbit
le *(m)* the
légume *(m)* vegetable
les the *(pl)*; them

lire to read
lit *(m)* bed
litre *(m)* liter
loin far
loisir *(m)* leisure
louer to rent
lundi Monday

M

ma my
madame *(f)* Madam
mademoiselle *(f)* Miss
magasin *(m)* shop
main *(f)* hand
maintenant now
mairie *(f)* town hall
mais but
maison *(f)* house
malade ill
manger to eat
marcher to walk
mardi Tuesday
mari *(m)* husband
matin *(m)* morning
me me
même same; even
mer *(f)* sea
merci thank you
mercredi Wednesday
mes my
mètre *(m)* meter
mieux better
minute *(f)* minute
moi me
moins less
moment *(m)* moment
monnaie *(f)* change
montagne *(f)* mountain
monter to go up
morceau *(m)* piece
moyen average
musée *(m)* museum

N

ne...pas not
ne...plus no longer; no more
neuf nine
noir black

Vocabulary

nom *(m)* name
nombreux numerous
non no
nous we; us
nouveau new
numéro *(m)* number

O

oeuf *(m)* egg
omelette *(f)* omelet
ou bien or else
ou or
où where

P

pain *(m)* bread
panneau *(m)* sign
par by
parce que because
pardon excuse me
parler to speak
partir to leave
partout everywhere
pas not
passer to pass
pauvre poor
payer to pay
péage *(m)* toll
penser to think
père father
petit small
petit déjeuner *(m)*
    breakfast
peu little
peut-être perhaps
plan *(m)* street map
plat *(m)* dish
plus more
plusieurs several
poire *(f)* pear
poisson *(m)* fish
pomme *(f)* apple
pomme de terre potato
porte-monnaie *(m)*
    purse
poste *(f)* post office
poulet *(m)* chicken
pour for

pourboire *(m)* tip
pourquoi? why
premier first
prendre to take
près near
pressé in a hurry
prix *(m)* price
problème *(m)* problem
proche near

Q

quai *(m)* river bank
qualité *(f)* quality
quand when
quartier *(m)* neighborhood
quatre four
que? what?
quel? which?
quel! what a . . . !
quelqu'un someone
qui who

R

regarder to look at
région *(f)* region
remercier to thank
rendez-vous *(m)*
    appointment
repas *(m)* meal
réponse *(f)* answer
rester to stay
riche rich
rien nothing
robe *(f)* dress
rôti *(m)* roast
route *(f)* road
rue *(f)* street

S

salade *(f)* salad
samedi Saturday
sauf except
seconde second
séjour stay
semaine week
sept seven
servir to serve
seulement only
si if; yes

Vocabulary

soeur *(f)* sister
soir *(m)* evening
soleil *(m)* sun
sortie *(f)* exit
sous under
souvent often
stationnement *(m)* parking
suffisant enough
sucre *(m)* sugar
suivre to follow
sur on
surtout above all

T

tabac *(m)* tobacco
tant pis too bad
tard late
tarte tart; pie
tasse *(f)* cup
tellement so much
temps *(m)* time; weather
thé *(m)* tea
théâtre *(m)* theater
timbre *(m)* stamp
tire-bouchon *(m)* corkscrew
toujours always; still
tout *(pl tous)* all; every
train *(m)* train
tranquille quiet
travail *(m)* work
traverser to cross
très very
trop too

U

un *(f une)* one
université *(f)* university

V

verre *(m)* glass
vert green
veste *(f)* jacket
viande *(f)* meat
ville *(f)* town, city
vin *(m)* wine
vite quickly
voici here is; here are
voilà there is; there are

voir to see
voiture *(f)* car
votre *(pl vos)* your
vraiment really
vous you

W

wagon-bar *(m)* bar (train)
wagon-restaurant *(m)* restaurant car (train)

Y

yeux *(mpl)* eyes

Z

zéro zero
zone *(f)* zone

Days of the Week

Dimanche—Sunday
Lundi—Monday
Mardi—Tuesday
Mercredi—Wednesday
Jeudi—Thursday
Vendredi—Friday
Samedi—Saturday

jour—day
matin—morning
après-midi—afternoon
soir—evening
nuit—night
tous les jours—every day
jours fériés—holidays

Months

Janvier—January
Février—February
Mars—March
Avril—April
Mai—May
Juin—June
Juillet—July
Août—August
Septembre—September
Octobre—October
Novembre—November
Décembre—December

Vocabulary

ILE DE LA CITE ET ILE ST. LOUIS

Palais Royal

RUE DE TURBIGO

R. DU LOUVRE

RUE BERGER

RUE DE RIVOLI

PONT NEUF

RUE DU PONT NEUF

BLVD. DE SEBASTOPOL

Palais du Louvre

Musée du Louvre

QUAI DU LOUVRE

AVE. VICTORIA

Pl. du Châtelet

Institut de France

Pont Neuf

Ile de la Cité
Palais de Justice

Pont
Notre Dame

QUAI DES GRANDS AUGUSTINS

Ste. Chapelle

BLVD. DU PALAIS

RUE DE LA CITE

Pont
St. Michel

Notre Dame

BLVD. ST. GERMAIN

RUE ST. JACQUES

RUE RACINE

BLVD. ST. MICHEL

RUE DES ECOLES

RUE MONGE

RUE DE VAUGIRARD

La Sorbonne

Palais du Luxembourg

Pl. Edmond Rostand

Panthéon

Maps

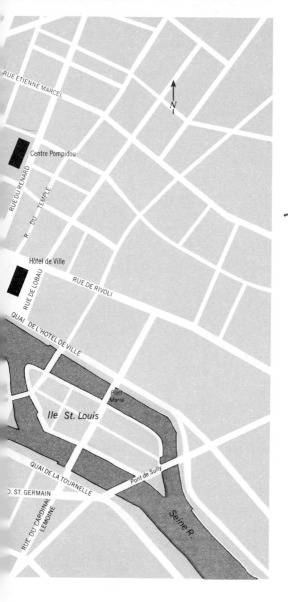

RUE ETIENNE MARCEL

N

Centre Pompidou

RUE DU RENARD

R. DU TEMPLE

Hôtel de Ville

RUE DE LOBAU

RUE DE RIVOLI

QUAI DE L'HOTEL DE VILLE

Pont Marie

Ile St. Louis

QUAI DE LA TOURNELLE

Pont de Sully

D. ST. GERMAIN

RUE DU CARDINAL LEMOINE

Seine R.

Maps

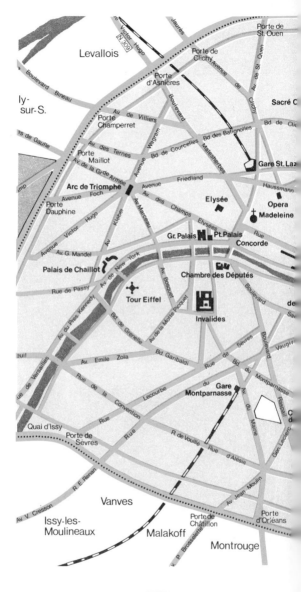

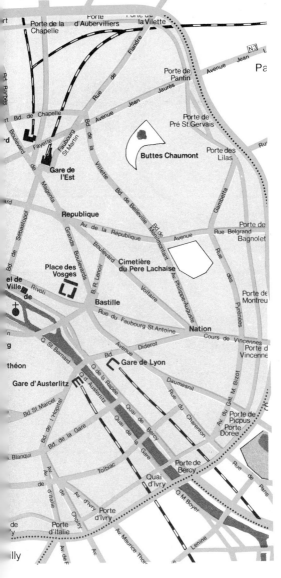

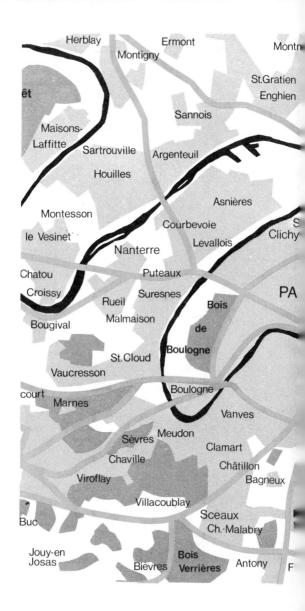

Maps

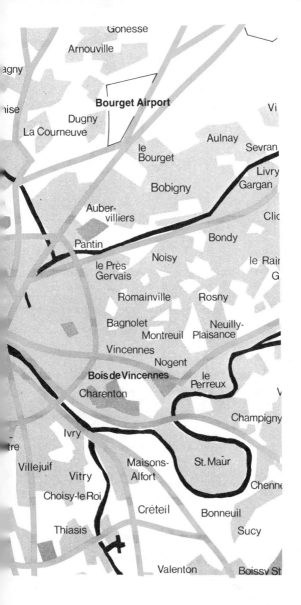

Gonesse

Arnouville

agny

hise

Bourget Airport

Dugny

La Courneuve

le Bourget

Aulnay

Sevran

Livry
Gargan

Bobigny

Auber-
villiers

Clic

Pantin

Bondy

le Près
Gervais

Noisy

le Rair

G

Romainville

Rosny

Bagnolet

Montreuil

Neuilly-
Plaisance

Vincennes

Nogent

Bois de Vincennes

le
Perreux

Charenton

V

Champigny

Ivry

tre

Villejuif

Vitry

Maisons-
Alfort

St. Maur

Chenne

Choisy-le Roi

Créteil

Bonneuil

Thiasis

Sucy

Valenton

Boissy St

Vi

Maps

CITIES IN YOUR POCKET

Barron's offers 12 fact-filled *Cities In Your Pocket* guidebooks for just $3.95 each: Atlanta (2534-2), Boston (3767-7), Chicago (3768-5), Hong Kong (3770-7), London (3760-X), Los Angeles (3759-6), New York (3755-3), Paris (3756-1), San Francisco (3758-8), Tokyo (3774-X), Toronto (2836-8), and Washington, D.C. (3757-X). They're in bookstores—or order direct at address below.

LEARN A LANGUAGE

Barron's leading travelers' language aids will make your trips more satisfying. All are available in bookstores — or order direct from Barron's Educational Series, Inc., 113 Crossways Park Dr., Woodbury, NY 11797, and list title and number. Add 10% ($1.50 minimum) for postage and handling.

French

Talking Business In French Translates 3,000 terms used in business and technology. (3745-6) $6.95
Now You're Talking French In No Time A 90-minute cassette of spoken French, 48-page audioscript and *French At A Glance* phrasebook. (7397-5) $9.95
Getting By In French A mini-course on two 60-min. cassettes with companion book. (7105-0) $16.95
Mastering French: Foreign Service Language Inst. Language Series Develops your fluency: twelve 90-min. cassettes with book. (7321-5) $75.00

German

Talking Business In German Translates 3,000 terms used in business and technology. (3747-2) $6.95

Now You're Talking German In No Time A 90-minute cassette of spoken German, 48-page audioscript and *German At A Glance* phrasebook. (7398-3) $9.95

Getting By In German A mini-course on two 60-min. cassettes with companion book. (7104-2) $16.95

Mastering German: Foreign Service Language Inst. Language Series Develops your fluency: twelve 90-min. cassettes with book. (7352-5) $75.00

Italian

Talking Business In Italian Translates 3,000 terms used in business and technology. (3754-5) $6.95

Now You're Talking Italian In No Time A 90-min. cassette of spoken Italian, 48-pg. audioscript and *Italian At A Glance* phrasebook. (7399-1) $9.95

Getting By In Italian Mini-course on two 60-min. cassettes with companion book. (7106-9) $16.95

Mastering Italian: Foreign Service Language Inst. Language Series Develops your fluency: twelve 90-min. cassettes with book. (7323-1) $75.00

Japanese

Now You're Talking Japanese In No Time 90-min. cassette of spoken Japanese, audioscript and *Japanese At A Glance* phrasebook. (7401-7) $9.95

Getting By In Japanese Mini-course on two 60-min. cassettes with companion book. (7150-6) $16.95

Spanish

Talking Business In Spanish Translates 3,000 terms used in business and technology. (3769-3) $6.95

Now You're Talking Spanish In No Time A 90-min. cassette of spoken Spanish, 48-page audioscript and *Spanish At A Glance* phrasebook. (7400-9) $9.95

Getting By In Spanish A mini-course on two 60-min. cassettes with companion book. (7103-4) $16.95

Mastering Spanish: Foreign Service Language Inst. Language Series Develops your fluency: twelve 90-min. cassettes with book. (7325-8) $75.00

TIPS FOR METRO USERS

The métro goes everywhere in Paris and, with the addition of the RER trains, to much of the surrounding areas as well. Special *semaine* passes—good for unlimited travel on the métro—are available to tourists. These can be bought at métro stations. Another money-saving ticket is the *carnet*—literally a "book" of tickets, 10 to a package. These are good for both métro and bus. Métro fares are 1 ticket unlimited length of trip. Bus fares go by zone.

* It's easy to take the métro to and from the airport. From Charles de Gaulle take the Roissy-Rail (RER, A-1). From Orly take Orly Rail (RER, C-2). You can transfer to a regular métro line once you're in Paris.
* Métro lines (there are 13 in Paris) go by the name of the first and last stop, so if you are at the Arc de Triomphe and you want to go to the Louvre, you get on the train marked "Direction Vincennes." All stations have maps posted, and all cars have maps of the line you are on. Transfers (free) are made at junctions labeled "*correspondance.*"
* After buying your ticket, put it through the machine at the entry gate. Remember to take it with you as you pass through; you may have to show it to an inspector. The métro has 2 classes. First class—the cars are yellow—is reserved from 9 A.M. to 5 P.M. for those with a first class ticket. If you're caught without one, you'll have to pay a stiff fine.
* Remember that trains do not run all night. The last one is about 12:45 A.M.; the first trains in the morning start about 5:30 A.M.